BECKY

BECKY

The heartbreaking story of
BECKY WATTS
by her father

DARREN GALSWORTHY

HarperElement
An imprint of HarperCollins*Publishers*
1 London Bridge Street
London SE1 9GF

www.harpercollins.co.uk

First published by HarperElement 2016

1 3 5 7 9 10 8 6 4 2

A catalogue record of this book is
available from the British Library

ISBN 978-0-00-817960-1

Printed and bound in Great Britain by
Clay Ltd, St Ives plc

MIX
Paper from
responsible sources
FSC™ C007454

FSC™ is a non-profit international organisation established to promote
the responsible management of the world's forests. Products carrying the
FSC label are independently certified to assure consumers that they come
from forests that are managed to meet the social, economic and
ecological needs of present and future generations,
and other controlled sources.

Find out more about HarperCollins and the environment at
www.harpercollins.co.uk/green

For my beautiful Bex

CONTENTS

FOREWORD

I've always enjoyed the outdoors. When I was growing up, my father would teach me all about the wonders of nature, and there was nothing I enjoyed more than pulling on my wellies and running outside to explore. To me, it was the only place where you could be free and let your imagination run wild. An open clearing would become a kingdom, a wooded area would turn into a secret, magical garden. A large tree would become my castle for the day. When I had children of my own, I taught them that their imagination was limitless. As they grew up to love the outdoors too, I rediscovered it through their eyes. For me, that was part of the magic of having children.

I still love taking long walks, but these days I tend to be alone. It gives me a good opportunity to think and to set the world to rights. I never feel completely alone anyway – everywhere I look I can see memories of my daughter Becky, from when she was a toddler, clutching her microscope to examine the bugs on the leaves, to when she was a teenager, examining her nail polish as we walked together, talking about her hopes and dreams.

Becky was at the beginning of adulthood when she was cruelly taken from us. She was just starting to figure out who she was, and who she wanted to be in the future. She was growing into a beautiful young woman, with a wicked sense of style and an attitude to match.

These days, I take a long walk whenever I want to feel her presence around me again. I often stroll slowly along the familiar winding lanes and sit down by the edge of a pond, enjoying the film reel of memories as they play out in my head. It's there that I usually have one of my many one-sided conversations with Becky.

'Hello, Bex. I hope you're happy and safe, wherever you are. I hope you're with my nan and she's showing you all the love she showed me when I was your age. I wish you were with me so much. I miss everything about you – your laugh, your sense of humour, even the way you would make fun of me all day long.

'I miss trying to embarrass you with my "dad dancing". I even miss the practical jokes you used to play on me – like the time you waited until I fell asleep on the couch and then you painted me with as much make-up as you could find. I wondered why the man at the door was looking at me so strangely when I greeted him, but when I heard you giggling from your room I knew instantly that you had something to do with it. I was horrified when I looked in the mirror and saw my red lips and bright blue eyelids – but you thought it was hilarious, and the sound of your laughter was enough to make everyone smile.

'I miss having fun with you when you were a little girl, scrunching up my face into all sorts of shapes just to make you collapse into giggles, baking cupcakes with you in the kitchen, and reading to you in bed. My favourite part of the day was always watching you fall asleep then kissing you goodnight.

'Bex, I even miss the rows we used to have. We were so alike, we used to rub each other up the wrong way, but we'd always end up rolling around with laughter. I miss the way you used to hurl yourself at me when you came in, winding me in the process. I miss you pulling my right arm around you and cuddling in. You could stay like that for hours, and I used to thank my lucky stars that you still wanted to do that, even when you were a teenager.

'Not an hour goes by that I don't think about you, Bex. From the moment I open my eyes to the moment I rest my head on my pillow at night, I see you. I see you in your room on your phone, I see you messing about with your friends at the front gate, I see you in our living room, cuddled up watching a film – you are everywhere. In a way, I'm glad because I don't ever want to forget anything about you.

'I try very hard not to think of the way you were taken from us, but it's difficult. All I ever wanted to do was protect you, and I've tortured myself that I wasn't there for you on that fateful day.

'I loved you so much, Becky – and you knew it too. You knew how to wind me around your little finger. I couldn't even tell you off for being naughty without telling you that I loved you first. I didn't want you to have any doubt about how loved you were. You are still loved so much – not just by me, but by your friends and the whole family. Now that you're gone there is a huge hole in our hearts.

'I try not to focus on our loss; instead I think about all the amazing memories we made together. I used to worry about you not making friends easily, but now I'm actually grateful that you didn't, because I became both your dad and your friend, and I will always treasure the time we spent together.

'So for now, until we meet again, my princess, I just close my eyes and imagine you running around with your brown hair – which always shimmered red when the sun caught it – a big smile on your face and a lot of love in your heart. Your laughter could cheer me up even on a dark day. And one day, I know I'm going to hear that laughter again. Lots of love, Dad x'

CHAPTER 1

BECKY

MONDAY, 23 FEBRUARY 2015

Appeal over missing schoolgirl: *Concern is mounting over the disappearance of Bristol schoolgirl Becky Watts. The 16-year-old was last seen by her stepmother, Anjie Galsworthy, four days ago after she returned to her home at Crown Hill, St George's, following a night at a friend's house. Mrs Galsworthy says she saw Becky at around 11.15 a.m. on Thursday and chatted with her before heading out. Becky's family and friends are growing increasingly worried as her disappearance is out of character. Her boyfriend Luke had been expecting to see her that day, but she didn't respond to his texts. Becky's mobile phone and laptop are missing too, but it appears she took no cash, clothes, makeup or anything else that might suggest she was going away for any length of time. Today, her father, Darren Galsworthy, and grandmother, Pat Watts, made a heartfelt public appeal for her return. Mr Galsworthy said: 'Becky, we just want you to come home. You're in no trouble at all – we just want to make sure you are*

OK. If you can, please give us a call or a text to let us know you are safe. We all love you and want you back home with us.' Police are working with the family. They've released a photo and description of the missing girl and a social media campaign is under way, with the hashtag #FindBecky.

The first time I peered down at my baby daughter Becky, my heart melted. She was a proper bundle of joy and cute as a button. As she gazed up at me from her cot, blinking rapidly to try to take in her new surroundings, I couldn't help but fall for her. At 6 pounds 12 ounces she was tiny, but I soon discovered that she had a good set of lungs for a newborn and could silence a whole room with her cries.

I adored Becky from that first moment, even though my feelings were tinged with uncertainty because I wasn't sure if she was really my child. Her mother and I had been in an on–off relationship that was veering towards 'off' at the time she was conceived. But as Becky grew up, she became more and more like her old man – so much so that it startled both of us at times. Her big hazel eyes were the same as mine, and as she got older she developed a lot of my mannerisms. The only difference between us was the fact that she was far better looking! I called her 'my beautiful Bex' because, to me, Becky really was beautiful – inside and out.

I was born and bred in Bristol and have lived here all my life. Some parts of the city aren't pretty, as I well know because I've made my home in some of the roughest bits, but in Bristol I have a strong sense of belonging. Bristol folk are some of the kindest, most genuine and supportive people you will ever meet, and I am proud of the city's brilliant community spirit. I simply can't imagine living anywhere else.

I was the first child in my family, born on New Year's Eve 1963, when the Beatles were at number one with 'I Want to Hold Your Hand'. I waited until 11 p.m. to make an appearance, so my parents, John and Sue Galsworthy, were staring down at my scrunched-up face as the clock struck midnight and everyone else across the country was welcoming in the New Year.

The next day, they brought me back from Southmead Hospital to their two-bedroom terraced house in Easton, Bristol. At that time Easton was one of the most deprived areas in the South West and it was multicultural, which was quite rare in those days. My family were among the only white people on our estate. Life in the 1960s in Bristol was quite tough for working-class people like us, and we had to struggle to make ends meet. My dad worked long hours as a machinist for a nuclear and defence engineering company, and my mum worked in a leather factory then later became an auxiliary nurse at an old people's home.

My little brother Lee was born on 15 August 1966, when I was two and a half. We shared a room and at first I quite enjoyed having a younger brother, but as he grew older he became a bit gobby, always getting himself into trouble with the other kids on our estate. Because I was the older one, I had to jump in to protect him, and I eventually got a reputation for enjoying a fight – all thanks to Lee!

The 1970s was the decade of strikes, which led to power cuts and huge piles of rat-infested rubbish on the streets because the bin men weren't collecting it any more. The economy was prone to inflation – it seemed as if every single time you went to the shops, prices had gone up. This led to workers demanding higher wages, which the government didn't want to pay, and as a result the unions started to call for all-out strikes. Three-day working weeks were introduced as businesses were only allowed to use electricity for three consecutive days each week, while there were regular power cuts for home users. This meant that the inside of our house was as freezing cold as the outside during the winter months – we had ice on the inside of the windows. I was taught to bake bread at school because the bakers were on strike, like everyone else, and I got in the habit of nicking coal whenever I spotted it just so we could light the fire at night to keep warm. Huddled together by candlelight in the evenings, Lee and I thought it was great fun – but, of course, we were young and didn't have any responsibilities. I imagine it was quite different for our parents, who had two kids to feed and keep warm.

My dad was the head of our household and extremely strict, as many fathers were back then. It wasn't uncommon to receive a beating with his belt if we were naughty. Sometimes if my brother was bad I'd be punished too, and vice versa, which didn't seem fair. Teachers were also allowed to beat pupils in those days. We were often hit with a bat, like a wooden paddle, in primary school, and when we got to secondary school a cane was used. I was quite an emotional kid, and it didn't take much to make me cry. When the teacher asked me if I wanted a telling off or the bat, I always chose the bat because I was used to getting beatings at home and knew I could take them. Strange as it may sound, to me words hurt more.

My mother wasn't the most maternal person and never stood up for my brother or me. She worked morning or evening shifts at the leather factory, and we would often come home from school to find her passed out on the sofa after drinking gin during the afternoon. I didn't realise she was an alcoholic until much later. I didn't really know what that was then, but I knew it was useless trying to get any sense out of her when she'd been drinking. Since she wasn't capable of making dinner, I learned to make food for Lee and me from an early age. At first it was just sandwiches I made from the food parcels donated to poor families by people at the local church. Later, I learned to make simple meals like egg and chips or sausage and chips, and I often made dinner for my father too. He was always in a better mood if there was food on the table ready for him when he returned home from work.

Money was incredibly scarce for our family. We didn't have a fridge – just a wooden cupboard in the back garden where we kept our milk. We were lucky enough to have a black-and-white television, but in those days there were only two channels and it took five minutes to warm up after you switched it on. Lee and I didn't have any toys but we made our own entertainment, playing in rubbish dumps and skips and hanging out with other kids around the estate. We never received any presents at Christmas from our parents – they didn't celebrate Christmas at all – but we knew that when we went to visit May, our grandmother on my mum's side, we would get spoilt.

Nan always had time for her grandkids and would be sure to feed us up because she knew we weren't getting enough to eat at home. I loved her dearly, and some of my best childhood memories involve her. On Tuesdays and Thursdays she picked us up to take us into town on the bus and she always had a bar of chocolate for us to share. When I was eight, she gave me the best present ever: my first proper bike. It was a bronze-coloured Panther bike, which was second-hand but still the best thing I'd ever seen. For years, Nan was the only source of love and affection Lee and I had, what with Mum's drinking and Dad's temper dominating life at home. I don't want this to sound like a sob story because others had it much tougher than me, but let's just say it wasn't the most comfortable, stable start in life.

My parents split up when I was nineteen, and my dad then married Denise in September 1985. Through Denise I instantly gained two stepbrothers – Kevin, who was three, and Ben, who was one. My father and Denise went on to have four children together – Sarah, Sam, Joe and Asa. I bonded with them pretty quickly, and to this day they remain among my closest friends. Dad mellowed with age and became a much gentler man than the one I had grown up with, so that today we have a good relationship. My mum died in 2010, from pneumonia, and sadly we never became close.

I had already left the family home by the time Dad remarried. When I was eighteen I moved out to live with my girlfriend, Angela Holloway, who was a year younger than me. We later got hitched, but the marriage only lasted three years. It was a case of far too much, too young, for both of us.

During the period when I was married, I used to babysit for the kids of some friends of mine, Mark and Verna West. One day, I arrived just as their other babysitter was leaving, and the minute I set eyes on her I felt as though I'd been struck by lightning. She was so gorgeous I could barely speak to introduce myself.

'I'm Anjie,' she told me.

'Darren.'

I felt electricity running all the way through my body, and I just couldn't take my eyes off her. She kept glancing at me too, while we chatted about everyday things like the kids we were looking after, where we lived, that kind of thing. It was the strangest feeling, but I just knew there was something special about her. It was as if kindness and light shone out of her, and it was the most powerful sensation I had ever felt.

However, I was married to Angela Holloway at the time and, after we got divorced, I heard that Anjie was seeing someone else, then in 1986 I heard she was pregnant. I just assumed it was a case of bad timing and nothing was going to happen between us. I never forgot about her, though.

I was twenty-two when Angela and I broke up. I had a few girlfriends after that but nothing too serious. I was concentrating on my career, and that didn't really leave me much time for a relationship. At the age of sixteen I had done a youth-training scheme in tyre-fitting and car maintenance, at eighteen I was taken on for an engineering apprenticeship at a company that made precast concrete products, and by my mid-twenties I was working as a sheet metal engineer for a firm called City Engineering. I was very serious about making enough money to have a better standard of living than I'd had when I was growing up. I wanted a decent place to live and enough food to put on the table, and I was prepared to put in the graft to earn them.

When I was twenty-nine, I met a girl called Tanya Watts, who was twenty-two and worked as a carer in an old-folks' home. She was with some friends in a local pub, and we got chatting, as you do. We seemed to get on well, I bought her a few drinks, and suddenly, almost before I knew it, we were in a relationship. We moved in to a flat in Cadbury Heath soon after meeting and settled into a life of working, going to the pub at the weekend, and taking the occasional holiday. Her mum, Pat, paid for us to go to Pembrokeshire for a week the first year we were together.

We didn't ever get married because the relationship always had problems, but I was excited when our son Danny was born on 19 February 1995. He came into the world at Southmead Hospital – same as his old man. When I held him for the first time I couldn't help but laugh because he was covered in fine black hair and looked like a baby chimp! I was thrilled to see that he looked exactly the same as me in my baby photographs. It was a very proud moment. I was overwhelmed that I had a son, and I swore there and then that I would always love and protect him.

Danny and I bonded instantly and I threw myself into being a dad, but I was working such long hours as an engineer that my time with him became sacred. Meanwhile, my relationship with Tanya was deteriorating fast. We began to fight about anything and everything, hurling hurtful comments at each other, often continuing rows into the early hours of the morning. I tried to shield baby Danny from as much of it as possible, but living with Tanya was getting harder and harder for me.

Sometimes she kicked me out of the flat after a row, and one night in January she told me I'd have to sleep in my car. I didn't sleep a wink all night long, and as I lay there shivering, I real-ised that Tanya and I being together was doing more harm than good. I couldn't see any way we could make it work in the long term, but at the same time I didn't want to leave my baby son, so I kept trying.

We got into a pattern: we'd have a big row, Tanya would kick me out, then I'd go back a few days later to see my boy and we'd try again. Danny was two years old before I eventually decided enough was enough. Tanya kicked me out after yet another row, and I moved into a flat my friend was subletting while he worked away from home. Two weeks later, Tanya called and asked when I was coming back, and I told her that the answer was never.

I was relieved that at last the decision had been made, but it was horrible being away from Danny. I missed him terribly. He was just at the stage of chatting away in a mixture of baby words and real words and I couldn't bear to miss any of it, so I persuaded Tanya to let him come to stay with me on the weekends. Hand-overs were difficult because the communication between us was in tatters by then, although I tried my hardest to be civil for Danny's sake. I paid my child maintenance, but still we often argued over money. It was difficult, to say the least, but Danny was precious and I treasured every single moment with him.

It was a tough time all round. The only thing keeping me going was the thought of seeing Danny at the end of each week. I worked all the hours under the sun to make ends meet. My father didn't teach me much, but he did teach me the importance of hard work. I've always been a hardworking man and I'm proud of that.

One Saturday night in October 1997, I was in my flat, with Danny asleep in bed, when Tanya knocked on the door. I opened it, expecting her to start an argument with me about something, but instead she was smiling and friendly. I'd had a few drinks by that stage and decided to let her in. One thing led to another and we ended up sleeping together. She left before the sun came up, and as soon as I woke I regretted what we had done. It was sending out all the wrong signals because, as far as I was concerned, the relationship was totally over.

I tried to forget about it and move on, but a few months later one of Tanya's female friends – she didn't say who she was – rang me while I was at work.

'Tanya's pregnant,' she blurted out. 'And you're the father.'

'And how on earth am I the father, then?' I demanded. 'Of course it's not my bloody child. She's just trying to mug me off.'

When I saw her next, as I was dropping Danny home the following weekend, she noticed my eyes wander down to her growing baby bump. I said I didn't believe it was mine.

'It is your baby,' she shrugged. 'You'll see.'

The months passed and I carried on having Danny at the weekends, as usual. Then, on 3 June 1998, I got a call at work from one of Tanya's friends to tell me that she had given birth to a baby girl. I thought it was nice that Danny would have a sister, but I still didn't believe the baby was mine, even though she was born roughly nine months after Tanya and I'd had that one-night reunion.

The day after the birth, I drove Danny up to the Bristol Royal Infirmary so he could meet his little sister. Tanya had decided she was to be called Rebecca, Becky for short. Danny was excited about it, and I didn't want him to miss out.

As we walked through the ward, Danny spotted Tanya and ran towards the cot where little Becky was sleeping.

'Don't wake her up!' Tanya warned as he peered over the edge. I was proud of how quiet and gentle he was for a three-year-old. I could tell he instantly felt protective towards his baby sister.

'Don't you want to say hello to your daughter?' Tanya asked me, and I sauntered over to the cot to have a better look.

Becky was a cute little thing, wrapped up tightly in a white blanket and with a little white cotton hat on her head. I didn't want to fall in love but I simply couldn't help myself. She was so adorable, I fell hook, line and sinker on the spot. It was overwhelming, just like the feeling I'd had when I first saw Danny. But was she mine, or was some other man going to come along and claim to be her dad? At that stage, I didn't know.

Tanya took Becky home a few days later, and we went back to the routine of me having Danny each Friday to Sunday.

'Why not take Becky as well?' she asked one Friday night when Becky was three months old.

I was reluctant, as I didn't want to spoil the time Danny and I spent together, but Tanya wouldn't take no for an answer.

'She is your daughter,' she insisted. 'You're going to have to start looking after her sooner or later.'

'We don't know that she's mine,' I pointed out. 'I'm not having her until I know the truth.' I'd thought about getting a DNA test, but it was expensive and at that time I didn't have the cash to spare.

Finally, Tanya said, 'You're not having Danny if you don't take Becky too.'

She knew she would win with that. I was backed into a corner, with no choice other than to take little Becky home with me. I could remember all the routines from when Danny was a baby: getting up in the night to feed her from a bottle, bathing her carefully in a little baby bath, and dressing her in her tiny clothes. It was during these moments that I started to look at her more closely, and I noticed her hazel eyes were starting to look exactly the same as mine. I melted inside when she beamed up at me, and my stomach filled with butterflies whenever she reached out to grab my finger. I've always been a complete softie at heart, and Becky was winning me over more and more every time I saw her.

I was out one weekend with the kids, Danny holding my hand and Becky, who was six months old, in her pushchair, when I bumped into Anjie on Kingswood High Street. I felt flustered but Anjie's face broke into a huge grin as soon as she saw me.

'Darren! How are you? I haven't seen you in ages!' she said.

Suddenly, I got the same rush of electricity running through me as I'd had ten years previously, when we first met, and I felt tongue-tied. I'd caught glimpses of Anjie over the years while she was out and about in Bristol – usually with her little boy – but we'd never had the opportunity to chat properly.

'Oh, you know – keeping busy,' I forced myself to reply, gesturing at the kids.

'They are very cute,' she said, the smile not leaving her face. 'Are you still with Tanya?'

'Oh no, not at all,' I answered quickly. I really wanted Anjie to know I was single. I was disappointed when she then told me she was in a relationship, although something in the way she talked about it gave me a hint she wasn't too happy.

We parted, promising that we would go for a drink and a good catch-up soon, and for the rest of the day I thought of nothing else but her. I'd honestly never had such strong feelings for anyone in my life, and the possibility that things might work out between us was incredibly exciting.

A few months later, I was in the pub having a pint after work when she walked in with her friend Kim. I could tell from the expression on her face that she was not in a good way, although she raised a smile when I asked if I could get some drinks in and join them.

'I was hoping to see you,' Anjie said, taking a seat. 'That's why I came here.'

It turned out that things were on the rocks with her boyfriend, but she hadn't had the guts to tell him yet. We had a few drinks and she came back to stay at my flat, just to clear her head. I said I was sorry she was having such a difficult time, although secretly of course I was delighted at the thought that she might soon be single. A few weeks after that night she broke up with her boyfriend, and we started seeing each other. I was over the moon.

Everything was so easy with Anjie. We instantly felt like we were two jigsaw-puzzle pieces that fitted together perfectly. She was warm, loving, gorgeous to look at and great fun to be with. I'd gaze at her sometimes and have to pinch myself because I couldn't believe my luck. One night, when we were cuddled up in front of the television, she looked at me and said something that stopped my heart beating.

'We were always meant to be together, you know,' she said. 'I always knew it would be you and me.'

It turned out that when we first met, Anjie had felt the same connection as I had. It felt like the most natural thing in the world for us to be together.

I soon realised that Anjie was the kindest person I had ever met. Most people have the ability to be kind, but with Anjie it just radiated from her. She was lovely to everyone she met, and could never do enough to help someone in need. She would spend her days helping elderly neighbours with their shopping and chores, and she loved being around children. I couldn't believe my luck that I'd found someone like her. As far as I was concerned, she was an angel on earth.

Because Anjie's previous relationship had been so troubled, she had taken the difficult decision to have her son, Nathan, stay with her mum, Margaret, during the week and come to her at weekends. Nathan was twelve when Anjie and I got together, and we decided that it was best for him to stay in the same school, which meant he had to stay with his nan, who lived five miles away. Anjie still saw him every day, though, because she used to walk over and take him to and from school, morning and afternoon, meaning that she had covered 20 miles by the end of the day. She was too broke to afford the bus fares.

Nathan didn't see anything of his biological father, so when she decided it was time to introduce us, I was keen to make a good impression, hoping I might become a father figure to him.

'Nathan, this is Darren,' Anjie said when we picked him up from his grandmother's one weekend.

'I haven't seen you since you were a little boy – you've grown loads since then.' I grinned at Nathan, but he regarded me suspiciously. I could tell straight away that he was possessive of his mother. The minute we got to Anjie's house, he wanted to play-fight with me in the garden. It took a few hours of play-fully throwing him around for me to break the ice with him, and that was it – we were fine after that.

It was time for Anjie to meet Danny, who was four, and Becky, who was not quite two. This was a different kettle of fish as both my kids loved her the second they set eyes on her. Danny immediately sat next to her and listened, all ears, as she read him a story, while Becky just gazed at her in awe. Anjie was a natural mother, through and through.

When Nathan first met Danny, he shyly invited him up to his room to play computer games. Danny was thrilled – he didn't have anything like that at home. Suddenly, a boy eight years older than him was inviting him to play on the PlayStation with him. That was awesome! They remained locked up in that room for hours, and we barely heard a peep out of them. I think Danny had always wanted an older brother, and Nathan provided someone for him to look up to. From then on, Danny adjusted to life as the 'middle child' in our family, which suited him just fine.

Becky was too young to play with Danny and Nathan, so she mainly spent her time with Anjie and me. She was quite a demanding child, who would scream at the top of her lungs for hours on end for no reason that we could ever work out. I'd had her checked out with a doctor and there was nothing physically wrong. It seemed as though she was just staking her claim for attention in the household. When we started feeding her solids instead of milk, she would scream in between spoonfuls of baby food because we weren't giving it to her fast enough. She was like a little monster sometimes – but I was still a doting dad and nothing was too much trouble.

At first, I would often take my kids out for one day every weekend to give Nathan time alone with his mum, because he seemed a little jealous when she was affectionate towards my two, particularly Becky. But Anjie was adamant that she wanted us to be a family and that we should do things together. When she said that, I gave her a huge hug. I would have done anything for my kids and I think they knew that. I wanted to give them a proper family life – the life I'd never really had – even if I could only do it at the weekends. Anjie wanted to give them a great home too, so that's what we set about doing. For the next fifteen years, all of our energy was put into making sure the three kids had a stable upbringing with plenty of love. And there was so much love in our house it was unreal.

Eventually, the kids and I were seeing so much of Anjie and Nathan that it made sense for me to move in to Anjie's house in Hillfields, which was just a few miles from where I had been living in Barton Hill. We then moved together to a new house in the St George's area. In both houses, Nathan had a room of his own, while Danny and Becky shared a room. During the week, the house was quiet as it was just Anjie and me, but at weekends it was like living in a madhouse with three kids running around, winding each other up and playing games. But we didn't want it any other way.

I still hadn't bothered to get a DNA test because I knew in my heart of hearts that Becky was my daughter. Tanya hadn't named me on the birth certificate, though, and I wanted things to be clear, so when Becky was two years old I decided to go ahead with the test. When the results eventually came back they proved that she was definitely my daughter. By then, I loved her so much I don't think it changed anything, but it did feel good knowing for sure that she was mine. I knew then that I would never, ever be forced to let her go.

CHAPTER 2

THE FIGHT

SATURDAY, 28 FEBRUARY 2015

Scores join search for missing Becky: *Police have ramped up the hunt for Bristol teenager Becky Watts after she mysteriously vanished a week ago. A forensics team has combed her home for possible clues, the police helicopter has twice scoured the surrounding area – including Troopers Hill Nature Reserve, which lies two miles away – and police divers have been carrying out specialist open-water searches at the pond in nearby St George's Park. Neighbouring forces from South Wales, Wiltshire, Devon and Cornwall, and Gloucestershire have now joined the operation, and police said yesterday that Detective Superintendent Liz Tunks, head of the major crime investigation unit, had taken over as senior investigating officer. Thousands of posters and leaflets have been distributed across the city, and there have been several public appeals for help by Becky's family, but so far to no avail. In a tremendous show of support and solidarity, scores*

*of volunteers have this week joined family, friends and
neighbours to sweep the city for any sign of the missing
schoolgirl. As time passes, hopes of finding her alive are
fading. Pleading desperately for the return of his daughter on
radio station Jack FM, Becky's father, Darren Galsworthy,
said: 'It's been absolute hell on earth. Someone out there
knows something. I just want my girl back.'*

After a gruelling week at work, I always looked forward to
spending the weekends with my family. The sixteen-hour days
I was doing as a sheet metal engineer would leave me completely
knackered by Friday evening, but there was nothing more
satisfying than picking up my kids for the weekend – Nathan
from his nan's and Danny and Becky from Tanya's house in
Cadbury Heath. It was easily my favourite part of the week. I
immediately felt that little bit lighter the moment I clapped
eyes on them.

Anjie and I would plan all sorts of activities for the kids:
bowling and Laser Quest (a kind of hi-tech hide and seek) for
the boys, or just simple trips to the park or beach. I was happiest when we were all together; it didn't really matter what we
were doing.

Around the age of two, Becky became a proper toddler,
prone to having loud tantrums. She'd never lost that powerful
set of lungs she'd displayed in hospital, and she demonstrated
them publicly on many occasions. When we went to a birds of
prey show, she screamed so loudly she upset all the birds.

'Will the family with the very loud toddler please leave, as
you are interrupting the show?' said an angry female voice over
the tannoy.

Anjie and I were mortified, and I tried to hide my embarrassment. I picked Becky up and stomped out of the building then plonked her down on the pavement outside, where she continued to scream and screech at me. To Anjie's horror, I sat myself down a few metres away and started making the same noises back to Becky. People didn't know what to think as they watched us screeching away. It certainly shut her up! I can laugh about it now, but it was a waste of the ticket price – a whole £18 I was never going to see again.

When Becky was three, we took the kids on holiday to Exmouth. Danny, Nathan and I armed ourselves with little fishing nets and went searching for crabs and limpets when, all of a sudden, Becky decided it was time for a tantrum. She stood on the sand a few metres away from us and screamed her head off. No amount of coaxing from Anjie or me could make her calm down, so in the end I picked her up, put her on her lilo and paddled her into the sea.

'If you don't start behaving, I'm going to let go and you'll end up over in France,' I warned, pointing to show her the direction.

She looked at my face, trying to work out if I was serious, and when I stayed deadpan she decided to calm down.

Maybe some of Becky's tantrums were about testing her own power, the way all toddlers do, but they were also a way of getting our attention because she was still not talking by then. She had been slow to walk and crawl, not finding her feet till well after her second birthday, and at two years old she wasn't talking yet – she didn't use recognisable words until she was well past her third birthday. I wasn't unduly worried at first because I know all kids pick up these skills at their own pace, but the tantrums meant she could be a handful at times.

She might have been demanding, but she was also an extremely affectionate child. All she had to do was look up at me and smile and she would have me wrapped completely around her little finger. She was always reaching up for a cuddle. Her favourite place to be was cuddled up with Anjie or me, or hanging with her arms around Anjie's neck. She was my princess and I adored her.

It always melted my heart when I spotted Danny and Becky peeping through the curtains at their mother's house, waiting for my car to pull up outside on a Friday evening. The minute they saw us turning onto their street, Danny would fling open the front door, and, as soon as she could walk, Becky had a habit of rushing out to greet us. This might have been cute but it scared me silly, as I had to pull over quickly and jump out of the car to make sure she didn't run straight into traffic.

As happy as the kids were to see me, Tanya was always less so. Communication between us as parents reached an all-time low after Anjie and Nathan came into my life. I tried to keep my cool and let things wash over me, but handovers remained incredibly tense, difficult times.

Becky and Danny would be very quiet when they first arrived at our place on Friday evenings. It was as if it took them a few hours to warm up and start enjoying themselves. I just assumed the pair of them were taking some time to get used to the new family unit, but Anjie had her doubts.

'Have you noticed how Becky has starting sitting on the sofa all the time in just one spot?' she said to me after we put them to bed one evening. 'It comes across like she's scared to move, like she's been told off for it. I had to plead with her just to come and play on the floor with me and Danny.'

'She'll come around,' I reassured her, but in the back of my mind I knew she had a point. Some weekends, the kids would be timid and jumpy, as if the slightest thing unnerved them. Once, when I went to pick them up, Danny was hiding underneath Tanya's kitchen table.

I tried to talk to Tanya about their behaviour but, to be honest, communication between us was too difficult. She just shrugged when I brought it up.

'Maybe they don't like being there with you and your new family,' she suggested. I knew it wasn't that because once they relaxed – usually by Saturday morning – they were giggling and laughing and having a great time.

Tanya and I often clashed over the state of the old clothes the kids were wearing when they came to us. Anjie and I went out and bought them new outfits, but the following week they would come back in the old clothes again. Once or twice, Becky didn't even have any shoes on when she got into my car, and I couldn't find a suitable pair for her in Tanya's house. Every time I raised the issue with Tanya, she threatened to call the police to remove me from her home. Despite the fact that I was paying child maintenance every month, Anjie and I were having to buy the kids loads of essentials every time we saw them. In the end, we kept the clothes we bought for them at our house, so at least they always had something nice to wear when they were with us.

On Sunday nights, when we got into the car for me to drive them both home, Becky would cry her eyes out the whole way, and cling to me like a limpet as I carried her out of the car and up the front path.

'Come on, sweetheart, it's OK,' I'd say as I tried to reassure her. 'You're going to see Mummy now and you'll come back to Daddy's house next weekend.'

No matter what I said, it was absolutely heartbreaking for me to leave her that upset. Danny never cried, but he would sigh and drag his feet.

I used to drive home to Anjie feeling terrible and trying desperately to understand what was going on. 'I know they like spending time with us and we have lots of fun together, but it's not just that. It's as if they don't want to go home,' I said to her in bed one night. 'Becky just didn't want me to leave. Something's wrong, Anjie.'

I didn't want to seem like an ex complaining, but eventually I was so worried I phoned social services.

'We'll look into it,' I was told, but as far as I could tell nothing happened. I called again and again, but I might as well have been hitting my head against a brick wall for all the good it did.

Then, in September 2001, when Becky was three and Danny was five, everything changed. I opened the door to a man who introduced himself as Dave and said he was a social worker. I invited him in and he wasted no time in telling us why he was paying us a visit.

'I have an update about your children, Daniel and Rebecca,' he said, and Anjie shot me a concerned glance. 'I'm sorry to have to tell you this, Mr Galsworthy, but the pair of them have been taken into care.'

I stared at him in shock, and my stomach tightened into a knot.

'Are the children OK?' Anjie asked him. She sounded panicked. 'Has something happened to them?'

'The children are fine,' Dave answered. 'I didn't mean to startle you. They are both fit and healthy, but we weren't sure they were being properly cared for at home with their mother so we deemed it necessary to step in. They'll be staying with a foster family until we decide what to do.'

I was horrified to think of children of mine being in care, being looked after by strangers. What had been happening to them at home?

'I want my kids to come and live here with me,' I said, and Dave nodded.

'I imagine you do, Mr Galsworthy, but it's now a case of reviewing their care and deciding on the best possible outcome. You'll have the opportunity to apply for custody, and you'll still have your regular access to them on weekends. It's important that Daniel and Rebecca maintain that routine and still see a lot of you. Their mother, Miss Watts, will also have supervised access to them.'

I was relieved that they could still come and stay with Anjie and me at weekends. At least they would have an ounce of normality throughout the whole thing. I could tell that Anjie was thinking the same thing, as her shoulders relaxed a little.

'So why can't they come to us straight away?' I asked. 'We have enough room to have them here during the week, and they are always properly taken care of when they're with us. Why can't you just arrange for them to live here?'

'It's a little more complicated than that, I'm afraid,' he answered. 'There will be a few court hearings about their care, and you'll be considered for custody. I imagine their mother,

Miss Watts, will be applying too. Until a decision is made, Daniel and Rebecca will need to stay with a foster family during the week.' It seemed part of the problem was that I hadn't been named as Becky's father on her birth certificate.

'So what you're telling me is, I now have to fight to get my kids?' I asked him. I could feel a wave of anger wash over me but I tried not to show it.

Dave nodded again. 'I'm afraid so.'

As soon as he left, Anjie and I looked at each other, still reeling from the news.

'I suppose we should just be grateful that they're safe,' Anjie said, and I smiled. She could always look on the positive side of things. I knew they would be treated properly in foster care, but that they would inevitably be confused and scared by all the changes in their young lives. I was desperate to have them living permanently with me.

When I saw the kids the following Friday, they rushed into my arms.

'Are you OK?' I asked Danny. 'Is it nice where you are staying?'

He just nodded and didn't want to talk about it. I explained that I wanted them to come and live with us, but that mummy wanted them as well and the social workers were going to decide what was the best thing. Becky clung to me like her life depended on it. Although she hadn't started talking yet, I knew she understood most of what was being said around her. 'We'll still see each other every weekend while they're deciding,' I reassured them. 'Just like before.'

For the next three months, Anjie and I lived and breathed the fight to get my children out of care. It was the first thing I thought about as soon as I woke up in the morning, and the last thing that passed through my mind before I fell asleep – if I managed to get any sleep at all. The number of sleepless nights I had worrying about the fate of Danny and Becky was unreal.

We saw Dave, the social worker, a few times after that, and I grew to really like him. He talked us through the whole process and kept us up to date with what we had to do to apply for custody. A brilliant family solicitor called Greg Moss, one of the best in Bristol, agreed to take on the case on behalf of the children, and it was good to know he was on our side.

We got dressed up and went to several family court hearings, only to discover that they were going to be adjourned to another date. It was irritating, as I had to book a whole day off work every time. Eventually, I had used up all of my holiday allowance for the year just to be able to attend a string of meetings that lasted five minutes each.

The hearings were nerve-racking for Anjie and me. We both knew we were more than capable of taking care of Danny and Becky full-time, but we had to prove that to the family court. We were put under the spotlight as they queried everything about us. They wanted to know why Nathan lived with his nan during the week, and Anjie had to explain tearfully that it was a decision she had made in the past when she was involved in a troubled relationship and it had seemed best for him to have stability. After Anjie and I got together, we all decided it was best for him to stay at the same school, which meant staying with his nan. Then they asked Anjie to take a parenting class, and she did so well in it that she was later approached by Bristol City Council, who asked her if she wanted a job teaching the classes! We had a good laugh about that.

I was so lucky to have Anjie through that whole difficult period, as I told her on many occasions.

'If it wasn't for me and my family, you and Nathan could have a peaceful life,' I said to her. 'Are you sure you really want all of this? You didn't sign up for it and I wouldn't judge you if you wanted out.'

But Anjie simply smiled at me. 'Your family is my family,' she said, squeezing my hand. 'I love you, and of course I'll stick by you, no matter what happens.'

That was just another example of Anjie being Anjie – she was the kindest person in the world.

Someone must have told social services that I was a heavy drinker, because they made me do a breathalyser test on a few occasions when I went to pick up the kids. It was annoying. Like most lads I'd had drunken moments in my younger days, but I hardly ever drank in that period. Still, I did the tests willingly to keep the peace and to prove I was a responsible parent. They also quizzed me on my job, my relationship with Anjie and Tanya, and what my relationship was like with the kids. It was exhausting and upsetting, but, with the help of Greg Moss, I did my best to prove that I was a hard-working man who would do anything to support his family.

When the children stayed with us at the weekends, Anjie and I tried to make it as normal as possible for them, often taking them out for the day to take their minds off everything. I was desperate for them to know how wanted they were and how much they were a part of our family. They seemed in bright enough spirits, and the foster parents they were with seemed lovely, so I knew they were being well-treated when they weren't with us. Their foster parents' own children were in the sea cadets, and they took Becky and Danny along for some of the outdoor activities, which they enjoyed, but it wasn't their home and Danny knew it.

'Daddy, why can't I live with you and Anjie?' he asked as I dropped them back at their foster home one Sunday evening. He always looked confused whenever I had to leave without him, and he would hug me hard as I said goodbye. 'I don't want you to go, Daddy,' he said, peering up at me.

It broke my heart, but I tried to reassure him. 'Anjie and I are doing our best to get you and Becky home where you belong. Don't you worry, son,' I said. 'In the meantime, you're going to stay with this nice family and have lots of fun. I'll see you soon, I promise.'

But Danny simply looked up at me with his sad eyes. Walking away from that front door while waving goodbye to my kids felt impossible sometimes, and I had to force myself to put one foot in front of the other. It just made me all the more determined to get them home with me, where they belonged.

Nathan was fourteen at this time, old enough to understand, so Anjie explained to him what we were doing and how important it was to get Danny and Becky out of care. He got on well with Danny and didn't seem to mind the idea of seeing more of him, but when we spoke about Becky coming to live with us he wrinkled his nose in disgust.

'I don't want her to live here with you, Mum,' he moaned. 'She's so loud and annoying.'

'She's only a baby, Nathan,' Anjie explained. 'She'll grow out of all that in time.'

We didn't pay much attention to Nathan's attitude to Becky at the time. There were eleven years between them and he was bound to be irritated by her demanding ways. He was also prone to getting jealous over his mother's affections. Now and again, he would get annoyed if Becky grabbed Anjie's hand, but we always reminded him that she was only little and needed more attention. We guessed that he would probably feel jealous about Becky and Danny coming to stay with his mother full-time, while he only stayed with us on the weekends, but we decided to cross that bridge when we came to it.

It was a long process, but in January 2002 the family court granted us an interim care order for Danny and Becky to stay with us full-time until the final hearing, and in March 2002 we were granted a residence order, meaning we were awarded full custody of them. When we opened the letter I threw my arms around Anjie in celebration. It was over, and we had won. My kids were staying with me. I don't think I've ever felt so relieved in all my life. I vowed to enjoy every future minute I spent with them.

That night, when I put them to bed in our house, knowing that I wouldn't have to drive them back to that foster home ever again, I spent longer than usual tucking them in and reading them a story. Becky was still too young to understand, but I explained things to Danny. 'You'll be living with Anjie and me now,' I said. 'You'll be sleeping here every night. No more living in foster care. That's all over.'

The relief on his face was obvious. He had taken it upon himself to look after his younger sister while they were in care – he was even given an award from social services at South Gloucestershire Council for being such a brilliant older brother. But that was far too much responsibility for a five-year-old to shoulder, so I think he was happy that, from that minute on, he could go back to being a kid again.

One Friday evening, not long after we were awarded custody, we drove Becky and Danny to pick up Nathan from his nan's house. As we waited outside for him, Becky looked out the car window and saw him coming towards us. She opened her mouth and, as clear as day, said the word 'Nathan'.

I swivelled around in shock, as did Anjie. It was the first distinct word she had ever uttered.

Nathan jumped in the car and looked round at us, puzzled by our stunned faces.

'What's the matter?' he asked.

'Becky just said your name,' I told him.

'Yeah, right!' he sneered. 'Becky doesn't even talk yet. As if she said my name!'

'Seriously, Nath, Becky said your name,' Anjie said. 'You should be flattered. She's never said anything before.'

Nathan turned to look at Becky, sitting there in her car seat, and he was obviously surprised.

We spent the rest of the day trying to get her to say it again, but she wouldn't.

CHAPTER 3
HAPPY FAMILIES

TUESDAY, 3 MARCH 2015

Despair for Becky's family follows discovery of dismembered body: *Shockwaves were felt across Bristol today following the discovery of mutilated body parts thought to belong to missing schoolgirl Becky Watts. Police believe the teenager's corpse, which was found at a house in Barton Court, Barton Hill, around a mile and a half from her home, had been cut up. Becky's family are said to be 'in hell' and 'completely broken' after hearing the harrowing news, which ends any hopes they had of seeing her alive again. Becky's dad, Darren Galsworthy, and stepmother, Anjie, described the latest development as 'too much to bear'. The grisly find, which is understood to have followed a tip-off yesterday evening, comes 12 days after the 16-year-old first vanished. The body was driven away in a private ambulance before a team of forensic experts went into the mid-terrace property. As officers continue their investigations, police have put up a white tent outside the house, which is close to a number of* *other properties that have already been searched as part of the operation. They've also seized a black Vauxhall Zafira. Today, police were granted a further 24 hours to question a 28-year-old man and a 21-year-old woman arrested over the weekend in connection with Becky's disappearance. Following the discovery of the body parts, they have arrested a further four people on suspicion of assisting an offender.*

From the minute we knew Becky and Danny were permanently staying under our roof, I felt deliriously happy. I know it sounds corny, but I just loved seeing everybody together like that. On weekends I'd jump out of bed and rush downstairs to make us all a hearty breakfast, then we'd go out somewhere in the car.

As soon as we got our residence order for Danny and Becky, Anjie and I rushed out to buy them some new bunk beds and things for their room. I grabbed a few cuddly toys for Becky and some games for Danny – although I knew he would probably want to spend most of his time playing on the PlayStation with Nathan.

Becky had a few favourite toys, but she mainly enjoyed playing with her dolls and doing arts and crafts. She would often rush over to show me something she had made for me, perhaps a clay model or a drawing. She occasionally asked me to play dollies with her. I tried it once or twice, but I have to admit I was never very good at it, so we usually ended up playing basketball in the back garden. From an early age she also loved books. Her favourite bedtime story was 'Little Red Riding Hood', and she used to make me read it to her almost every night. Once she was staying with us, she began speaking more and more, until she was chatting so much that we forgot she'd ever been slow to start.

For Becky's fourth birthday in June 2002, I spent the best part of a week making her her very own playhouse in the garden. I had to tell Becky I was building a shed, as she kept peeking around the back door to see what I was doing. I got some aluminium sheets from work and carefully created a miniature house, complete with windows and doors. It had a latch on the door, windowboxes full of flowers, and a velux window on the roof. Inside, I laid lino and arranged a little table and chairs, her dolls and a play cooker. I painted everything pink and purple, Becky's favourite colours, and piled her presents inside for her to wake up to on her birthday morning.

When the day arrived, I carried her out to the back garden and pointed at the little house.

'That's yours,' I said. 'I made it for you.'

Becky furrowed her brow and looked at me suspiciously. 'No, Daddy, you told me that was your new shed.'

'I said that so it could be a surprise,' I said, laughing. 'It's far too small for me – it's your very own playhouse. This is your birthday present. Look – all your other gifts are inside!'

It took a moment for the penny to drop, and then Becky beamed with delight and squirmed out of my arms. She ran straight into the house and sat down to open the rest of her presents. Later that day, she dragged poor Danny in there to play 'house' for hours. He even had to eat his tea in there with her! He was less than impressed, but he could see it was worth it for the look of joy on Becky's face.

That night, when I tucked her into bed, she smiled up at me in her adorable way.

'Have you enjoyed your birthday, sweetheart?' I asked.

She nodded sleepily before muttering, 'I love you, Daddy,' and nodding off. Those were the moments I lived for every day.

Our lives had been completely put on hold while we fought for Becky and Danny to live with us, so that summer I wanted us to have as much fun as possible. I pushed my overdraft right to its limit and I added quite a bit to my credit card bill too – but it didn't matter, because finally we were all together. That July, the five of us went on a week-long holiday to Littlesea, Weymouth. I bought a second-hand caravan and we pitched up in a big green field and spent hours and hours of quality time together. During the days we played adventure golf and tennis, and I taught Becky and Danny to swim. In the evenings, we made a campfire and toasted marshmallows over it. Once the kids were asleep, Anjie and I had a drink under the stars.

One night, I looked across to see her smiling at me.

'Well, that's it now, love,' I said. 'It's the five of us together from now on. Lots more memories to make.'

As she reached across and squeezed my hand, I couldn't remember ever feeling happier.

There were always going to be some teething troubles, bringing together three kids with such a big age gap between them, but on the whole it wasn't too bad. Danny and Nathan got on fine from the start, but Becky continued to get on Nathan's nerves sometimes. One of his hobbies was painting Warhammer fantasy models. He used to sit at the coffee table in the living room for hours on end, carefully painting these miniature fighters from make-believe worlds with paintbrushes that were so well-used they only had two or three bristles left. He was brilliant at it, and I was always impressed by his patience – much more than I've ever had! Sometimes he would try to get us all involved, and Anjie, Danny and I would do our best, squinting down at the little figurines and trying to keep a steady hand. However, little four-year-old Becky wasn't so careful. Once, she toddled over to see what we were doing, grabbed a model, dunked it in a pot of paint and held it out to Nathan, smiling proudly. Of course, she had ruined the model completely and Nathan was furious, but her eagerness to please him from an early age was there. Becky clearly adored him.

As time went on, Becky grew more and more attached to Anjie, and one day, when she was five, we realised she didn't entirely understand the relationships in our 'blended family'. I'd been on the phone to Tanya and I'm afraid the conversation had got a bit heated. After I hung up, Danny looked across at me from where he was sitting on the sofa.

'Who was that?' he asked.

'Oh, just your mother,' I answered.

'Do you have to speak to her like that?' he asked. Danny always protected his mother. I think he just wished we would all get on with each other, which is only natural.

'She's playing silly buggers yet again,' I said. 'You should have heard the way she spoke to me.'

Becky – who was lying across Anjie's lap – grinned at Danny. 'My mum's better than your mum! My mum's better than your mum!' she sang, trying to tease him.

Danny looked at her, incredulous. 'My mum *is* your mum!' he shouted. 'Oh Becky, you are stupid. She's your mum too, you idiot.'

Poor Becky looked crestfallen. She looked at me first, uncertainty in her eyes, and then up at Anjie. 'He's lying, isn't he?' she asked.

Anjie glanced at me, a worried look on her face. We'd always known the moment would come, but we'd never really sat down and talked about how we were going to handle it.

'You're my mum, aren't you?' Becky continued to Anjie, desperate for it to be true. 'Did it really hurt when I came out of your tummy?'

I knew we had to tell her the truth, so I decided to grab the bull by the horns. I crouched down next to Becky while Anjie wrapped her arms around her. Becky sat, listening silently as I explained that Tanya was her mum, not Anjie.

'You never actually came out of Anjie's tummy, darling,' I said soothingly. 'Danny's right, you've both got the same mum.'

Suddenly, Becky let out an ear-piercing scream. She burst into tears, looking utterly devastated. Anjie tried to console her, but she squirmed away and bolted up the stairs to her bedroom.

As soon as the door slammed behind her, Anjie burst into tears too. 'I wish she *was* mine,' she sobbed. 'She feels like she's mine.'

'I know, love,' I said, giving her a hug. 'She'll be OK, I promise.' I hated seeing Anjie upset almost as much as I hated seeing any of my kids upset.

But Anjie knew how to handle it. She went upstairs and gently knocked on Becky's door. I heard Becky let her in – and that's where they stayed for the rest of the day. They cuddled up together, talking, reading and watching television. I brought them their dinner on a tray that evening, and then at night

Anjie slept in Becky's bed with her. That seemed to do the trick because the next morning she was right as rain.

She came bouncing down the stairs and beamed up at me the way she always had. 'I've got both a mum and an Anjie,' she chirped. 'And I love my Anjie.'

Sometimes, she'd come out with stuff like that – things that completely melted my heart. From then on, she drew pictures of the whole family together, and when she was finished she held them up proudly to show Anjie and me.

'Look, Daddy,' she said. 'I've got two mums, two brothers and a dad.'

'Yes, you have,' I said, ruffling her hair. 'Aren't you the luckiest girl around?'

Her relationship with Anjie went from strength to strength after that. They spent a lot of time together, baking, shopping, and sewing – all the things that mothers and daughters normally do. Anjie had always wanted a daughter, and now it seemed that at last she had one.

In 2003, Becky started at Summerhill Primary School, where Danny was already a pupil. It was just a few streets away from where we lived, and we hoped that she would settle in quickly and enjoy her time there. Instead, she screamed her head off when Anjie tried to leave her there, with the upshot that she had to hang around and help the teachers, just to make Becky stay. At home she had always been fearless, but at school we were surprised to find that she seemed to struggle to bond with most other kids. She had one close friend, called Hope, and she also became close to her cousin, Brooke, Anjie's sister's daughter, who was three years older than her. She might only have had two friends, but Becky was fiercely loyal to them from the start, something she shared with her old man.

When the summer holidays arrived it was always the start of a chaotic but fun-filled time in our house. We didn't have a lot of money, so we never went abroad, but we always went off in the caravan for a week or two. We'd start by picking Nathan up, complete with his massive rucksack, then get on the motorway to our destination of choice, usually Brean Sands, Weymouth or Minehead.

As soon as we got there, Danny and Nathan would be off, getting up to mischief as all boys do, and Becky would beg to go to the swimming pool. She was a proper water baby. She adored swimming, and by the time she was five she was incredibly confident in the water. She could happily spend all day in the pool at our campsite, and it was always a nightmare getting her out again. She loved it so much I built a 25-foot-long and 12-foot-wide pool in our back garden for her to splash about in. Her feet couldn't touch the bottom but she was absolutely thrilled, and every day when it was warm enough she'd strip off straight after school, tug on her swimming costume and jump in.

Becky's favourite place to go on holiday was definitely Butlin's. She loved it there, because there were so many things for kids to do that they never got bored. It was great for Anjie and me too, as the kids could entertain themselves, leaving us with some valuable adult time.

By the time Becky was five, Nathan was sixteen and old enough to babysit her and Danny while we went for a drink. He liked to earn some pocket money and show us how grown up he was. I was proud of the effort he made with his siblings on these occasions. He even volunteered to take Becky into the ball pit a few times to thrash around in the colourful plastic balls, and he often took Danny on the water slides. I remember one occasion in particular that always makes me chuckle. Anjie and I were in the pool with Becky, waiting for the boys to come down the slide, and we noticed that they were taking an awfully long time.

'What on earth is the hold-up?' I muttered to Anjie. Then I noticed that Nathan was laughing – holding onto his sides with laughter, in fact – while six-year-old Danny had a face like thunder. After a while, they came back down the steps, with Danny looking like he might burst into tears.

'What's the matter, boy?' I asked, thinking some kid had picked on him. 'Why didn't you come down the slide?'

'Some fat woman got stuck.' Nathan howled with laughter. 'They sent everyone back down the steps. They've had to call for help to get her down.'

We all watched with amusement as they tried to drag this poor woman down the slide by her feet. Danny was upset to miss his turn on the slide, but he saw the funny side in the end and he had another go later. I know it sounds odd, but that is one of my favourite memories of us on holiday as a family: all five of us standing there, laughing at something silly.

One of the best things about Bristol is that there are loads of family friendly events held all year round. One of our favourites was the Bristol Balloon Fiesta. Becky loved watching the hot-air balloons take off and fill the sky, and all three kids adored the fairground. Nathan always took Becky and Danny on the rides for me because I was far too petrified to get on them myself. As an engineer, I could see everything that could possibly go wrong with the mechanics of a ride. It would make me feel sick just watching, but I couldn't bear to spoil their fun by banning them from going on.

'I'll just wait here, Bex. Nath will take you,' I'd call, waving them off. I usually stood, rigid with fear, for the whole three minutes while they whizzed around, screaming their heads off with delight.

Of course, life with children isn't always about treating them – I had to do a great deal of teaching and coaching too. When Becky was six years old I taught her to ride a bike by slyly removing her stabiliser wheels before she climbed on. I gave her a shove and was thrilled when she sailed off down the path without them. Of course, as soon as she realised they were missing she fell over with a look of surprise and confusion on her face.

'My wheels have fallen off, Daddy!' she shouted, but she soon got up and tried again. She was always a very determined character.

When she started learning her times tables at school, I would test her while she was on her trampoline in the back garden. She would bounce up and down while I sat on the step and shouted out: 'Five times three? Six times four?' That was our unique way of doing homework!

Becky was never happier than when she was outside, and she and I loved going for long country walks. Although Bristol is a busy city, it is blessed with lots of countryside around about and some fantastic public parks. One of our favourite places for a stroll was St George's Park, which wasn't far from our house. Becky would pull on her wellies and trot along by my side, her little hand in mine, but she did insist on stopping every five minutes to examine any flowers or bugs she could find. She loved climbing trees or fishing for tadpoles in the pond with her fishing net. We would collect them in jam jars and watch as they turned into frogs – something my father used to do with me.

Becky wasn't the type of girl who was afraid of insects. When she caught head lice at school – an ongoing battle for Anjie and me, as she was always coming home with a new crop of them – she'd ask me to show her the little critters I combed out of her hair. She was fascinated by them, examining them under her microscope and even labelling them as 'my little friends'. It made me shudder with disgust, I have to say.

As she got older, her personality just got stronger – complete with an attitude on occasion! Once, when she was six years old, she finished her dinner and waited expectantly at the table for dessert. I realised that I didn't have anything else to give her, as I hadn't done the food shopping yet. I was hoping that she would get bored and play with her toys, as Nathan and Danny had done, but she stayed at the table, staring at me.

'Daddy, where's my pudding?' she asked sweetly.

'Sorry, Bex, no pudding tonight,' I said. 'Daddy hasn't been to the supermarket yet.'

The dismay on her face was almost comical. 'No pudding?' she exclaimed. 'But I ate all my dinner!'

'You can have extra pudding tomorrow for being a good girl,' I said, chuckling.

I didn't expect her to react so violently, but she threw herself dramatically from her seat and ran out of the room, returning a few seconds later with the phone.

'This is child abuse,' she announced. 'I'm phoning Childline.'

I couldn't help bursting out laughing, which only infuriated Becky more.

'I'll do it, Daddy!' she shouted, waving the phone in the air. 'I'll call them and tell them you wouldn't give me any pudding.'

That just set me off even more, of course.

Becky couldn't stop herself cracking a smile, and soon she was in stitches too – that's just how it was with us. Even when one of us started out genuinely annoyed about something, in the end we'd both be falling about in hysterics.

Becky enjoyed trying to push me to the limit, as all kids do. In particular, she liked to set me 'challenges', something she started when she was as young as four. We were both very stubborn, and the father–daughter rivalry between us was hilarious to witness. Becky would set me at least one 'challenge' a week and, not wanting to be beaten, I would try my best to complete her mission before setting her a challenge too. Anjie would just roll her eyes and leave us to it.

Becky's challenges included making me do cartwheels, backflips and handstands. Now, I was 14 stone at the time and had quite a large belly, so the sight of me trying to spin myself around and land on my feet again was not pretty. Becky would howl with laughter at my failures then gracefully demonstrate the move herself.

Much later, my challenges to her included eating an entire blazing hot curry without pausing for breath (she was in her teens by this time, I hasten to add!). I labelled this the 'Atomic Curry Challenge', and Becky was so keen to win she even ate a whole red chilli to top it off. Afterwards, she had to drink about a gallon of milk to cool her mouth. I recorded that particular challenge on my phone while shaking with laughter, and that video has come to mean so much to me.

Becky absolutely loved animals, and we spent many family days out at Bristol Zoo and various wildlife parks. No matter what animal it was, she adored them all. By the time she was thirteen she had so many little animals living in her room it was like something from a Disney film. She had a terrapin, a rabbit called Buster, two white rats, two Siberian dwarf hamsters and three regular hamsters.

Becky designed a three-storey mansion for Buster to live in, which took me a week to build. It had a room for his food, a sitting area, a bedroom and another level on top with a glass window. It also had stairs to the ground floor so he could run around outside in his very own little garden. Never did any rabbit live in such luxury! Despite this, Becky then decided that Buster should come inside to stay with her and the other animals in her bedroom. It was ridiculous in the end – the smell from the cages became overpowering and we had to shout at her to move Buster outside again. Of course, she had promised at the outset that she would look after the animals and clean out the cages, but guess who ended up doing it? That's right, Anjie and me.

Eventually, Becky asked us for what she called a 'real' pet, and we took her to Bristol dogs' home. Surprisingly, there was a litter of kittens there and she ended up staring at one kitten for so long that we let her have him. He was jet black except for four white paws and a white chin, and she called him Marley.

In the dogs' home, Marley appeared sweet and innocent-looking, but as soon as he came in the front door of our house he started causing absolute mayhem. We soon realised he was a complete psycho cat. He would climb the walls and curtains and claw his way around the furniture. Of course, Becky thought this was hilarious. One of his favourite games was to hide until I walked past, then he would jump out and land on my back, his sharp claws digging into my flesh. He would hang on for dear life while I ran around trying to shake him off. It was almost as if Becky had trained him to do this, because she would roll about in fits of laughter while I grappled with him.

Marley was very much Becky's cat. He never showed the rest of us any affection whatsoever, but he would purr and gaze up at Becky lovingly. He liked his freedom during the day but would always go into Becky's room for a cuddle in the evenings, probably terrorising the hamsters who were huddled behind the bars of their cages.

During my childhood, Christmas was always a disappointment, so I made a huge effort for my own children. Anjie and I would pull out all the stops to decorate the house and make it as festive as possible. She would bake lots of treats and, every Christmas Eve, I would dress up as Santa. I'd put on a padded red-and-white costume, complete with little spectacles and a big white beard, making Anjie and Nathan giggle. I would wait until Danny and Becky were drifting off to sleep before sneaking into their rooms with their stockings, which were bursting with treats. If they were already asleep, I'd quietly sing Christmas songs and jiggle about in order to get them to stir. I'd watch them breathing fast in their excitement and trying to stay as still as possible when they realised 'Santa' was there.

After the presents were opened on Christmas morning, we'd visit my nan, May, who had more treats for everyone, then return home so I could cook our Christmas dinner. The children would spend the afternoon playing with their new toys, and Anjie and I would have a drink and toast another good year.

We discussed having children of our own many times, but Anjie had previously suffered an ectopic pregnancy, which left her with only one fallopian tube, and it just didn't happen. We paid for fertility tests and considered having IVF, but the cost was so high that we eventually decided against it. That's why it was so lovely that Becky became like the daughter Anjie never had. It was a huge part of why they were so close. The way we saw it, we had three healthy children between us, so we just counted our blessings. We were happy and that was the main thing. I felt like the richest man in the world.

CHAPTER 4

MY BOY

WEDNESDAY, 4 MARCH 2015

Schoolgirl Becky Watts's stepbrother charged with her murder: *The stepbrother of Bristol schoolgirl Becky Watts – whose mutilated body parts were discovered earlier this week – has been charged with her murder. Nathan Matthews, 28, lived with his girlfriend, 21-year-old Shauna Hoare, not far from a house in the Barton Hill area where the teenager's remains were found by police on Tuesday, almost a fortnight after her disappearance. The couple, both of Cotton Mill Lane, were first arrested in connection with the case four days ago before being re-arrested on Monday on suspicion of murder. Yesterday afternoon, detectives were given a further 24 hours to interview them, before charges were brought against Mr Matthews this afternoon. Mr Matthews is Anjie Galsworthy's son from a previous relationship. Miss Hoare, who goes by the name Phillips on social media, was charged at the same time. A photo of the pair wearing fancy dress emerged today and has been spreading quickly on social* *media. Both were remanded in custody overnight and are due to appear at Bristol Magistrates' Court tomorrow morning. Police have also been given more time to question another three men and a woman arrested on suspicion of assisting an offender.*

As time went on, my relationship with Nathan blossomed and we became much more like father and son. Nathan didn't ever see his biological father, so he began to look up to me for advice and support as he hit his teenage years. I knew this was a huge responsibility, so I vowed to try my hardest to instil a sense of right and wrong and to teach him the importance of hard work.

Nathan's main interest was computers. He was brilliant with technology, and I was always amazed at how fast he was with a keyboard. He was forever sorting out things for his mum and me on the computer, and he knew all about the latest gadgets and computer games, much to Danny's delight. Despite the eight-year age difference between them, Danny and Nathan were thick as thieves. They would spend almost every weekend in Nathan's room, playing on the PlayStation and generally larking about. Occasionally, they invited me in to play with them as I passed the bedroom door. I quickly learned, however, that they only got me involved so they could laugh at how terrible I was. I would get really wound up trying to play the car-racing games, and the pair of them would crease up in hysterics whenever I crashed. Even Anjie would get in on the act, standing by the door and commenting on how rubbish I was. Nathan was very competitive and liked to try to beat me at everything. On the rare occasions when I actually won a game against him, he would sulk for hours afterwards. He could be a bit of a sore loser!

As well as trying to beat me at computer games, Nathan would enjoy trying to outwit me in other ways. He was always trying to get one up on me and would tease me mercilessly, but I would give as good as I got. It was all friendly banter. Nathan had a good sense of humour and enjoyed having me as a sparring partner. As time went on, he would try to get Danny and Becky to join in, and then the three of them would gang up on me. He particularly used to enjoy writing messages on my car when it was dirty. I often found things like 'Watch out, blind old fart driving' on my back window, while Danny, Becky and Nathan rolled around laughing.

Nathan wasn't always so cocky, though. Now and again he still needed his parents. Once, when he was twelve years old, he caught the bus to Kingswood – about a mile from where we lived – to spend his birthday money on a computer game. After buying the game, he forgot which bus to catch home and burst into tears. I received a frantic call from his mother and raced from work to pick him up. He looked a little sheepish when he saw me, but he was very relieved.

When they weren't cooped up in their room, Nathan and Danny liked to go out on their bikes, so when Becky was old enough to keep up, the whole family often went for long rides on the Bristol and Bath Railway Path, which is specially for walkers and cyclists. Although Nathan wasn't into team sports, he was interested in shooting and archery. I had a couple of air rifles and an archery kit, and the two of us used to spend hours in the back garden together, messing about with them. We challenged each other to hit various targets and competed to get the best score. When he was thirteen I bought him his very own air rifle for his birthday, and I've never seen him so happy. He wanted to go out and shoot with it immediately, and soon grew to be pretty good at it.

Much like Becky, Nathan was a bit of a loner at school. Despite being quite a confident kid, he didn't make friends easily, so when he was fourteen I enlisted him in the Army cadets. I had done this myself at his age and thoroughly enjoyed it. It taught me a lot of self-discipline and gave me a sense of pride, and I thought it would do the same for Nathan. Of course, he already had an interest in guns, so he was thrilled when I suggested the idea. I think he was hoping he would make some friends there too – which he did. Being in the cadets gave Nathan a good sense of being a part of the community, as they were always out and about fundraising and doing charity work, such as packing bags for customers in supermarkets.

After a few months he got the opportunity to go away to camp with the squadron on Salisbury Plain, a military training ground. He was thrilled and couldn't wait to go, so I agreed to give him a lift there.

'Thanks for the lift. See you soon, Dar,' he said, jumping out of the car with his heavy rucksack on his back.

I chuckled as I waved him off because I knew from experience what he would have to endure in the week ahead. He had 5.30 a.m. starts, 10-mile treks and lots of drill-training to look forward to. But I also knew that he would have a great time with his new friends; it would do him a world of good.

When I picked him up at the end of the week, he looked absolutely knackered. He slumped into the passenger seat of the car, unable to raise the energy to speak.

'You look wiped out, son,' I commented. He simply nodded in reply, and went straight to bed when we got in. After a few days of recovery, he was full of beans again, and I overheard him telling Danny how much he had enjoyed it.

'It was amazing,' he said, as they sat on his bed. 'We got to shoot with real guns and everything.'

'Wow!' Danny said, hanging on his every word. Danny really looked up to his older brother, and I felt a little surge of pride that Nathan had enjoyed doing something I had loved when I was a kid. He stayed in the cadets for three years and then joined the Reserves for another two years after that.

At school, Nathan was quite average, never academically brilliant. He was probably best known among his fellow pupils for his wheeling and dealing – buying computer games and sweets and selling them on at a profit. When he was coming to the end of his time at his secondary school, The Grange in Warmley, his grades started to slip. Anjie and I grew concerned about his GCSEs, so we paid for a private tutor for six weeks to give him some extra help. It worked – Nathan's marks improved dramatically and he managed to pass six of his exams.

As a reward for the turnaround in his grades, the school gave him three tickets to watch a Bristol Rovers match. As a family we weren't really into football, but Nathan, Danny and I went to watch the game together and, surprisingly, we had a blast.

'Now look, boys,' I said as we stood in the family section of the stadium waiting for the game to begin. 'That man over there is the referee and he will constantly make the wrong decision. We don't like him.'

'No, we don't,' Nathan agreed.

The three of us spent the whole game shouting colourful abuse at the referee. It was hilarious but, looking back, it's a complete wonder that we didn't get thrown out.

During the months leading up to Nathan's sixteenth birthday, he nagged Anjie and me for a moped, so finally we agreed to pay for him to do his compulsory basic training (CBT). Beforehand, I took him to buy some leathers and a helmet. I had owned multiple motorbikes in my lifetime, and was keen to impress on him that safety comes first.

'You will get a bike one day,' I told him as he tried it all on. 'But let's start with the protective kit, shall we?'

On his birthday I drove him to take his training and his CBT test. It was a viciously cold day in January, and as I dropped him off I wished him luck. While he was doing it, I waited in the car. It took hours and hours, but I didn't want to drive home just in case he needed me.

At last, he appeared and started to walk towards my car looking really ill. He was pale as a sheet and I could tell he was frozen to the bone. The intense training followed by the test had completely exhausted him.

I held my breath as he got into the car sighing. I was worried that he hadn't got through it but he turned to me with a huge grin on his face.

'I passed!' he shouted, and I punched the air in delight.

'Well done, son!' I said. 'Yes! Now let's get you home to warm up. You look like you've got hypothermia.'

The pride I felt at that moment was so immense, it couldn't have been any greater if he was my biological son. I was just delighted for him. As a surprise, I had secretly spent around £2,000 on a moped, which was waiting for him at home. I quickly phoned Anjie and told her the good news. She knew that her job was to wheel the bike out of the shed and into the garden for Nathan to see when we got back. It was all wrapped up and ready, in the hope that he would pass that day.

When we jumped out of the car, Anjie and I grinned at each other, waiting for Nathan to see his bike. To our disappointment, he walked straight past it.

'Hot cup of tea please, Mum,' he muttered to Anjie. He didn't even look at the moped.

'Here's your bike, Nath,' I called. 'It's all legal. You're free to ride it now if you want.'

He turned and looked at the moped for a few moments before answering. 'Nah, I'll go out on it tomorrow. Thanks Dar, thanks Mum.'

The poor sod was too frozen to think about anything other than getting warm again. I didn't blame him, to be honest. Once indoors, he sat in front of the gas fire for the rest of the evening, trying to get the feeling back in his hands and feet.

The next day, however, he woke up and immediately got dressed in his leathers, ready to jump on his new moped. He asked Anjie to take pictures of him posing next to it, and he was beaming as he zipped off down the road. He looked so happy and confident. I felt really proud of him that day, and I could tell Angie did too.

After that, Nathan rode his bike all over Bristol, and he made some new friends as he met other moped owners. I used to laugh as I saw them all riding past the house together, as if they were in a pack.

When he left school, Nathan trained as an electrician at City of Bristol College, and owning the moped helped him to get an evening job as a delivery boy for Domino's Pizza. He also worked at Sainsbury's on weekends. At that point, he was showing all the qualities I had wanted so much to give him. He was hardworking, dedicated, and he was earning his own money.

'He's like a mini-me,' I bragged to Anjie as we watched him ride off to work one day. She couldn't have been prouder of her son, and I was chuffed to bits with the man he was becoming.

A few months later, Anjie called me in a blind panic while I was at work. She was such a blubbering mess that at first it was hard to make sense of what she was saying.

'Nathan's been in an accident,' she said, sobbing down the phone. 'Someone drove out of a junction and straight into him.'

'Is he all right?' I asked, my heart missing a beat.

'Yes, but he's in hospital,' she said. 'He was taken from the scene by an ambulance, but his bike is still by the side of the road. Can you go out and find it?'

'Right, OK, love,' I said. 'Try not to panic.'

Nathan had been riding through Kingswood at about 35 mph when some idiot drove straight into him. He was thrown over the bonnet of the car on impact and ended up crumpled on the road, screaming in pain. His handlebars had smashed into his stomach and he had snapped his wrist as he landed but, other than that, he was OK. I silently thanked our lucky stars that I had made clear to him the importance of wearing appropriate protection while out riding. His helmet and leathers probably saved his life that day.

I left work immediately. My friend Andy Collins drove me in his van to search for the moped, which we discovered on the side of the road. I was horrified because it was completely folded in half. I felt sick as I loaded it into the back of the van, thinking about how much worse the accident could have been.

Later that day, we went to collect Nathan from hospital. He was in pain and feeling very sorry for himself.

'Come on, boy,' I said putting my arm around his shoulder. 'Let's get you home. You've had enough excitement for one day.'

'I thought he was going to have a go at me about the state of the bike,' he told his mother, who laughed.

'You are far more important to him than any bike,' she replied. 'Darren cares about you – he doesn't give a damn about the bike. That can be replaced – you can't.'

'Oh.' Nathan replied. 'All right, then.'

I think he needed reassurance every now and again that, as far as I was concerned, he was my son. He gave me a little more respect for a while after that, before we reverted to our normal relationship, which involved lots of banter and teasing of each other.

When Nathan turned seventeen, he asked if he could learn to drive a car. I was fully behind this, because Anjie and I had been shaken up pretty badly by the moped incident. I figured that he would be a lot safer in a car. We paid for lessons with a driving instructor because I knew I would never have the patience to teach anyone. Many moons ago, I did once try to give Anjie a driving lesson, and the hour I spent in the car with her scarred us both for life!

Nathan was so keen, he took to driving like a duck to water. He had absolutely no problems at all. When it came to his practical test, I drove him to the test centre and waited for him, and once again he walked out of there grinning like a Cheshire cat.

'Let me guess – you passed?' I asked.

He nodded in reply.

'Well done, son,' I said, starting the engine. 'I'm proud of you. You're doing really well – but you're still not driving *my* car!'

Nathan always underplayed his successes and would never let on that he was pleased I was proud of him, but you could see it on his face. He couldn't stop smiling all the way home. Within a few weeks, he rushed out and bought his first car – a sporty-looking white Renault Clio – with the money he was earning from his three jobs. I was less than impressed with this purchase, as when I gave it a test drive I could tell it was falling apart. The gearbox was on its way out, the clutch only engaged when my foot was a couple of inches off the floor, and there was rainwater leaking in, causing the electrics to fail.

'This car is junk,' I told Nathan, but he just crossed his arms and huffed at me.

'I like it; it looks cool,' he replied. It turned out to be one of those things I needed to let him find out for himself. After a few days he started moaning his head off about the car not running properly.

'That's what happens if you don't listen to your old man,' I told him, making things ten times worse.

Nathan had a few cars after that. His pride and joy was a black Vauxhall Astra, which cost him £6,000. He was completely in love with it. He would spend hours polishing and tinkering with it in front of our house. And then, one blazing hot day, when he had only had it for two months, I accidentally did something I'm not proud of.

The pollen count was unusually high so my hayfever was really bad. I was driving home after doing some errands when I was suddenly blinded by a strong burst of sunshine and had a sneezing fit, both at the same time. I tried to pull onto my drive-way, but instead of hitting the brake, I slammed my foot on the accelerator and smashed straight into the front of Nathan's new car. I was mortified.

Nathan managed to get it fixed thanks to his insurance, but I wasn't his favourite person for a while after that, and I can't say I blamed him.

Working on cars ultimately proved a bonding experience for us, though. Nathan had been completely obsessed with them from the very first moment he got behind the wheel. I knew quite a lot about motorbike engines so I was able to get to grips with a car engine pretty quickly, and we spent a lot of time tinkering with our respective cars on Sundays. It wasn't uncommon for us to be working on a car all day long, while Anjie brought out drinks and snacks for us. It's those Sundays that I really cherished with Nathan. As he approached eighteen we got a lot closer. In many ways I had more in common with him than I did with Danny. Danny was such an easy kid that you never knew he was there, but he preferred hanging out with his friends to his dad. As he matured, Nathan still remained pals with Danny, and he started to make more of an effort with Becky. When I watched him, I often thought that Anjie, his nan and I had all done a good job of raising him. I looked forward to seeing what he would make of his life.

The day he turned eighteen, I knocked on his bedroom door in the morning to give him a card.

'Happy birthday, son. I'm taking you out for a pint tonight,' I told him.

Nathan had never drunk or done drugs as a teenager – none of our kids did, as we wouldn't tolerate that sort of behaviour – so he looked genuinely excited to go out for his first pint.

Our first stop was The Pied Horse, my regular haunt, and as soon as we got there I ordered a pint and put it in front of him.

'Big moment, this – your first legal drink.' I winked at him while he took a sip. 'Happy birthday, boy.'

We spent the next few hours playing darts and pool, just him and me. I took him to three more local pubs before we went home and he enjoyed himself immensely, but he proved to be a bit out of his depth. After about eight pints, he was completely hammered and staggering as we headed home together. We tried to keep quiet as we got in, but we almost woke the whole house as we crashed through the front door.

When I got into bed, Anjie sat up and whispered, 'What have you done to my son, Darren?'

I laughed. 'He did it to himself, Anj. He'll be suffering in the morning.'

And, sure enough, I was right. I woke up bright and early and started cooking the family a fry-up, when a bleary-eyed Nathan walked down the stairs.

'All right, boy?' I asked him, chuckling. 'Bit worse for wear, are we?'

'I'm dying, Dar,' he croaked as he slumped on the sofa.

'I've got just the thing for you. This will sort you right out,' I said, handing him a plate loaded with food.

Nathan took one look at the greasy fry-up in front of him and turned green. He looked at me in alarm, handed back the plate and bolted up the stairs to be sick. I was laughing so hard I almost dropped his breakfast on the floor. It took him three days to recover fully, and it was something I brought up during our banter for years after. I hadn't set out to make him ill, but as far as I was concerned it was a valuable lesson for him to learn.

Even though he was officially an adult, Nathan still occasionally needed his old man to help get him out of scrapes. A few months after his eighteenth, I was driving over to pick him up in Warmley when I spotted him standing outside one of the shops, waiting for me. I was just about to toot my horn to get his attention when I saw a six-foot-tall guy suddenly grab him by the throat and push him against a nearby wall. I didn't have to think twice: I swerved the car into the kerb and turned off the engine before sprinting across the road.

There was a girl standing nearby, screaming, 'That's not him! Get off him!'

'What the hell do you think you're doing to my son?' I bellowed, before using all my strength to yank the guy off him and punch him hard in the jaw. He dropped to the ground and I turned to Nathan.

'Get in the car,' I yelled, and we legged it. The guy was bigger than both of us put together, and I didn't want to risk finding out what he might do when he got back up again.

Once I had driven away, I turned my attention to Nathan. He was visibly shaken.

'You all right, son?' I asked. 'What was all that about?'

'No idea,' he replied. 'I don't even know the guy.'

I was fuming that anyone would dare touch him when all he was doing was standing innocently in the street. As we drove back, Nathan turned to me.

'Thanks, Dar,' he mumbled.

'You don't have to thank me,' I answered. 'I was only defending my boy.'

That's exactly what Nathan was to me – my boy. To him, I was the only father figure he had ever known. We'd had our ups and downs, but on the whole I thought we had a good father–son relationship. Our blended family showed time and time again that DNA meant nothing. We supported and looked out for each other no matter what.

Although we generally got on well during Nathan's teenage years, we also locked horns sometimes. All teenagers tend to behave appallingly from time to time, and Nathan was no exception. One of these incidents occurred when his nan Margaret and granddad Christopher went away for a few days. Unbeknown to us, Nathan decided to have a huge party in their house, inviting all his friends.

Anjie received a frantic phone call from him the next day.

'Don't be mad, Mum, but I had a party last night and it got out of hand,' he blurted out. 'You have to help me put it right.'

Anjie hung up the phone and looked at me, shaking her head in despair. 'We're going over to my mum's house,' she said. 'Grab some bin bags.'

When we got there, I couldn't believe what I was seeing. It was a complete bombsite. The inside doors were completely ripped off their hinges, the sofas were slashed, there were picture frames smashed on the floor and fag butts stomped into the carpet. There was the telltale stink of spilled alcohol and pools of vomit everywhere. I felt sick just looking at it. The worst thing was, Nathan's nan was due to get home that evening.

'We haven't got enough time to clean all this up!' I shouted. 'What the hell were you thinking?'

'Please,' he pleaded in desperation. 'I have to fix it. *Please* help me.'

It was obvious that Nathan was completely bricking it, so I started to feel sorry for him and we agreed to help. Luckily, I had my toolkit in the car, so I managed to fix a few of the doors while Anjie and Nathan got to work cleaning up. We spent a whopping nine hours in that house trying to sort it all out. I smuggled away dozens of bags of damaged items and rubbish in the boot of my car. We did a pretty good job, but Nathan still had to face the music when his grandparents got home. There were too many broken items to pretend it never happened.

'Sorry, boy, but you have to face them on your own,' I said when we had done all we could. 'The rest is down to you now.'

Needless to say, Nathan had an almighty tongue-lashing from his grandparents when they returned. Strangely enough, after that Anjie and I never accepted his offers to look after our house while we were away!

Nathan was eighteen when he started seeing his first girlfriend, but it only lasted a few months. He often complained to us that all her friends were male rather than female. Despite his confidence around his family and close friends, I think he was quite insecure when it came to girls. He certainly seemed to get jealous very easily.

When he and his girlfriend broke up, Nathan started to act very oddly. He insisted that she owed him money, and he used to hang around outside her house in his car. Anjie and I were horrified when we heard he had been moved on by the police.

'Will you stop stalking her, boy?' I said angrily when he got home. 'You're being creepy. Just walk away, Nathan. Sort yourself out.'

'She owes me £400, Dar,' he mumbled.

To be honest, I think the money was just an excuse. I think he would have hung around stalking her anyway. It ended up with Margaret, his nan, having to go and talk to her mum about it, as his former girlfriend was starting to feel afraid of the way Nathan was acting. We were worried about his behaviour too, although we just thought it was a phase he would grow out of.

For the most part, he did seem to grow out of being weird around girls, but none of his girlfriends seemed to last very long. I don't think that's at all unusual for guys in their late teens, but there was another incident when Nathan was nineteen that both annoyed and worried me at the same time.

I was working on my car in the driveway one day when he pulled up outside the house. I glanced into his car and saw four very young girls sitting inside. At a glance I could tell they were no older than around twelve. They were all giggling.

'Who the hell are they?' I asked Nathan, thinking this was a prank and he was trying to wind me up.

He looked at me blankly. 'Oh, just some girls who wanted to go for a drive.'

I couldn't believe that he had picked up some random young girls off the street and driven off with them.

'What are you playing at, boy?' I demanded. 'I don't know what's going on here, but this is odd. They're children. Get in the car and take them back to wherever you found them. Take them back to their parents.'

My reaction made Nathan laugh at first, but when he realised I wasn't joking he shrugged, got back in the car and drove off. I assume he took the girls home, but we didn't see him for a few days after that, as he was back at his nan's and he refused to talk about it afterwards.

I couldn't get my head around why he'd thought it would be a good idea to take some young girls out in his car, and I eventually decided that he had done it to wind me up. A niggling little doubt was planted, all the same. Did he have some weird ideas about girls? Eventually, I decided he was just a normal teenager trying to find his way in the tricky world of relationships with the opposite sex.

CHAPTER 5

BECKY'S
TEENAGE YEARS

FRIDAY, 17 APRIL 2015
Hundreds gather to say goodbye to the 'Angel of Bristol',
Becky Watts: *Hundreds turned out this morning for the*
funeral of Bristol teenager Becky Watts. Almost two months
after the schoolgirl's disappearance and brutal death horrified
the city, people came together to celebrate the 'shy but
big-hearted' teenager's young life with a fitting send-off –
thanks in part to £11,000 of donations towards the service
from far and wide. Mourners and supporters – some wearing
T-shirts featuring a photo of the 16-year-old – lined the streets
outside St Ambrose Church, showering the horse-drawn
carriage bearing her coffin with pink roses as it passed. With
the church packed to the rafters, scores more watched
proceedings on a big screen outside as a moving service
included stories of Becky's younger days and her great
kindness. Her father, Darren Galsworthy, paid an emotional
tribute to his daughter, through the Reverend David James.
He said: 'As you look down from heaven, just look at what

your short life has achieved – not bad for a shy girl. You will
forever be in our hearts and thoughts. Rest in peace, Angel of
Bristol.' Following the service, people cried and clapped as
Mr Galsworthy released a dove into the skies above her coffin,
before the family left for a private burial at Avonview Cemetery.

Becky had a hard time starting secondary school. Hope, her only friend from Summerhill Primary School, went to a different secondary, and she struggled to make any new friends. She was confident at home, but painfully shy around other kids. Even when we were away on holiday and there were lots of other children running around, Becky wouldn't mix with them. She was never very good at introducing herself into friendship groups and reading other children's body language, so as a result she was often left out their games. She'd just spend a lot of time on her own, or with her family.

Anjie and I hadn't been particularly worried about this when she was at primary school because she had Hope, and she was also close to her cousin, Brooke, but from the minute she started secondary school, Becky found herself the subject of teasing by several different groups of girls. I suppose her lack of self-confidence made her an easy target.

I didn't know anything about it until a few months into the new term. When she came home from school one afternoon, Becky threw her bag on the sofa and plonked herself down next to Anjie, as she always did.

'Hello, love,' I ventured. 'Had a good day?'

She shrugged in response.

'Why don't you ever bring any of your new friends to the house?' I asked, and to my surprise Becky burst into tears.

Anjie and I looked at each other warily. 'Oh no,' she said, putting her arm round Becky. 'What's wrong?'

'I don't have any friends,' Becky sobbed. 'Nobody likes me.'

I was gutted for her. I had been hoping that after years of being a bit of an outcast at the primary school, she would come out of her shell a little when she got to secondary school. It seemed it wasn't going to be that easy. We talked to her for ages that evening, trying to boost her confidence, telling her that she was a lovely girl and it wouldn't be long before everyone else realised it.

Danny was in the same school so I secretly asked him if he and his friends would keep an eye out for any trouble if they saw her in the corridors, and we crossed our fingers and hoped it would get better in time.

But it didn't. One evening, I came home to find Anjie and Becky cuddled on the sofa again, Becky's eyes red from crying.

'What's happened?' I demanded, horrified, and Anjie shot me a worried glance.

'We'll talk about it later,' she said firmly.

I nodded and left them to it. Anjie was always much better at handling stuff like that than I was. Once she had calmed down, Becky went up to her room and Anjie came into the kitchen to have a chat with me.

'Becky's still being bullied,' she said. 'They are picking on her looks, her weight, everything. She had her brand-new jacket ripped off her back today.'

'I'll take the day off work tomorrow and go to the school,' I said. Frankly, I felt like finding the culprits and giving them a piece of my mind, but Anjie shook her head.

'*I'll* go and speak to the school,' she said. 'And if that doesn't work, I'll send you in later.'

That's how it worked with us. Anjie was the calm, collected parent while I tended to be more like a bull in a china shop. I must admit, her approach often worked better than mine, but I couldn't stand the idea of anyone treating Becky like that. It made me feel sick to my stomach.

Anjie spoke to staff at the school, who promised to look into it, but still Becky was coming home in floods of tears almost every day.

'Why don't people like me, Dad?' she said, weeping, time and time and again.

It's a heartbreaking thing for any parent to hear. We all want our kids to be popular in the outside world, but it's difficult to give advice on how to fix things when they get off on the wrong foot. I felt frustrated and powerless that I couldn't wave a magic wand and make it all better. I didn't know how to answer her increasingly desperate questions except to reassure her that she was a lovely person and things would work out in the end.

'Why am I so fat and ugly?' she muttered whenever she caught sight of her reflection in a mirror.

I didn't know where that had come from. Becky was extremely pretty and in no way overweight. At eleven years old, she had the normal amount of puppy fat for a girl of her age.

'You are absolutely perfect,' I told her, looking straight into her eyes, but I could see my words didn't mean much. It wasn't my acceptance she craved.

Anjie and I went up to the school several more times to speak to the staff about what was happening, but if anything our intervention made things worse. When the teachers got involved, the girls who were bullying Becky vowed to make her life hell. It wasn't long before their bitchy comments about her weight started to take their toll.

I was getting ready to do the weekly food shop one Saturday afternoon when Becky bounded down the stairs and handed me a shopping list.

'What's this, Bex?' I asked.

'It's a list of the foods I want to eat from now on,' she said. I glanced at the list and saw it was just loads of low-fat, ready-made meals.

'OK, love,' I said doubtfully, 'but this is crazy. You're not fat at all and these meals aren't particularly good for you.'

I must admit that this was shaky ground for me as a man. I've never really understood why women link their weight to their self-worth, and I found myself struggling to find the right things to say to make Becky feel better about herself.

'Dad, I just want to lose a bit of weight,' she said. 'That way I won't get bullied any more.'

I didn't see the harm in humouring her for a little while. If she needed to feel that she was regaining control over the situation by losing a few pounds of puppy fat, then so be it – even though buying the ready-made meals she wanted virtually doubled our food bills. I tried to encourage her to eat healthy foods too, but after a few weeks I noticed that she wasn't even finishing the ready meals I was buying for her. I walked into the kitchen one evening to find her scraping the last of her chicken curry meal into the bin.

'What are you doing, Bex?' I asked. 'Those meals cost money.'

'I'm just full, Dad,' she said quickly, before pushing past me and running up the stairs to her bedroom.

Anjie told me later that Becky had confided that she wasn't losing weight as fast as she wanted to. Obviously, she thought that by eating a few spoonfuls less, it would speed up the progress.

'Hopefully it's just a silly phase,' I said to Anjie, but deep down I was getting very worried. She was still only eleven. Wasn't that a little young to be spending so much time stressing out about her weight?

Soon, it became obvious that Becky was getting obsessed about it, staring at herself in the mirror, weighing herself and eating less and less every day.

'I'm not losing enough weight,' she moaned to us one evening after she had spent the past half hour glumly pushing food around her plate.

'You look fine, love,' Anjie said, reassuring her, but Becky just shook her head.

'I need to do some exercise too,' she announced. 'Dad, will you help me?'

'That's not a bad idea, Darren,' Anjie said brightly.

I had a multi-gym and punchbag in my workshop, which I used regularly, and I thought getting some muscle tone might make Becky feel better about herself and give her a healthier approach to weight loss.

'We'll get you some boxing gloves, Bex,' I said. 'But the golden rule is that you need to actually eat in order to be able to exercise. Food is fuel, OK?'

'Got it,' Becky said, beaming at me. 'Food is fuel.'

For a few months, Becky's attitude to her weight improved. She spent a few hours a week practising her boxing with me, and at mealtimes she ate every last mouthful. She started toning up, and I could see that getting stronger was making her more confident. I was pleased with this progress – I wanted her to understand that it was better to be fit and strong than a skinny size zero – but obviously the girls at school had their own ideas, as they carried on tormenting her just as much as ever.

A few months after Becky turned twelve, I came home to find Anjie waiting for me in the kitchen. She looked angry.

'I had a call from the school,' she said. 'They wanted to know why we are pulling Becky out of school in order to home-school her. They asked if there was anything they could do to change our minds.'

I was flabbergasted. We had made no such decision – we'd never even considered it. Becky had obviously lied to her teachers to try to get out of going to school.

When we confronted her, Becky burst into tears again.

'I'm sorry I lied, but I have no friends there. Nobody likes me,' she sobbed. 'Please can I be home-schooled? I don't ever want to go back there.'

'Come on, Bex,' I said gently. 'You have to go to school. We can't afford to home-school you. You'll get past this, I promise. The bullies will soon get bored, and then they'll turn their attention to someone else.'

But that wasn't the answer Becky wanted to hear. She turned and fled to her room, slamming the door behind her. Anjie and I looked at each other in despair. We were at our wits' end as parents. What more could we try? We talked long into the evening, trying to come up with solutions. Move her to another school? Wasn't that giving up? And what if the same thing simply happened again?

From then on, we started getting letter after letter from the school, saying that Becky hadn't been turning up for lessons. They even threatened legal action against me for failing to make her attend.

'I could go to prison for this,' I shouted, waving one of the letters at Becky when she came in one night. She just shrugged at me. I was at a complete loss as to what to do. I had a job to go to, so I couldn't march her into school and physically make her stay there all day.

After a while, the school agreed to separate Becky from the other pupils and teach her on a one-to-one basis, in what they called 'The Pod', which was a teaching hut where they gave classes to pupils who were struggling to fit in. She seemed to adapt far better to this method of teaching, although her attendance was still an issue.

In the meantime, her obsession with weight loss began spiralling out of control. She started slipping back into her old ways, and soon she was making excuses to skip meals altogether. She kept hounding me for a boxing session as soon as I got in from work, but it didn't take much for her to get dizzy suddenly or even faint, because there was no food inside her. She had to give up exercise, and before long even getting up from a chair seemed like too much hard work for her. She looked ill and painfully thin, and I grew more and more desperate.

Every time Becky looked as if she was going to faint, Anjie and I jumped to our feet in panic. I was turning into a nervous wreck, but Nathan, who had been scornful of Becky's obsession with weight loss from the start, laughed at our reaction.

'She's obviously just doing it for attention,' he sneered. 'Stop giving her the attention and she'll soon stop all of this. Look at her – she's enjoying it.'

He made things worse on occasion by taunting Becky, saying she was fat, and, needless to say, his comments upset her even more. It really wound me up when he came out with that kind of thing, but I just put it down to sibling rivalry and jealousy over the fact that Anjie and I were concerned about Becky. Even though Nathan was twenty-three while Becky was just twelve, he could still be immature when his mother showed affection towards his little sister.

I had to take him to one side a few times in order to have a quiet word.

'Becky is seriously ill,' I explained, 'and you are not helping. Some support would be nice, Nathan.' But he just shrugged and sloped off.

Almost every day, Becky and I had a war at the dinner table as I tried to get her to eat. I pushed food towards her, only for her to shake her head and try to leave and head up to her room.

'Listen, Bex,' I said, 'it's time to stop this now. You've lost enough weight. I don't care if I have to sit here for three days, you are eating this meal.'

But Becky would just shake her head. Nothing I did got through to her. I'm ashamed to admit that I ended up losing my temper on many occasions, out of sheer frustration.

'You're making me fat!' she screamed.

'I'm not making you fat – I'm keeping you alive!' I shouted back, upon which Becky burst into tears and ran off to her room.

Anjie in particular found it very upsetting, and she would often start crying as soon as Becky was out of sight.

'I think we need to accept that this isn't a phase any more,' she sobbed, and I nodded in agreement.

The next day, I woke Becky and told her we were paying a visit to the doctor.

'You don't have a choice, I'm afraid,' I said as she opened her mouth to argue. I pulled back her duvet cover and ordered her to get dressed.

When we got there, the doctor tried to reason with her. 'You are underweight for your height and age,' he told her. 'If you don't start eating more, we'll have to admit you to a specialist clinic.'

'I'll eat,' Becky promised him, but I knew my daughter well enough to realise that she didn't mean it. For the next few weeks, it was the same old story, again and again. I sat across the table from her, trying to make her eat a proper dinner. Now and again, she would humour me by swallowing a few spoonfuls of food, but never enough to make me believe we were making progress. Neither Anjie nor I could get through to her, and the situation was starting to push me to breaking point.

'Can't you see you're killing yourself?' I shouted at her as she stared at the food on her plate. But it didn't do any good. She didn't appear to care any more. She claimed that the sight of food made her feel sick. I grew increasingly desperate as I watched her wasting away, her cheeks hollowing and her limbs shrinking to nothing but skin and bone. She was too weak to go to school. She could have collapsed at any time.

We called the doctor again, and he sent Becky's notes to specialists at the Riverside Adolescent Unit – an eating disorder and mental health facility for young people. Because Becky had previously spent time in care, social services had to be involved as well, which I hated.

During Becky's first assessment, they weighed and measured her, and when I saw the numbers on the scales my mouth dropped open in shock. She weighed just 5 stone 3 pounds. We learned that the average for girls of her height and age was 6 stone 8 pounds.

Anjie and I stared at each other in dismay, but when I glanced over at Becky, I was angry to notice that she seemed almost happy about how little she weighed. That's when I realised how much this obsession had messed with her mind.

At that appointment, the doctors officially diagnosed Becky with anorexia. My heart sank. She was just twelve years old! Her body hadn't even finished developing and she was starving herself.

Listening to her assessment was difficult. We told the specialists that her periods – which she had only had for a year – had stopped completely. They explained that it was because her body was in 'shut down' mode. She always felt freezing cold because she didn't have enough meat on her bones to keep her warm.

Anjie and I were silent as we drove home, still reeling from the shock of how little Becky weighed.

'I knew she had lost a lot, but I never thought it was that much,' Anjie whispered to me. 'How did we let her get like this? I'm scared stiff, Dar.'

I must admit, I was too.

As part of her treatment plan, Becky was required to attend two hours of counselling each week with a child psychologist. Anjie and I went with her to these sessions, where she was encouraged to talk about her feelings surrounding body image and food. She struggled at first to open up to a stranger, and it was hard not to jump in and speak for her, but eventually Becky started talking. She told the counsellor about the bullying she suffered at school, and how she wanted to be thin so she would fit in.

When Becky was asked about her family, she immediately snuggled into my side and I put my arm around her.

'I feel safe at home,' Becky confided. 'That's where I feel most confident. I only feel safe when Anjie and Dad are there, though. I don't feel safe on my own, or with my older brother Nathan.'

I looked at her, not understanding what she meant. Nathan and Becky got on all right most of the time, although there was a huge rivalry between them. We knew Nathan was jealous of Becky's relationship with his mother and often accused her of wanting to be the centre of attention, but we'd hoped that attitude was easing off as he was in his twenties.

'You don't need to be scared of Nathan, sweetheart,' I said. 'He's your brother! He won't ever hurt you. Besides, if he tried, I would protect you, wouldn't I?'

'How would you be able to, Dad?' Becky asked, a strange little smile on her lips. 'You're getting older now.'

'Cheeky bugger,' I chuckled.

To be honest, I thought Becky was just being silly when she spoke about Nathan like that. He could be arrogant and sometimes a bit nasty, but I knew that he would never hurt Becky or Danny. We were a family.

After a few weeks in which Becky showed no improvement, a social worker and a specialist from the clinic came to visit her at home.

'Becky, we'd like to show you around the unit tomorrow, to give you a proper tour of the facilities,' the specialist said, smiling at her. 'As you aren't getting any better, we'll need to admit you. You'll stay with us until you've recovered.'

Becky's eyes opened wide and she looked at Anjie and me in horror.

'I'm not going to stay in Riverside,' she blurted out. 'I don't want to go there. You can't take me away from home. My dad won't let you.'

'There's nothing your parents can do about it. I'm sorry, but you have no choice. If you don't eat, you'll have to come and stay at the clinic for a while,' the specialist explained. 'You'll get proper support there. We can help you.'

Becky looked at me, waiting for me to say something.

I sighed. 'Bex, I can't stop them taking you,' I told her gently. 'We've tried everything we can to make you better, but it's just not working, sweetheart. If you're not going to eat, then Riverside is the best place for you.'

'I'll eat! I promise!' Becky's eyes filled with tears. 'I don't want to be away from you and Anjie. Please don't let them send me away. I'll start eating properly, I swear.'

Even though the social worker and specialist didn't seem totally convinced, Becky's extreme reaction at the thought of being separated from her family persuaded them to reconsider and leave her at home for a little while.

'We'll be back if there's no improvement in the next couple of weeks,' the specialist told us before she left. 'This is all up to you now, Becky.'

Becky nodded frantically. She looked terrified at the idea of being away from home. I could see she was shaking.

That night, she wrote out another of her shopping lists for me to take to the supermarket the next day. As well as some microwave meals, she added pizzas and pasta, foods she hadn't touched in months. When I got home with the shopping, she immediately grabbed a ready-made lasagne and stuck it in the microwave.

'That's the attitude, Bex,' I said, feeling a huge weight start to lift from my shoulders. Maybe this is the turning point; maybe she would get better now, I thought. Her eating problem had put a massive strain on both Anjie and me over the past few months. As parents, it's your job to feed your children, and when you don't manage it, for one reason or another, it feels as though you are failing. We had grown to dread meal times because of the stress of watching Becky push her food around her plate rather than raising it to her lips, but, to our delight, she ate every last bit of that lasagne. It was a struggle for her because her body had been starved for so long that I think her stomach must have shrunk, but she forced herself to finish her food. The threat of being taken away from her family had jolted our little girl into action, and from then on she went back to eating three proper meals a day, plus snacks.

Becky was tasked with putting on a couple of pounds a week, and she was weighed regularly so the unit could monitor her progress. Within eight months – just before her thirteenth birthday – she got back to a healthy weight. Once she had enough energy to exercise, we started boxing again so she could get fit. Although it was a long, slow process, her whole attitude to her weight and her relationship with food became a lot better.

Her thirteenth birthday came at the end of an agonising two years. To mark the occasion, we bought her a huge chocolate cake, and I had tears of pride in my eyes when she cut herself a massive slice. I cannot describe the massive relief Anjie and I felt knowing that our girl was going to be OK after all. We hoped that she could live like a normal teenager from now on.

Becky's confidence had always been low, and the counsellor told us that she appeared to have developed social anxiety around the time she was being bullied at school. She was too shy to get on a bus or go shopping by herself, but once her anorexia was firmly under control, her confidence slowly started to grow. When she got to the third year of secondary school – year nine – she started mentoring the younger kids in year seven. Usually, the older kids in the final year of school would take on mentoring duties, but Becky had been bullied so badly that she desperately wanted to look after the younger pupils.

If she noticed a young kid looking upset or lost in the hall-way, she would rush over to see if they needed help. She even hung out with a few of them during breaks and at lunchtime, so they didn't have to be alone. The school gave her an award for her mentoring and for being the most kind-hearted pupil. She knew from experience how difficult it was to fit in, so she wanted to do all she could to help others in the same position she had been in. I was extremely proud when I heard about what she was doing, and I was pleased that she was using her own struggle in such a positive way.

Unfortunately, Becky had missed so much schooling because of the bullying and the anorexia that she had slipped far behind the rest of her year. After discussion with her teachers, we decided we had no choice but to pull her out of mainstream education and place her in a special facility for pupils who had missed school due to serious health problems. She started at the Bristol Hospital Education Service when she was fourteen. I was on tenterhooks waiting to hear how her first day went because I knew how much she struggled with new surroundings and meeting new people. The last thing we wanted was for her to have problems fitting in at another school, at such a crucial point in her education.

When I came home from work that night, Becky was watching television.

'What was your first day like, Bex?' I asked tentatively.

'It was pretty good, actually,' she said, smiling, and I sighed with relief.

It soon went from 'pretty good' to 'great'. Becky settled in nicely at her new school and even made two new friends – Adam and Courtney. The three of them seemed to gel instantly, and soon they were constantly hanging around at our house. For once, Becky had her very own friends, and they were good friends at that. The three of them looked out for one another, and I honestly couldn't have wished for two nicer people for her to spend time with.

Once she was better, I no longer had to treat Becky with kid gloves, and she and I sometimes had blazing rows. She was a typical teenager and, now and again, she wound me up to the point where I would lose my temper and yell at her over something as basic as tidying her room. She would yell back, and once we had locked horns, neither of us was willing to back down. Whereas Anjie always tackled Becky in a placid way, I regressed to teenage level, and we would yell at each other for ages. To everyone else this was funny because we were so alike, but neither of us would admit it. Anjie used to laugh her head off as she watched the pair of us yelling at each other.

'You are like mirror images of each other,' she said, chortling during the chaos one evening.

'I'm not like her!' I shouted, and at the same time Becky insisted, 'I'm not like him!'

That immediately set us off laughing, which is how our arguments usually ended. They would flare up suddenly, and end just as quickly amidst snorts of laughter.

In time, Becky started having boyfriends, but I made no secret of the fact that I hated her dating. In my eyes, she was far too young, and I was a typical over-protective father. Whenever she brought a boyfriend home and introduced us, I practically snarled in their direction, so they ended up terrified of me. When she was fifteen she started going out with a lovely boy called Luke – the only boyfriend of hers I actually liked. He was blond, blue-eyed and a perfect gentleman, both caring towards Becky and polite to me.

When she turned sixteen, Becky confided in Anjie that she was thinking about having sex for the first time. The two of them disappeared for ages into Becky's room to discuss it. Of course, being the highly suspicious dad I was, I leaned against the door, trying my best to eavesdrop.

'The most important thing is that you're ready,' I heard Anjie telling her. 'If anyone tries to push you into it when you're not ready, they aren't good enough for you. If someone really likes you, they will wait.'

'Right, OK,' Becky replied, and I could tell she was embarrassed. 'You don't really need to tell me this stuff, Anjie.'

'I absolutely do!' Anjie replied. 'It's all part of the job. Now, do you know how everything works?'

'Of course I do,' Becky said indignantly.

But Anjie knew as well as I did that Becky could be a little emotionally immature. Her lack of schooling meant that she sometimes needed things explained in full, so Anjie launched into a comprehensive guide to sex. When she finished, she was met with silence.

'I didn't know he's supposed to put it *inside* me,' Becky finally said, sounding horrified. 'I thought he was just going to put it *on* me.'

I had to cover my mouth with both hands to stop myself laughing. I quickly moved away as fast as I could to the other side of the house. Needless to say, I think Becky got a bit of a shock that day and decided that sex might not have been for her just yet.

As her GCSEs approached, she started to consider her options for the future. Her strongest subjects were English and Art, but for a while she was dead set on becoming a vet because of her love of animals. As time went on, however, she decided that interior design was more her thing. Becky's talent for drawing came from me. She would spend hours designing her ideal house, complete with the decor and furnishings. She would also watch television programmes such as *DIY SOS* religiously.

I fully supported her aspirations, as I truly thought she'd be good at design, and I told her that I was happy to work every hour under the sun so that she could go to university or college and achieve her dream. From a young age, Anjie and I had always told the kids that, with hard work and determination, they could be anything they wanted to be.

CHAPTER 6

SHAUNA

FRIDAY, 13 NOVEMBER 2015

Nathan Matthews and Shauna Hoare jailed for killing schoolgirl Becky Watts: *Cold-hearted killer Nathan Matthews was today locked up for at least 33 years for the brutal murder of his teenage stepsister Becky Watts. His girlfriend and accomplice Shauna Hoare was given 17 years for charges including conspiracy to kidnap and manslaughter. Sentencing judge, Mr Justice Dingemans, told 28-year-old Matthews that he wouldn't be eligible for parole until he was 61 at the earliest, and broke down in tears as he paid tribute to Becky's family's dignity in the face of such horror. It marked an extraordinary end to a dramatic and emotional five-week trial, which heard how Matthews had suffocated Becky during a violent struggle in her bedroom in what the prosecution described as a sexually motivated kidnap plot. He dismembered her body, packaging the eight parts into bags and suitcases that he later tried to hide in a garden shed. Before the warped pair were told of their fate, the court heard powerful victim impact*

statements from Becky's family. In the words of her father,
Darren Galsworthy: 'The heartless, cold and calculating
perpetrators of this despicable act of evil can never be
forgotten or forgiven. These family members sat in our home,
knowing what they had done, and watched my very public
descent into madness and despair. They said nothing, but
continued to pretend to help us, showing no emotion at all.'

In June 2011, Anjie woke up one morning and said something that marked the beginning of a difficult new phase of our lives: 'Darren, I can't see.'

I opened my eyes groggily to see her sitting bolt upright on her side of the bed, blinking and waving her arms around frantically.

'I can't see anything – I'm blind!' she screamed, sounding terrified. I jumped out of bed and knelt by her, waving my hand in front of her face. Her eyes looked vacant as she stared straight ahead.

'Are my eyes open?' Anjie shrieked, and I swallowed hard, panic rising in my chest.

'Yes, love, they are. Try not to worry. Let's get you to a doctor.'

I tried to keep my voice calm for Anjie's sake but I was totally confused. How does somebody go to bed at night with 20/20 vision and wake up in the morning blind?

I helped her get dressed and we drove to the hospital. All the way there my brain was working overtime, trying to figure out what could possibly have happened, but outwardly I remained calm and practical, telling her that there must be a simple explanation.

The doctors in A&E were as baffled as we were. They told us that Anjie's eyes looked healthy, and they carried out loads of blood tests to try to determine what was going on.

As we waited in the treatment room, I gripped Anjie's hand tightly. What if she was permanently blind? What would it mean for the family? I was the only one who worked in our household, but if I quit my job to care for Anjie I wasn't sure how I would pay the mortgage.

After a while, a doctor came back to talk to us. 'I'm afraid we don't know the cause as yet,' he said. 'Every blood test so far has come back normal. We will need to investigate further, but in the meantime it's important that you go home and try to get some rest.'

We were baffled by this. If the doctors didn't know what to do, that meant there was no treatment, which meant it might not get better. I had never heard of anything like this before, and we simply didn't know what to do except struggle through the days. I helped Anjie as much as possible and waited for the doctors to come up with an answer.

Thankfully, a few days later, when she woke, Anjie could make out shadowy shapes, and gradually her sight began to return to normal. Each day she could see a little more clearly than the day before, and within six weeks it was as good as it had ever been. I wondered if the loss of sight might have been a reaction to the stress we were under while dealing with Becky's anorexia. You hear of psychological trauma causing physical symptoms. But I was wrong. It turned out that it was just the beginning of something far, far worse.

As soon as Anjie's sight returned fully, other parts of her body started to go wrong. She was physically exhausted and needed to sleep twice as much as she had before, then about six months later her legs started to feel weak. When she tried to stand up from a chair, they sometimes gave way beneath her, causing her to fall back onto the seat. She got wobbly walking around the house and became nervous going out on her own in case she collapsed somewhere. We were back and forwards from the doctors every week seeking answers, but still they couldn't tell us what was going on. I was panicking. Why couldn't someone at least give us a diagnosis?

After nine months, we were called in to see a specialist, who told us that Anjie had multiple sclerosis – a condition which affects the nerves in the brain and spinal cord, causing problems with muscle movement, balance and vision.

'What's the treatment for it?' I asked straight away.

'I'm afraid there is no cure,' he told us, 'but MS sufferers react in different ways. The symptoms may get better or worse, depending on how your body handles the disease.'

We were devastated. Anjie had always been the fit and healthy one in the family. She was the one who dragged us all out for long bike rides, and she used to walk miles every day. It seemed desperately unfair that she should be struck down by this awful disease and faced with an uncertain future.

We tried to be as positive as we could, but the symptoms continued to worsen. She dragged herself around the house by holding onto doors and furniture, but any objects left on the floor could trip her up. Nathan was very worried about his mum and used to yell at Becky if she left any of her stuff lying around on the floor or the stairs, which I thought was hypocritical since he often left his own belongings all over the living-room floor.

It was alarming for all our children. Anjie had been their shield, the person who protected them, but now the situation was reversed and she was the one who needed protecting.

Anjie tried her best to get on with life, but it was clear to see she was struggling with her limitations. She would get frustrated quickly and often burst into tears when she couldn't manage something she'd have easily done before, like reaching a plate down from a high shelf or cooking a meal. When we went out she couldn't walk any distance at all, so we got a wheelchair and took turns to wheel her round the park or to the shops.

Every time Anjie got upset, I struggled not to burst into tears myself. The woman I loved – a woman who had always been a force to be reckoned with – was slowly deteriorating, and there was nothing I could do to stop it. All I could do was look after her. I was still going to work most days, but I would rush home as soon as I could to prepare an evening meal and see what Anjie needed.

Becky was great at fetching cups of tea and helping her in and out of her wheelchair, but Danny had moved out early in 2011, just after his sixteenth birthday, to go back to live with his mum, Tanya. It was during the period when we were struggling with Becky's eating disorder, and I think that was hard for him. I kept nagging him about his unwillingness to go to college or get a job, so that was obviously a factor too. He had always felt protective towards Tanya and maintained a relationship with her. I was obviously hurt by his decision at the time, and it meant that the pressure was on Becky and me to look after Anjie. And, given that Becky had just recovered from her illness, it was mostly down to me, with help from Nathan whenever he popped in.

'You don't have to worry, my love,' I told Anjie as I helped her into bed one evening. 'I'll always be by your side.' And I meant it. Anjie had been my rock for many years and now it was time for me to be hers.

Back in 2008, when Nathan was twenty-one, he had announced that he was bringing a new girlfriend home to meet us. He didn't tell us anything about how they had met or what she was like, but simply said that her name was Shauna.

I was out on the driveway working on my car when they pulled up outside the house. As I wiped my hands and looked up, my first thought was that Nathan was trying to wind me up. In the passenger seat was a young girl who didn't look a day over fourteen. My mind flashed back to the time I had to tell him to take those twelve-year-old girls home to their parents, and as I watched Nathan get out of the car, I waited for him to erupt into laughter at my expense. The girl was so young it had to be a joke, but Nathan simply looked at me, straight-faced, while she got out of the car. She was dressed in a little black skirt and a revealing top. The style was very provocative for someone so young, and I found myself instantly alarmed by her appearance.

I'm the sort of man who gives people a chance. I like almost everyone unless they give me a reason not to, and I don't consider myself in a position to judge others for their appearance. But there was a look about that girl that made me wary.

'Who's that?' I asked Nathan as he started to walk towards me.

'Oh, that's Shauna – my new girlfriend,' he answered nonchalantly.

'Are you trying to get yourself arrested?' I asked angrily.

Nathan looked stunned at my reaction. 'Relax, Dar. She's nineteen …' he started, but I held my hand up to stop him.

'I can tell she's not nineteen, boy. I'm not stupid. Get her back in that car and piss off.'

'What? You can't stop me going into my mum's house,' he answered, reddening with embarrassment.

'Your mum doesn't pay the mortgage – I do. So I think you'll find I can,' I replied, standing my ground. 'Seriously, Nathan – get going!'

He stared at me for a moment, then must have decided it wasn't worth fighting over any further, because he turned and walked back towards the car.

I was annoyed at Nathan for lying to my face like that. I could tell from her babyish features and slight figure that the girl was nowhere near nineteen. I watched as Nathan told her they were leaving. I couldn't hear what they were saying, but she was obviously upset about it, looking very much like a petulant teenager.

I was determined never to allow Nathan to bring underage girls into my home. The way I saw it, Anjie and I had fought hard to get Becky and Danny out of care, and I wasn't going to let Nathan scupper all of that by having an inappropriate relationship under my roof. My children finally had a normal, settled family life, and I didn't want to give social services any reason to question the way I was raising them.

I glared at Nathan until he and Shauna got back in the car and drove off, then I went inside to wash my hands.

'Did you see the girl that idiot boy just tried to bring in here?' I complained to Anjie. 'He tried to tell me she was nineteen but there's no bloody way that girl is nineteen. What the hell's wrong with him, hanging out with kiddie girls all the time? I told him to sling his hook.'

'All right, Dar, calm down,' Anjie began, but I interrupted her.

'She's a wrong 'un,' I said. 'I can tell she's trouble.'

'Maybe you're just being an overprotective dad,' she replied. 'You don't even even know her yet.'

Anjie always tried to see the good in everyone, sometimes naively so.

'There's something about her I don't like, Anj,' I replied. 'She's far too young for him, for a start. She's just a kid.'

Anjie was worried because she didn't want to upset Nathan if he was serious about this girl, but she didn't argue with my judgement.

We didn't see Nathan for a few days, but when he did eventually come over to see his mum, he was moody and sullen with me.

'Is your attitude problem something to do with your new girlfriend?' I asked him.

He glared at me. 'Why can't I bring her over?' he asked.

'If you can show me Shauna's birth certificate to prove she's over the age of consent, I'll give her a chance,' I replied. 'But I am not risking letting an underage girl into my house when we know social services are keeping an eye on Becky and Danny.'

He shrugged and turned his back on me. He continued to see her for the next year, but there was no further attempt to bring her to the house until one day in 2010, when Nathan arrived at the front door waving a birth certificate. I looked at it and saw that Shauna had just turned sixteen. I had been right when I'd guessed that she was underage the first time he brought her over. Nathan was a full seven years older, which to me seemed too much of an age gap at that stage of their lives, but I couldn't refuse to let Shauna into the house now that she was sixteen.

A few days later, I arrived home from work to find Anjie, Nathan and Shauna in the living room, having a cup of tea and making small talk. I wasn't in a great mood, I must admit. There were redundancies being handed out at work and I was waiting to find out my fate.

Shauna gave me a big smile as I walked into the room and jumped up to introduce herself. 'Hi, I'm Shauna. It's really nice to meet you.'

I was surprised at how polite she was, compared to the stroppy teenager I had seen the day Nathan first brought her over.

I nodded in reply, and instantly felt awkward. I'm not the sort of man who enjoys chit-chat. That was Anjie's area of expertise.

After a few minutes I decided to leave them to it, and busied myself by cleaning out the rabbit hutch and doing some general tidying up. I went upstairs to speak to Danny and Becky, but after a while I decided that I had to go back downstairs and be sociable.

When I returned, Nathan was phoning for a takeaway and Anjie and Shauna were watching television. They seemed to be getting on all right.

'Will you come and help me in the kitchen, Darren?' Anjie asked when she saw me lingering in the doorway.

'She's a nice girl,' Anjie whispered to me once we were out of earshot.

I growled in response. I still didn't like the idea of them as a couple. They whispered and giggled to each other when we were in the room, which to me was just plain rude. All in all, there was something creepy about Nathan when he was around her.

'Come on – you said you'd give her a chance,' Anjie reminded me.

She was right – I had promised, and, to be fair, Shauna had been very polite so far. But I was still unsettled when I went back to the living room and saw her and Nathan cosied up on the sofa. I had a gut feeling that they were not good for each other.

I spent the rest of the evening being aloof and keeping my distance, but as time went by I got more used to seeing Shauna hanging around the house, and eventually I started to warm to her. To be honest, she gave me no reason not to. She was well-mannered and Nathan clearly adored her. I couldn't snub her completely because of a silly gut feeling.

I did once ask her about her relationship with Nathan. 'You're very young, Shauna,' I said. 'Why are you looking at guys Nathan's age?'

She seemed shocked by my bluntness, but shrugged. 'I like him,' she said.

We learned that before she had even reached school age, she had been taken into care and had then been bounced from foster home to foster home while she was growing up. She hadn't had anyone fighting for her the way Becky and Danny had when I was struggling to get them out of care, and that made me sympathise with her. At the age of thirteen she'd moved in with her mother, with whom she was still living.

Anjie welcomed Shauna into the family straight away, as she always did with any of the kids' friends. Danny wasn't bothered, mainly because he was usually out with his mates, but Becky, who was twelve at the time and just recovering from her struggle with anorexia, saw Shauna as a potential friend.

I could tell Becky looked up to Shauna, and hoped to win her over. Problem was, Shauna didn't seem to want to be friends with someone so much younger, and she could be quite dismissive. But the more cool and indifferent Shauna was to Becky, the more eager Becky was to make friends with her. We often saw this in her. She kept pursuing people she wanted to be friends with even when they were horrible to her. We suspected it might have been something to do with the disruption of her early months in foster care.

Once Becky had conquered her eating disorder, she discovered fashion. I gave her a monthly clothes allowance, but she preferred to buy her clothes online because she didn't have the confidence to go into shops. Boohoo.com was her favourite site. The only drawback to buying clothes online was that she couldn't try them on first, so she would often order a top or shoes only to find when they arrived that they didn't fit or she didn't like them. Frustratingly, she wouldn't send them back for a refund. Instead, she would offer them to Shauna.

'Would you like these?' I heard her ask once, holding out a pair of jeans. 'They don't really look right on me. You can have them if you want.'

Shauna snatched the jeans away from Becky and inspected them before throwing them on the sofa next to her handbag. 'I'll take them off your hands, if you like,' she replied coolly.

I was gobsmacked that someone who was so polite to Anjie and me could be so ungrateful when she was given a gift. On that occasion I bit my tongue, and I hoped that Becky had learnt her lesson.

But she hadn't. A few weeks later, I had just come home from work and chucked my bag on the floor near the door when I overheard Becky talking to Shauna in the kitchen.

'I've got this leather coat you can have if you like, Shauna,' Becky said.

I drew in my breath sharply and listened. I wasn't going to tolerate Shauna being rude to Becky again.

'OK, I'll have it – but only because I'm doing you a favour,' Shauna replied.

I barged through the kitchen door to see Shauna holding the coat in her hands.

'I heard that,' I said. 'Bex, take that coat back upstairs. It's not Shauna's. I paid for it and you aren't giving it away.'

Becky looked embarrassed as she took the coat back, and Shauna just glared at me.

'If you're going to look at me like that, Shauna, you can get out of my house,' I snapped. 'You've got five seconds. Go on – get out.'

Nathan and Shauna stormed out of the house, and Anjie came into the kitchen to see what was going on. I turned to Becky.

'Bex, you have to stop giving things away,' I said. 'Shauna's so ungrateful, she never even thanks you. She's getting all this stuff from you and she's being a right cow about it.'

Becky shrugged. 'I just wanted us to get on,' she replied. 'I want her to be my friend.'

It broke my heart to hear Becky talking like that. Her desperation for friends really upset me. I glanced at Anjie, who was clearly thinking the same as me as she wrapped her arm around Becky's shoulder affectionately.

'Come on, Bex,' she said. 'Let's go and watch a film together.'

We didn't see Nathan and Shauna for about a week, and I was a lot cooler with her after that, once I'd seen how offhand she could be towards Becky. Around this time, I was largely preoccupied with looking after Anjie as her legs were getting weaker and she was struggling to cope around the house, but I did start to notice a change in the relationship between Nathan and Shauna. He started becoming snappy with her, and I could tell he was jealous of any time she spent with her friends – especially if they were male. It reminded me of the way he used to be with his first girlfriend, back when he was eighteen. I think Shauna made him feel insecure, and she played on his jealous nature, teasing him by telling him that she was going out without him, and flirting with other men in front of him. I thought it was yet another sign of her immaturity.

As a result of all this, Nathan started becoming possessive and controlling. He wanted to be in control of her smoking, ordering her to give him money whenever she had a cigarette because he claimed he was helping her to quit. He also controlled her money – not that they had any between them. He became stroppy and negative when she was around, and we never saw him on his own any more; wherever he went, Shauna was there too, like a shadow.

When Nathan was seventeen he was forced to leave his electrician apprenticeship because the firm closed down, but he kept himself busy with various takeaway-delivery jobs. He didn't look for another full-time job, as he complained about having a bad back. He went to the doctors, where he was eventually diagnosed with fibromyalgia. This is a disease in which abnormal levels of certain chemicals in the brain cause the nervous system to trigger pain signals all over the body. Nathan claimed he'd had pains during his school days, but now it had got so bad that he was unable to work.

I was disappointed about this and, to be honest, a bit sceptical, because it seemed to me he'd been doing fine until Shauna came along. Previously, Nathan had always been on the right track with his attitude to work and earning his own money, but soon he was doing next to nothing. Once he was no longer in full-time work, I had to lend him money now and again to help him out. I never begrudged it if he needed it, but I noticed that his attitude started to change for the worse. The less he had to do, the less he wanted to do.

Nathan and Shauna seemed to be at our house all the time, and more often than not we would have to feed them. I was working from 7 a.m. until 7 p.m. just to make ends meet, so I started to feel that they were taking advantage of us. Now and again, I'd mention it to Nathan, but he never seemed bothered.

'Why don't you go out and get a proper job, Nath?' I asked him. 'That way, you can afford food to feed yourself and your girlfriend, instead of mooching from me and your mum all the time.'

'I can't work, Dar. I've got a bad back,' he moaned.

I was astounded. Within months, Nathan had gone from being a hard-working lad with the world at his feet to a lazy, useless lump who was living off other people. He stopped shaving, and sometimes he looked (and smelled) as if he hadn't washed or changed his clothes for days. The difference in him was unreal. Becky often joined in my criticism, calling him a lazy scrounger, and that didn't go down too well. I suspected that the real reason he didn't want to go out and work was that he didn't want to let Shauna out of his sight, but I had no way of proving it.

Nathan also got ruder and more arrogant every time I saw him – even to his own mother. He had always adored Anjie, so this change in attitude to her, at a time when she was struggling to cope with her MS, was a real worry.

Once, when I was in the next room, I overheard him telling Shauna that Anjie was 'a fucking idiot'. It made my blood boil so I charged in, all guns blazing, to tackle him about it.

'How can you say that about your mum, who has always been kind to you, who's always bent over backwards to help you? What on earth has happened to you, Nath?'

He shrugged, with a sneer on his face like he didn't give a damn what I said. I felt as if Anjie and I were losing touch with the boy we had been so proud of.

They didn't often stay over with us. Mostly, they slept at Shauna's mum's house, as she had a granny annexe on the side of the house where they could have some privacy. Then Shauna got pregnant, and they went on the list for council accommodation. When they told us the news, my attitude towards her changed. She was expecting my grandchild, which meant she was part of my family. No matter what I had thought of her previously, I was determined to help and support the pair of them as much as I could.

I hoped that becoming a father would force Nathan to grow up and find regular work before the baby arrived, but as usual he didn't seem interested. It was disappointing that he failed to recognise the big responsibility he was going to have once he was a parent, but I just had to hope he would realise it eventually – perhaps when he saw his little one for the first time and experienced that huge rush of love I had felt when I saw Danny and Becky as newborns.

Anjie and I looked forward to becoming grandparents, and Becky was delighted when we told her she was going to be an auntie. However, Nathan's attitude towards Becky was becoming more and more aggressive. He didn't seem to be able to tolerate her at all. Once, when Becky was excitedly talking to Anjie about the baby, Nathan suddenly turned on her.

'You,' he snarled, pointing at her, 'are not going anywhere near our baby.'

We were all stunned into silence, and Becky's eyes filled with tears. I felt my heart hammer in my chest, and I couldn't stop myself from reacting. I yanked him up by the collar and dragged him into the kitchen.

'What is wrong with you, boy?' I shouted. 'What are you doing speaking to Becky like that? She hasn't done anything to you. She's just a kid.'

Nathan just glared at me in response. I looked at his sullen face and realised I had no idea what demon had got into his head. He was a far cry from the boy I had raised. Something in him had changed, and I didn't know what to do to fix it. I just had to hope that the lessons we had drummed into him when he was younger would win over in the end, and he'd go back to being a decent person again.

* * *

Shauna went into labour, and the first thing Nathan did when her waters broke was drive her to our house. Anjie and I had just finished our breakfast when he burst through the front door, and as soon as we saw his panic-stricken face we knew it was time.

'She's in labour,' he said, panting.

Anjie went to check on Shauna while I called my boss and told him I wouldn't be coming in to work that day because my grandchild was being born.

Shauna was having contractions every ten minutes; we timed each one.

'You've got ages yet, love,' I said soothingly. 'There's no rush.'

Shauna nodded, accepting that I knew what I was talking about, but Nathan glared at me.

'How the hell do *you* know we don't need to rush?' he demanded. The pressure was clearly getting to him. He looked frantic.

'Because it's her first baby, you idiot,' I replied. 'Relax, will you? I've had kids of my own, you know. Trust me – she's got loads of time.'

We timed the contractions all day until the evening, and when she was down to just four minutes between each contraction I drove Anjie, Nathan and Shauna to Bristol Royal Infirmary. Anjie held Shauna's hand during the six-hour-long delivery, after which I got to look at my grandchild for the first time. Because of subsequent events, I can't name the baby here or give any details such as gender or appearance, but obviously it was a very precious time for Anjie and me. Nathan looked absolutely stunned. I hoped that meant that the reality of his new role as a father was starting to dawn on him.

Two days later, Shauna and the baby were allowed to come home from the hospital. She looked absolutely knackered when I went to pick her up, but she did thank me politely for coming, saying that Anjie and I were like the family she'd never had.

'Not to worry, my love,' I said. 'You get in – you've done your work.' I felt warm towards her at that moment, I must admit. She had handled the labour and birth really well, showing a lot of courage for one so young.

That day was filled with joy as everyone welcomed the new arrival. We all stayed indoors, passing the baby around and making cooing noises. Becoming a grandfather was like becoming a dad all over again. The love I felt for Nathan and Shauna's child hit me like a tidal wave, and seeing my family happy together filled me with contentment.

From then on, Shauna was one of us and, much to my surprise, Nathan settled nicely into being a father. It seemed to give him a bit more of a purpose to his life. He completely doted on his new baby and spent a lot of time dressing, feeding and playing with the child. During the pregnancy the council had given them a house in Barton Hill, not far from where we lived, and I helped them kit it out, giving them a sofa, a bed, and lots of other essentials.

Nathan and Shauna having a baby made me think more about the importance of family, and about how much I wanted Anjie to be my wife. For years we had planned to get hitched, but financial restraints, plus the fact that we had always been so busy raising the children, meant that the right time had never come along. When she got ill, the chances seemed even more remote, but I really wanted to throw an event to get the whole family together, including Danny, Becky, Nathan and Shauna.

In August 2013 I decided that I was going to make it happen. I sold all three of my motorbikes and banked six months of overtime wages, then I paid a visit to the local church – St Ambrose – and asked the vicar for the first date he had available. When he told me they had a cancellation at the end of the month, I was thrilled – but nervous as well. I hadn't told Anjie of my plans, and now I had just three weeks to plan a wedding. I handed him a cheque to save the date, and pegged it back to the house as quickly as I could.

When I got in, the first person I saw was Becky.

'Bex, I've got some exciting news,' I said, grinning at her. 'Anjie and I are getting married in three weeks – but she doesn't know it yet.'

Becky opened her eyes in shock and beamed at me. 'That is brilliant news! Well done, Dad,' she said. 'What can I do to help? I've got some brilliant ideas for colour schemes.'

'First things first,' I chuckled. 'I suppose I need to ask Anjie.'

When I told Anjie I had booked the church for our wedding, she smiled up at me.

'I just hope I can walk down the aisle,' she said, looking down at her wheelchair.

I grabbed both her hands. 'I don't care how you get down the aisle, my love,' I said. 'I want you to be my wife.'

We decided that Becky, her cousin Brooke, and Shauna should be our bridesmaids, while Nathan and Danny would be the joint best men. Because Nathan and Danny were such different characters, I gave them different responsibilities on the day. Danny was the quieter one, so he would be the ring bearer, while Nathan was more confident, so he would make the speech. Both boys were chuffed when I asked them. It was my way of showing them how important they were to me. We also agreed to have a flower girl and a pageboy as a way of including some of Anjie's little nieces and nephews.

Since Becky had an eye for fashion, we decided that she would be in charge of choosing Anjie's wedding dress, the bridesmaids' outfits, the waistcoats for the men, and the flower girl and pageboy outfits. She also took responsibility for the flowers. She was thrilled and got to work straight away, choosing some beautiful dresses in her favourite colour – baby blue – and ordering garlands made of fresh flowers for the bridesmaids. She also ordered a made-to-measure wedding dress, complete with a little lace jacket, for Anjie. It was stunning, and I was really proud of her eye for detail.

On Saturday, 31 August 2013, Anjie slowly but steadily walked down the aisle in front of 200 guests while holding on to her stepfather Christopher's arm. I couldn't help but turn around to take a peek as she made her way towards me and I had a big lump in my throat because she looked absolutely breathtaking.

As we said our vows to each other, I was overcome by emotion. I was amazed that I had managed to make a life with someone as kind-hearted and wonderful as Anjie. We told each other we would always be there for one another, surrounded by our kids and everyone we loved. Out of the corner of my eye, I could see Becky beaming at us. It may sound clichéd, but it really was the best moment of my life.

That evening, before the reception, we snuck off home, got out of our formal wedding clothes and slipped on some Shrek and Princess Fiona costumes – complete with bright green body paint. Nobody knew about our plans, so when we got back to the hall everyone gasped in shock then burst into shrieks of laughter. I remember thinking that I had never heard so much laughter at a wedding before.

Anjie was in great spirits that day, and she even managed to get up for our first dance. I held her tightly as we danced to 'How Deep is your Love' by the Bee Gees, then the DJ played Smash Mouth's 'I'm a Believer' from *Shrek*, the movie, to go with our costumes. As we danced, I glanced over to the corner of the room, where Becky was sitting with some friends, including Brooke. Nathan, Danny and Shauna were sitting with them too, all in a crowd. It was fantastic to see everyone together and getting along well. You could tell from their faces that they were having a brilliant time, and that meant the world to me. As long as my family were happy, I was happy.

'This is it now, love,' I whispered to Anjie, who was also looking over at our brood. 'My life is complete.'

'Best day of our lives,' Anjie smiled back. And it was.

Life settled back to normal pretty quickly after the wedding. Anjie's condition was not getting any better, so in March 2014 Shauna agreed to become her carer. She couldn't get a regular job because of the baby, but this way she could help Anjie while I was at work and earn a little bit of money, and she could bring the baby with her. I was finding it tiring to hold down a job and be Anjie's carer as well, so it seemed like an ideal solution – only it didn't turn out that way. Shauna did a bit of cleaning and washed a few dishes, but she wasn't much help to Anjie otherwise. We soon guessed that she was only doing it in order to claim the carer's allowance.

Nathan's attitude towards Becky returned to its usual one of sibling rivalry after the wedding. The more confidence she gained, the more he tried to destroy it. I often told him he was far too old to behave like that, but it got more and more extreme.

One of his tactics to wind Becky up was jumping out and scaring her. This started off as a harmless joke, but soon he was jumping out at her constantly. He would also grab her shoulders and scream loudly in her face. Becky complained about it all the time, but I didn't take it too seriously at first.

When I witnessed him doing it one time, I was surprised to see how menacing he was towards her. Becky almost jumped out of her skin and looked terrified. I hadn't realised how much he scared her until I saw her face that day.

'Cut it out, Nathan. You're scaring her,' I said, but Nathan just fell about laughing.

'I'm only winding her up,' he replied.

But something about the glint in his eye left me a little uneasy – and a glance at Becky showed that she found the situation anything but funny.

CHAPTER 7

THE DAY THAT CHANGED OUR LIVES

I'll never forget the last time I saw Becky alive – a few ordinary hours that now, as I look back, conjure such fierce emotions. It was Tuesday, 17 February 2015, and I came home from my job as line manager at Power Electrics, Warmley, to find Becky and Anjie in the house. Becky was mooching about, dressed in a fleecy blue onesie, because it was half-term and she didn't have to go to school. That girl had about seven onesies, one for every day of the week. If she was leaving the house she always looked immaculate – she had a real talent for doing her make-up and hair – but when she was in the house with us she didn't bother making much of an effort. She preferred to slob around.

It was cold and dark by the time I trudged through the front door. I saw Becky fleetingly as she was heading upstairs to her bedroom.

'Hiya, Dad,' she said, smiling as she passed me.

'Hello, my girl,' I replied, dumping my bag on the floor and walking into the living room to check on Anjie.

Every night, I had the same routine. I'd get home from work and cook tea for whoever was around, followed by doing the washing up – Shauna had long since stopped bothering. Then I'd sort out Anjie's and my packed lunches for the following day, have a shower and help Anjie shower, and then finally check my emails and plan my work schedule for the next day. I'd usually finish off by having a cigarette and watching television for half an hour before heading to bed.

Becky spent most of the time in her bedroom, like any other teenager. She had a flat-screen television in there, which she would watch while cuddling up with one of her many pets. I was always careful not to disturb her when she was in her bedroom. I knew that sixteen-year-olds needed their privacy, and Becky, more than anyone else I knew, needed her own space. She enjoyed having her own room after years of sharing with Danny, and it became her haven. It was the one place where she felt completely safe.

At about 10 p.m. Becky came downstairs while I was in the garden room having a cigarette.

'Dad, can you make me a pizza?' she asked.

I groaned. Becky would always leave eating until late at night, when I was ready to go to bed.

'I swear, you always pick the exact time I am ready to hit the sack, Bex,' I muttered as I walked over to the freezer. 'What sort of a time to eat is this?'

'Thanks, Dad,' she said, grinning. 'Can I have some garlic bread as well, please?'

Becky knew that she would always get her way with me when it came to food. We had a freezer specially for her, full of all the stuff she liked, and because of her years of anorexia, I never refused to cook her whatever she wanted. I was just glad she was eating and hadn't relapsed into her old ways.

'You've got me wrapped around your little finger, haven't you? Go on, get upstairs. I'll bring it up to you when it's done.'

She smiled at me before bolting up the stairs once again.

When her pizza was ready, I carried it up on a tray with her cutlery, and put a tea towel over my arm to make myself look like a waiter.

'Your room service, ma'am,' I said loudly outside her door.

I could hear Becky giggling as she opened the door. 'Thank you, kind sir,' she said sarcastically as she took the tray from me.

'I'm off to bed,' I said. 'Enjoy your pizza. Goodnight, Bex.'

'Night, Dad.' She smiled at me and closed the door, but not before I noticed that she was in the middle of watching *Jackass*. It was her all-time favourite programme, and she would watch it for hours on end, giggling uncontrollably.

I sloped off to bed, but I didn't sleep well that night. At around 3 a.m. I woke up to the sound of Becky's television down the hall. She had obviously fallen asleep with it on. I crept out of bed carefully so I didn't wake Anjie and tiptoed down to Becky's door. She was cuddled up in bed, fast asleep. She had her onesie on and a green jumper of Anjie's. Becky was always borrowing clothes from Anjie, and she would even nick things from my wardrobe as well. She particularly liked my baggy baseball tops, which she said were comfy to wear.

'How on earth can you sleep with this bloody thing blaring away?' I muttered as I gently removed the remote control from her hand and switched the television off.

If I had known that would be the last time I would ever see my beautiful girl alive, there's so much more I would have done. I would have stroked her hair, told her how much I loved her and how beautiful she was. I would have cuddled up beside her and stayed there all night long, watching her sleep.

Instead, I quietly shut her bedroom door behind me before getting back into bed and falling into a deep sleep.

The next morning, I got up at 6 so I could shower and get myself ready for work. I usually started at 7.30, so I was always out of the house before anyone else was up. That day was no exception – it was work as usual. When I got home that night, Anjie told me that Becky was sleeping over at her friend Adam's house. We often let Becky sleep over at her mates' houses, because she only had a few close friends and we knew them and their parents quite well. We'd often have her friends over to stay at ours too. All the mums and dads used to call it 'kid-share' because we took it in turns to look after them.

Thursday, 19 February was just like any other day. It was Danny's birthday, but we weren't seeing him because he was going to a party. We had celebrated with him the previous weekend, when I had given him some birthday money. I went to work bright and early, and Anjie had a hospital appointment booked for late morning. She remembers Becky knocking on the door at 8.30 a.m., wanting to be let in.

'Sorry, Anj,' she explained as Anjie opened the door. 'My key still isn't working.' She went straight up to her room. She had been complaining that her front-door key hadn't been working for a few days, and I hadn't got round to checking it.

At around 11 a.m. Anjie's mum collected Anjie to take her to her appointment. When Anjie returned to the house at

12.45 p.m., she noticed Nathan's car in the driveway. He and Shauna were in the living room, watching television and playing on their phones. They had let themselves in with a key Anjie had left for them under our wheelie bin.

As far as Anjie could tell, Becky wasn't in the house. This wasn't out of the ordinary. She was a typical sixteen-year-old, so if she wasn't at home it usually meant that she was out with one of her friends. Shauna confirmed that she had heard the front door slam earlier while she was out in the garden having a cigarette.

A few hours later, Becky's boyfriend, Luke, came by looking for her, and Shauna answered the door. She went upstairs to check Becky's room, and when she returned she shook her head.

'Nope, she's not in her room,' she told him. 'She went out earlier, I think.'

Luke turned to Anjie. He seemed confused. 'That's strange. She hasn't replied to any of my texts. That's not like Becky. We were supposed to meet up.'

'I'll tell her to get in touch with you as soon as she comes in,' Anjie promised.

'OK, thank you, Anjie. Speak to you later, then,' replied Luke, before walking off.

When Becky didn't return home that night, we all assumed that she was staying at a friend's house, as she had done the night before, and thought nothing more of it. Becky would often sleep over at a mate's without a moment's hesitation. Sometimes she wouldn't even bother to grab a change of clothes.

Shauna and Nathan stayed at our house until about 7 p.m., watching television and chatting to Anjie.

The following day, Friday, 20 February, my alarm went off and I went to work. At about 2.30 p.m. Anjie phoned me, sounding worried.

'I don't mean to alarm you,' she began. 'But Becky's friends are all here, and Luke is here, and nobody has seen her since Thursday morning. I can't get hold of her on the phone, and nobody knows where she could be. I rang Tanya and Danny, but they don't know either. Have you heard from her? Do *you* know where she is?'

I fell silent for a moment, racking my brains about the last time I saw Becky. It was on the Tuesday night, curled up in bed in her onesie. Alarm bells started ringing in my head.

'I've got no idea. I'll be home as soon as I can,' I said, before hanging up.

I ran into my manager Lee Zanelli's office.

'I've just had the strangest call,' I blurted out. 'My daughter's gone missing. All of her friends are sitting on my sofa and it seems none of them have seen her in days.'

For a moment Lee looked at me, stunned, before speaking.

'Do you want to try looking at her Facebook, see if you can find anything?' he suggested.

I logged into my Facebook account to check her page but saw nothing that indicated where she might be. I also tried to call Becky's mobile phone, but it was turned off, so I left her a message.

'Becky, can you call me back and let me know where you are? Thanks, love.'

I turned to Lee. 'I'm sorry, mate, but I've got to go,' I said. I could feel my blood pressure rising, my heart thudding in my chest.

'No problem, Dar – just get out of here,' Lee urged. 'Don't worry about things here. Go and sort it out. I'll let everyone know. Just go and find your daughter.'

I raced home, driving as fast as I could, and within thirty minutes I was pulling up outside the house.

When I walked into the living room, it was full of people: Anjie, Nathan and Shauna, and Becky's friends Adam, Courtney and Teela – a new friend from school – as well as her boyfriend, Luke. All their faces had the same expression – anxious and confused.

Luke explained that he had grown more and more concerned that Becky hadn't been in touch all day Thursday, so he'd decided to phone Anjie the next morning. Her friends also had no idea where she was, and everyone had come round to the house to see if she was here.

I didn't know what to think as I looked at each of them in turn. Becky always chose to spend her time with the same people – and all those people were sitting in my house.

'Right, let's get our heads together,' I said. 'When did we all last see her?'

'I saw her on Thursday morning when she left my house,' Adam volunteered, and Luke said that he had been in touch with her by text later that morning, adding, 'She was supposed to meet up with me yesterday afternoon, but then I didn't hear from her again.'

'I saw her before I went to the hospital, but she was gone by the time I got home,' Anjie said.

Shauna piped up. 'She left the house while you were at the hospital. I heard the door slam on her way out.'

We established between us that Becky had left the house at around 11.15 a.m, before Anjie returned from her appointment at 12.45 p.m.

As I called her phone again, I noticed that my hand was shaking.

'Becky, it's your dad,' I said. 'We are getting worried about you now. All your friends are here. Can you please call or text one of us to let us know you're safe?'

I hung up the phone then turned to Courtney. 'Can you come up to her bedroom with me?' I asked. 'Let me know if there are any clothes missing?'

She nodded and jumped to her feet. I knew Courtney and Becky were so close that she would instantly be able to tell if Becky had taken anything of significance with her. Courtney checked through her wardrobe and I glanced around the rest of her bedroom. It all looked pretty normal to me. Courtney noticed that Becky's blue puffer jacket was missing. She also noticed that Becky had left her make-up behind.

'She never goes anywhere without her make-up, Dar,' she said, looking worried. 'All her bags are here too, and she always has a bag with her.'

The onesie she had been wearing a few nights earlier was missing, as well as Anjie's green jumper. We also realised that her phone and laptop were missing, but Becky never took her laptop out of the house. Nothing made sense.

I walked back into the living room, sat down and took a deep breath. It was 4 p.m. and she'd not been seen for well over twenty-four hours.

'I think it's time to call the police,' I said. I grabbed my mobile and dialled 999.

'Hi, my name is Darren Galsworthy and I need to report a missing person,' I said as soon as I got through. It felt so unnatural for those words to be coming out of my mouth.

'It's my daughter. Her name is Rebecca Watts, and she's sixteen. She was last seen yesterday morning. She's 5 foot 1 inch tall, with long brown-red hair. She's particularly vulnerable as she finds it hard to read people. She never goes anywhere on her own. She's painfully shy – she won't even get on a bus alone.'

'Could she be at a friend's house?' the police officer asked.

'She doesn't have many friends and the ones she has are all sitting on my sofa right now,' I told her. 'She's always with her friends, at school, or at home with us. She doesn't ever go anywhere else. Nobody knows where she is. This is incredibly unlike her. Please help us.'

I felt my voice crack, and Anjie reached out to squeeze my hand tightly.

'OK, Mr Galsworthy, thank you for the information. We'll send someone round to your address as soon as we can,' he said, before ending the call.

I felt helpless. The only thing I could try was to phone Becky's mobile again.

'Please, Becky,' I begged, 'I'm so worried about you. Please come home. Please call me.'

As I hung up, everybody looked at each other anxiously. There was nothing to say. All any of us could do was wait. Anjie started crying quietly.

'You guys should probably get home,' I said, turning to Becky's friends. 'I don't want your parents worrying too. Thank you for coming over, and let us know if you hear anything at all. Becky is so lucky to have you lot as her friends.'

They nodded solemnly and filed out. I found myself pacing up and down the room, a bag of nervous energy. I couldn't relax. I needed to feel I was doing something, being useful, so I put my shoes on and went out to knock on every door in our street, asking if any of the neighbours had seen Becky, or if she had walked past the day before. But none of them had. When I returned, Shauna was in the garden room, smoking a cigarette and playing on her phone, and Nathan was crouched on the floor, watching as my grandchild charged around the living room.

I turned to him. 'Nathan, I want to put something up on Facebook about Becky.' He looked up at me as I added, 'Can you help?'

I was useless with Facebook and social media in general. I didn't have to use them for work and hardly any people my age used them to keep in touch, so I didn't really understand how it all worked. Whenever I did have to go on Facebook for something, I always asked Nathan and Shauna to help me.

Nathan slowly got to his feet. 'No problem,' he said, sitting down at the computer. 'We'll need to find a picture of her to put up and then we can post an appeal.'

Huddled together, we looked through Facebook and our phones to find a good photo of Becky to use.

'How about this one?' Nathan suggested, showing me a selfie-style shot of Becky taken from her Facebook page. 'It should be clear enough.'

'Yeah, good idea. Do that,' I said. Out of the corner of my eye I saw Shauna come into the room and sit down on the sofa. She was still playing around with her phone. I wondered if maybe she was looking for a good picture to use as well, but she didn't say anything.

'Right, that's uploaded,' Nathan said. 'Now we have a picture of her, we just need to write something above it, Dar. What do you want to write?'

I leaned over and told him what to say as he typed: 'PLEASE SHARE. Missing sixteen-year-old girl. Please private message if you have seen her or know anything.'

'That should do it,' Nathan said as he posted the message. 'People should be able to share it round for you now.'

'Thank you, Nath,' I said.

'No problem,' he replied, going over to sit down by Shauna.

Two police officers arrived to talk to us at about 6.30 p.m. We told them everything we knew: that Anjie had seen Becky before she left for the hospital, and that Shauna and Nathan had heard Becky's music on in her room when they'd arrived at the house.

'I heard the music being turned off and the front door slamming shut,' Shauna added. 'But I didn't actually see her leave.'

'Did you have a fight or argument with Becky in the hours leading up to her disappearance?' one of the officers asked me, and I shook my head.

'Not at all,' I replied. 'The last time I saw her was Tuesday night. I came home from work, she watched television, and I made her a pizza. I left for work the next day and she slept over at a friend's house the following night. Everything was calm and completely normal.'

They turned their attention to Anjie. 'What frame of mind was Becky in when she returned home after sleeping at her friend's house?' they asked.

'She seemed fine,' Anjie said. 'She was a bit grumpy because her front-door key didn't work, but that was it. She came home and went straight to her room. That wasn't unusual for her, to be honest.'

I wanted the police to organise search parties and get the whole force out looking for her, but they seemed to think that she had probably gone off with some new friend we didn't know about and would be back before long. That's the impression I got, anyway. I suppose that might be the case with most missing teenagers, but I knew my daughter, and I knew for sure that wasn't what had happened.

Once the police had left, Nathan and Shauna took their little one home, and I sat in front of the computer, staring hard at the screen, as if the answer might pop up there any moment. Tanya and Danny rang to ask for an update, but we had nothing to tell them. From time to time, Anjie offered me a cup of tea, but I refused everything. I couldn't focus on anything other than where Becky was.

The fact that she was missing had started to spread across Bristol. My family and friends started to share my Facebook post far and wide, and lots of people started to text or call to see if there was anything they could do to help. In total, the post was shared 887 times. I appreciated that they all wanted to help, but I didn't know what to say to anyone. *Please just find her!* was my only thought.

As the night went on, my imagination ran wild, and I started to imagine all the different scenarios Becky could have found herself in. Maybe she had been walking over to meet Luke and got attacked, beaten, then left for dead. Maybe she had been raped. Maybe my beautiful daughter had been kidnapped by a gang. Perhaps she had been dumped on a roadside, thrown out of a car. Perhaps she was tied up, unable to scream for help. She could have been out there, cold, frightened, and needing her dad. My heart felt as if it was going to explode out of my chest. I needed to find my girl.

As I worked myself up into more and more of a state, the voicemails I left on Becky's phone became increasingly frantic. I imagined that I was leaving messages for someone who had kidnapped her.

'If you have my daughter, let her go or I will kill you,' I said, raging down the phone. 'Let my daughter go. I want my girl back in one piece. I will kill anyone who hurts my daughter. I promise you, I will get to you, and when I do, you're dead.'

When Anjie heard me making my threats to my daughter's imaginary kidnappers she burst into tears. I hung up and ran my fingers through my hair despairingly. I knew I was acting crazy, but the worst thing about the situation was not knowing if my girl was safe or not.

'If she came back hurt or angry, or there was something wrong,' I told Anjie, 'then we could deal with it. We could fix it. As a family we can do anything, and I know we could take care of her. I just want her back, Anj.'

'I know, love,' she said, wrapping her arms around me. 'We all want her back.'

That night, I didn't sleep a wink. Anjie went up to bed as the stress was making her MS symptoms worse. She was so exhausted it was difficult for her even to speak. I didn't join her because my mind was too busy to contemplate sleep. I stayed up all night, searching Facebook and trying to find some answers, with no luck. Becky's friends were constantly messaging me, asking for updates, and I felt wretched as I had to tell them, over and over, that I didn't have any news.

I kept walking into Becky's room, looking for clues as to where she had gone, staring at her belongings.

'Where are you, Bex?' I asked out loud, trying hard to focus and put myself in her shoes. But it was no use. I couldn't think of anywhere she would go on her own.

The next morning, I posted on Facebook again: 'Please, if anyone has seen or heard from my daughter just let me know she is safe. She went missing on Thursday, 19 February at 11.15 a.m. She hasn't been seen by any of her friends. I'm really scared now. I want her home.'

Once again, the message was quickly shared by friends and family – including Shauna. Everyone wanted to help find Becky.

That day, I felt too paralysed by fear to wash, drink or eat anything. All I could do was stare at the computer screen and make phone calls to friends and family – anyone I could think of who had ever known Becky. Lots of friends knocked on the door, wanting to know if they could help and to check if Anjie and I were all right. But everyone who entered the house seemed like a passing blur to me. If they weren't Becky, I wasn't interested.

I felt as if I was having an out-of-body experience, looking in at all the distress, heartache and desperation. It was like watching somebody else act out my life – like watching a film, almost. I felt suffocated by thick, heavy black clouds. Waves of despair engulfed me relentlessly. The minute I managed to breathe and think clearly, another wave came crashing in. But despite how helpless I felt, I still had hope that Becky would come home unharmed.

Over and over, I imagined her walking through the door, hugging me and apologising for worrying everyone. Laughing it off, saying there had been a big misunderstanding.

'If she comes home, I'm never leaving her side ever again,' I told Anjie that night. 'We can do something special, together as a family. I always want her to know exactly how much we love her.'

'She already knows how much we love her, Dar,' Anjie replied. 'She's always known.'

'I'll never tell her off for leaving her stuff lying around again if she comes back to us, Anj,' I said as I choked back tears. 'I'll spend the rest of my life making her happy.'

That set me off and I started sobbing. Anjie wrapped her arms around me, but there was no comfort to be had. The sobs hurt my chest and didn't bring any easing of the tension, but once I'd started, it was hard to stop.

At last, we went up to bed and got under the covers. Anjie drifted off to sleep, but for me it seemed impossible. I would slide into unconsciousness for a matter of minutes then suddenly wake up again, realising that the nightmare I was having wasn't a nightmare after all – it was my reality. I doubted that I would ever sleep again. How could I when my daughter was out there somewhere and needed me?

I'm not a religious man, but I got up, went into Becky's room and knelt down at the foot of her bed. I clasped my hands together as hard as I could and started to pray.

'Please,' I said, 'bring my girl home to me. It doesn't matter if she's damaged. Just bring her home. I'll sort her out, and I promise I'll take care of her for the rest of my life. *Please.*'

I wasn't even sure which god I was praying to, but I prayed as hard as I could.

The more time that passed, the more I felt in limbo, not knowing whether my daughter was alive or dead – I was becoming increasingly desperate to find out.

CHAPTER 8

THE SEARCH

On Saturday, 21 February, two police officers visited the house and introduced themselves as Detective Constable Russ Jones and Major Crime Investigation Officer Jo Marks. They told us that they were our assigned family liaison officers – FLOs, for short. As they introduced themselves, I noticed that Jo was a little more reserved than Russ, who spoke quite bluntly about the situation and what was going to happen next.

I was so fraught with worry over Becky's disappearance and anger over the failure to find her that I struggled to take in a lot of what they were saying, but Anjie nodded quietly. She seemed to be listening a lot more intently than I was.

'We'll be taking swabs of her DNA today,' Russ said. 'We'll get it from places such as her toothbrush. It'll help us with the investigation. We'll also need to look around the house if that's OK with you, just in case we find anything that could help us.'

All I could do was nod helplessly. Anjie reached over and squeezed my hand. I felt as if I was trapped in a nightmare, and all I could do was watch it play out before my eyes.

A few minutes later, about eight officers arrived at my home, ready to take DNA samples and search for clues. I opened the door for them grimly.

'You can come in, look at whatever you want, take whatever you like,' I said. 'But the real search should be out there, not in here. We know for a fact that Becky left the house and didn't come back. She's out there somewhere, and you need to get out and find her.'

Jo looked at me sympathetically. 'There could be vital clues here as to why she hasn't come back, Mr Galsworthy. I know this is hard for you, but try not to worry. We know what we're doing.'

Jo's compassion disarmed me a little, and I waved the officers through the door so they could do what they needed to.

It transpired that Becky had left the house with her laptop and her phone, but didn't take any clothes, make-up or a tooth-brush. It didn't make any sense to me. If Becky had wanted to run away – not that she ever would – she would have made sure to take those items. It just didn't add up.

The following day, Avon and Somerset Police put out a public appeal for help to find Becky. They also said that they were planning to hold a search in the next few days.

I sat with Anjie on the sofa, watching the news reports into Becky's disappearance with my stomach completely tied up in knots. Hearing the reporters talk about 'Missing Bristol teen-ager Rebecca Watts' made me feel sick. I imagined that to everyone else listening at home, it sounded like another silly teenager who had run away to give her parents a fright. But that was my daughter they were talking about, and she was a girl who was too scared of the outside world ever to run away from home. She would never knowingly cause us so much worry and upset. You know your own, and she was simply not that kind of girl.

Every newspaper in the local area and some nationals, too, began picking up on the police appeal. Becky's face was plastered all over their websites, and the appeal was being shared across Facebook. Social-media users were starting to use the hashtag #FindBecky to link to the campaign. I couldn't help but wonder what I had done in my life to deserve this appalling, gut-wrenching despair.

Every hour that passed felt like a lifetime. My family descended on the house, worried about Becky and also about us. My brothers Sam, Joe and Asa, my sister Sarah, my dad, John, and my stepmother, Denise, all came round wanting to help.

I was sitting at the computer and Anjie was on the sofa when, one by one, they filed through the front door. Denise rushed straight over to give Anjie a cuddle, and Sam and Sarah crowded around me.

'Right, Dar, what can we do?' Sam asked, with a determined tone. 'We're here to help and we're not leaving until we've done something useful.'

'We've told all our friends, and they've told all their friends,' Sarah added. 'Everyone's willing to get out there and look for Becky. We need to print off some leaflets and get this going properly. We need to find her.'

That just set me off again. I began to sob as Sam and Sarah took my place at the computer and started designing leaflets and posters to put up around Bristol. They searched for a good picture of Becky, wrote the words, and, within minutes, we were printing hundreds of them. My printer didn't stop all day long.

Sam and Sarah handed the posters to Joe and Asa, and they took to the streets, sticking them up all over the area. They got their friends involved, and soon the whole of the city was plastered with pictures of Becky's face. They even started giving leaflets to people in cars as they pulled up at traffic lights.

Everyone was buzzing with nervous energy. Joe and Asa were in and out, collecting fresh batches of leaflets and posters, while Sam and Sarah kept printing more and more. Nathan and Shauna were back and forth to the house too, making sure Anjie was OK and generally keeping an eye on what was going on, and we spoke with Tanya and Danny regularly to keep in touch.

I slumped in a chair in the garden room and lit a cigarette. Anjie followed me in there so I lit one for her too. I noticed that my hands were shaking and I clenched my fists tightly to try to stop.

I looked at Anjie properly for the first time in days – she looked exhausted. I no doubt looked even worse.

'We're never going to see her again, are we?' I blurted out, choking on the words.

Anjie looked at me in shock. 'Of *course* we'll see her again,' she cried, grabbing my hand. 'You have to believe we will find her.'

At that moment, I thought I heard Nathan laugh and say something in the living room. It sounded like he was mocking what we had just said, but I quickly dismissed it. I hadn't slept in days so I was hypersensitive to everything, and my house was completely chaotic as people wandered in and out. I truly felt as if I was going mad.

All I could think about was Becky. Was she safe? Was she freezing or hungry? The weather was bitterly cold and there had been days of relentless rain lashing down on the roof of the house. If she was out there she would be soaked to the skin by now. She might have been ill.

Anjie squeezed my hand again. 'Darren, don't lose hope,' she said. 'You know what I think? She's met someone and gone off with them, not realising the worry she's putting us through. She can be very naive – you know that. She *will* come home. You can't give up hope.'

I looked at her, and then wrapped my arms around her for a hug. I didn't believe a word she was saying, but at that moment I appreciated her saying it. Anjie had always been my rock, and it was amazing the way she could always be positive, even at desperate times like that.

The next morning, Monday, 23 February, I logged onto Facebook again.

'Still no news,' I wrote. 'The police have turned my house upside down looking for clues. What fresh hell will we go through today?'

I considered what Anjie had suggested – that Becky might have gone off with somebody – but it seemed so unlike her. She was the kind of girl who couldn't even go up to the till in a shop. An hour later, I decided to try a different approach, just in case.

'Bex, if you can see this, please come home,' I wrote on my Facebook wall. 'We're heartbroken. We need you in our lives. You won't be told off and you can make as much mess as you want. I won't say a word, I promise.'

As I posted it, I sighed. It was worth a shot – anything was.

Later that day, the police told me that they wanted to hold a press conference so we could appeal directly to Becky to come forward. They wanted me to speak, as well as Pat, Becky's grandmother on her mother's side.

Even though I didn't really believe that Becky had gone off of her own accord, I agreed to do the conference, as it gave me a sense of actually doing something to help the police with their investigations.

Russ and Jo took us to a police station in the St Philips area of Bristol, where we met Detective Inspector Richard Ocone, the officer leading the investigation. We were taken into a cramped room, where there were about fifteen journalists and lots of photographers and TV cameramen. We were told to sit down, and to speak directly to the camera while reading the statement we had prepared with help from the police.

I took a deep breath, and started to read from the sheet in front of me, feeling very nervous.

'Bex, if you're watching this, please come home,' I started. 'We love you so much, and whatever you think, we can sort anything out, it doesn't matter. Just come home. And if any of her friends are hiding her – you're not doing her any favours. Just tell the police. Just tell the police and bring her home safe.'

I glanced down at my statement to read the next part, but the words started to go blurry.

'Sorry, I can't,' I said, my voice cracking. I tried my best to regain my composure, but it was no good. I stared hard at the table before admitting defeat.

'You're going to have to do it, Pat,' I said. 'I'm sorry.'

Pat nodded and swiftly took over.

'Hiya Bex, it's Nan,' she said. 'You can see your dad is a broken man. Please, if you don't want to come home yet just let someone else ring or text. And if you're a bit worried about coming back because of all this hullabaloo, come and stay with me for a few days. You know I have a spare room. You're so loved, and I don't think you believe it, but you really are.'

Pat paused for a second, looking over at me. I was trying my hardest not to cry.

'Look at your poor dad,' she added. 'Please come home. Or whoever is sheltering her – do the right thing. Thank you.'

DI Ocone said, 'Firstly, I want to say directly to Rebecca – you are in no trouble. All we are concerned about is your wellbeing, and we just want to make sure you are OK. If you can just call home, call one of your friends or call us, we can work with you to help work through any issues you are facing.

'I would also ask anyone who might know where Rebecca is to come forward and let us know. This is completely out of character for Rebecca, to leave without telling her family or friends – especially if she is not planning on coming home.'

As we drove back to the house, I allowed myself a faint hope that whoever had my girl would find it in their heart to let her go after seeing the state I was in. I knew Becky would never disappear on purpose. Somebody had to have her. Somebody out there knew where my daughter was. And when I discovered who that was, I was coming for them.

The next day, police began searching the local area and speaking to residents in the surrounding streets. They also started combing the woodland and open spaces nearby – the places I used to take Becky when she was a little girl. They carried out searches of neighbours' gardens, outhouses and the local nature reserve.

Meanwhile, I did a telephone interview with Jack FM, a Bristol radio station, about Becky's disappearance and the toll it had taken on our family. The police said it would be a good idea to talk to various different media outlets because the more people who knew about Becky, the better. As the presenter started asking me about my daughter, I tried to hold back the tears which had already started to fill my eyes. More than anything, I wanted to drum home how shy Becky was, and that what had happened was completely out of the ordinary for her.

'She's very shy and timid,' I told him. 'Not around us and her closest friends, but anyone outside of that and she wouldn't be able to talk to them. As I have told the police, she can't even go up to a till in a shop.

'She couldn't even ask for a bus ticket. She would rather walk than get on a bus and ask the driver for a ticket. This is how shy and reserved she is. So this just doesn't add up. None of her clothes are missing, her wash bag is here, her toothbrush is here, her make-up's still here. She would not leave the house without all her make-up on, looking nice.'

When he asked me how I was feeling, my voice cracked as I tried to reply.

'It's been absolute hell on earth,' I said. 'I've not been able to eat or sleep since she's gone missing. We just need her back home. Someone out there knows something. I just want my girl back, that's all. I just want her back.'

Then I took a moment to speak to my daughter, in the hope that she could somehow hear the interview. 'Bex, if you are able, just come home,' I pleaded. 'You aren't going to get told off or anything. Just come home. We need you home here. You are a total part of our life.'

The media attention on our family was ramping up. There was a huge amount of interest in us, and whenever I looked outside I could see a huddle of reporters and photographers, waiting for a few words or a picture of us. Most times when I left the house I was accompanied by a police officer or a member of my family, but I stopped now and then to give a quote to reporters. I knew that they had a job to do, and the more publicity we got, the more it was going to help us find Becky. All the same, I couldn't help feeling that the press attention was invasive. I kept thinking to myself that Becky would have hated being in the spotlight like that.

After the radio interview, I resumed my position at the computer. I had never spent as much time on Facebook as I did during those days. I sat there for hours, sharing pictures of Becky and anything else I could find – including the video of us doing our 'Atomic Curry Challenge'. I ended up watching that video over and over again. I couldn't take my eyes off Becky, laughing and joking around, being cheeky to her old man. I would have given anything to be in that moment with her once again, rather than sitting at my computer watching her helplessly, tears rolling down my cheeks.

That night, I lay in bed, hoping to get some sleep but knowing that it probably wouldn't come. My mind was exhausted, full of gruesome images of what might have happened to Becky. Mostly, I imagined that she had been kidnapped and raped. I knew there were some vile people in the world, and maybe my little girl was out there somewhere and she needed me. I got up in the middle of the night and stared hard at myself in the bathroom mirror. I looked wretched, my eyes red and swollen, with huge bags underneath.

'Where is my daughter? Where is she?' I asked out loud, staring at my reflection like a madman.

The next morning, on Wednesday, 25 February, in desperation I posted something on Facebook that I believed could help us find Becky, or at least get people thinking. Becky, Anjie and I were so close, we practically lived in each other's pockets. As I always did the family food shop, Becky would ask me to pick up stuff she needed – including personal items. I knew that she was having her period the week she went missing, as she had asked me to get some tampons for her. I was becoming more and more anxious about what might have happened, who might have taken her and what they might have done to her, and I was going to stop at nothing to find out, so I wrote: 'This is a message to all wives, mothers and girlfriends. It was my baby girl's time of the month, so if you have washed any blood from your partner's or son's underwear and they can't explain it, please report it. Please imagine: if this was your child, what would you do?'

The next day, some of the newspapers ran the message and described it as 'disturbing'. I was furious at the idea that my post might be seen as anything but a desperate dad appealing to the public for any information possible. Perhaps some other fathers don't have the same relationship with their children, but Becky and I were close enough for me to know when she was having her period. Looking back, maybe it was a little odd, but while I was in the agonising grip of despair and frustration it made perfect sense.

Joe and Sam had organised a public search that Wednesday, to run alongside the police investigation. They appealed on social media and through the press for people to help.

A few hours before the search was due to get underway, Russ and Jo came round to speak to Anjie and me.

'We'll need to bring a forensic team into the house to do a more thorough search, if that's OK,' Russ said. 'It means that you guys will have to stay somewhere else tonight. If you pack an overnight bag, we will take you somewhere now.'

'Why do we have to leave our home? I don't understand,' I complained. She obviously wasn't there so why were they looking in the house? The thought flashed through my mind that maybe I was a suspect. I knew they'd interviewed Luke, Adam and all Becky's friends, but there was no question of them being anything to do with it. I supposed they were just being thorough, but I wished they would focus on finding her instead of investigating the family.

Anjie and I threw together a change of clothing, our pyjamas and toothbrushes, and we were taken away in an unmarked police car to a hotel in the centre of Bristol. Our car and computer were going to be examined as well, so we couldn't use them. I knew the police were just doing their jobs and they needed us out of the way, but it wasn't a pleasant experience being turfed out of our home like that. Photographers bustled around the gate, taking pictures of us as we left. I stopped to give a quick quote to a reporter, who asked me what I thought of the public's attempts to help us find Becky.

I said, 'I'm very grateful for the support from the public. The search was organised by my brother, and I hope lots of people turn out for it. I can't say anything else right now, as I have to go.'

I wanted to join the search because I was desperate to feel like I was doing something useful. I had spent hour after hour sitting at the computer and on the phone, and it had started to take its toll on me. I needed to be out there, physically looking for my little girl.

I asked Anjie to wait by the phone while I went to meet all my side of the family, who had gathered at the bottom of our street. To my amazement, around a hundred people turned up. Nathan and Shauna weren't there, but I assumed it was because they had to look after their kid. When I thought about it, I realised that they hadn't done much to help since Becky had gone missing, but, to be honest, they weren't really the type to pitch in and help other people. That's just the way they were.

I was humbled that afternoon by the amount of people who did want to help my family. Neighbours and strangers alike seemed genuinely concerned about where Becky might be, and it made me grateful and proud to be a Bristolian. My bosses – Jeremy, John, Lee, Andy and Tony – even let all my colleagues take the day off work to join the search party. I felt completely indebted to them for that.

Sam and Joe split everyone into groups and coordinated them so that each group took on a different patch in the city. It was a freezing cold day, but people were resilient; they wrapped up warmly and got on with it. We walked miles that day. We combed every public park, every residential street, and we stopped every single person that we passed. We gave out hundreds and hundreds of flyers, all with Becky's beautiful face on them. Every time I pushed one into somebody's hand, I made sure I met their eyes with mine. I wanted them to understand how important it was that we found Becky and brought her home safely.

'Oh, you're the father of the poor girl,' a woman exclaimed as I gave her a flyer, and I nodded. To my surprise, she threw her arms around me in a touching display of compassion.

'I hope you find her,' she said.

I was amazed that Becky's disappearance had touched people so deeply. It frequently brought me to tears that day.

As we trudged across all sorts of terrain, I turned to my brother Joe.

'Thank you for everything, buddy,' I said, and he put his arm around me reassuringly.

'We'll find her, Dar,' he vowed.

I wished so hard that I could believe him, but at this point I was losing faith fast.

'I don't think I've ever felt so desperate and low in my whole life,' I confided, and he looked at me sympathetically and nodded.

'Just don't give up yet, Dar, all right?' he replied, giving me a squeeze. 'The worst thing we can do now is give up.'

We didn't stop looking until every last leaflet had been handed out and we had walked as far as we possibly could. At the end of the search a number of items were handed to police officers, including a pair of shoes, a notebook, a jumper and a blue T-shirt. Someone also spotted a bag buried in a hedge, covered in leaves, which was examined by forensics officers that night.

When I got back to the hotel, Anjie was anxiously waiting for me.

'Did you have any luck?' she asked hopefully, and I shook my head.

'Not really, love,' I said, taking her hand. 'Lots of people were out there helping us, though.'

'Nothing here either,' she sighed, pointing to the phone. 'Do you want something to eat or drink?'

I shook my head. I couldn't remember the last time I'd been able to eat more than a few mouthfuls of food or drink more than a sip of cola. I could tell I was losing weight rapidly, because when I got dressed all my clothes felt looser, but the idea of eating was unappealing. I couldn't taste food. Our desperate need to find Becky completely consumed me, and anything else seemed pointless.

Our hotel stay was extended from one night to two, and then three, with police saying that we couldn't return home because they needed more time to examine the house. We only had one change of clothes and nothing else, so Russ and Jo gave us £100 to buy some new clothes, and the force also paid for our food and drink while we were at the hotel, as well as giving us a hire car to use.

Everything was surreal. I hated not being able to walk into Becky's room and feel her presence around me. I worried that if she returned home, as unlikely as that now seemed, she might panic when she realised that Anjie and I weren't there. Most of all I hated just sitting in that hotel room, waiting and waiting, with nothing to do but watch television and pace up and down.

Over the next few days, forensic officers continued to comb our home for clues, and specialist sniffer dogs were brought in. Avon and Somerset Police enlisted the help of other police forces from South Wales and Wiltshire, and the searches were stepped up. They even went as far as wading through ponds in the nearby public parks. A laptop was discovered in woodland,

1. Becky was six when this picture was taken in summer 2005 at home in Crown Hill.

2–3. Becky is eight here, in her usual position around Anjie's neck. This picture was taken on the beach on a family holiday in Weymouth. Becky loved swimming in the ocean – she was a proper water baby.

4. This picture was taken during a family holiday at Cofton Holiday Park, Dawlish, during the summer of 2003. Becky is four here, Danny is seven and Nathan is fifteen. We went to Dawlish often as the kids enjoyed it so much.

5. In winter 2009 Bristol got completely covered in snow. Becky was ten and absolutely loved it. We played out for hours and this snowman was built in a field opposite our home in St George's.

6. Ten-year-old Becky and me at Bristol Zoo in 2009. Becky loved animals so much, she used to beg us to take her there. It was one of her favourite places to go.

7. Another family holiday in Dawlish, during the summer of 2007. Becky is eight here and we spent the day at the beach.

8. Becky, aged ten, in summer 2009 on the day she brought her cat Marley home from Bristol Dogs and Cats Home. He was a tiny kitten and very cute – however, he soon grew to be a large, feisty cat!

9–10. Becky is twelve in these pictures. She was in the middle of her struggle with anorexia. It was a very difficult time for us all as she wrestled with her eating disorder, and we were so relieved and proud of her when she managed to beat it.

11. My lovely wife Anjie and me on our wedding day in August 2013. One of the best days of my life and one of Becky's favourites too – she was beaming all day.

12. Becky as a beautiful bridesmaid at our wedding. She had chosen all the bridesmaids' dresses in her favourite colour – baby blue.

13. Flowers, teddies and tributes are left outside our home after Becky's death. The public were a huge support to us during those horrible first few months.

14. A horse-drawn carriage takes my beautiful Bex to her final resting place in April 2015. The funeral was funded by the people of Bristol and it was an amazing send-off for an amazing girl.

15. I release a single white dove for Becky at her funeral in April 2015. I broke down the minute it flew away – a very emotional moment.

16. Me and my family waiting to speak to the press after the guilty verdicts were delivered at Bristol Crown Court in November 2015. The trial was an extremely anxious and emotional time for us all, but we stood together as a unit.

17. This is my favourite picture of the two of us – it shows our relationship as father and daughter beautifully. It was taken by Anjie as we took a country walk together on holiday in Cornwall when Becky was thirteen.

not far from our home, and for a short while they thought it could be a breakthrough in the case – but it was soon discounted. The main thing the detectives said they were concerned about was that there had been no sightings of Becky whatsoever after she had left our house. It seemed incredibly odd and mysterious that not one neighbour, not one passing motorist had seen her that morning, and she wasn't in any CCTV footage, either. How could she just have vanished?

On 27 February, Russ and Jo took Anjie and me to the police station to get some extra details from us. They took us into separate rooms, and I spoke to a few different detectives, who quizzed me on my family's dynamic. I was confused by this line of questioning. I had expected more questions about Becky, but instead the officers seemed intent on focusing on the rest of us.

They started by asking me how our family worked, who was related to whom, and then they starting asking if we all got on with each other.

As well as asking me what my relationship with Becky was like, they quizzed me on Anjie, Nathan, Danny and Shauna, and how they interacted with her.

'Do Nathan and Becky get along?' they asked, and I shrugged.

'They fight occasionally, like any siblings do,' I answered. 'Nathan used to get jealous of Becky's relationship with his mum, which is natural.'

I thought again before adding, 'Becky is quite disapproving of Nathan and Shauna being in the house all the time. She thinks they scrounge off us financially and in terms of getting fed. Half the time, I agree with her.'

'And what about Shauna?' they asked.

'Shauna and Becky get on all right,' I said. 'Shauna is like family to us now. She's always around the house with our grandchild.'

They seemed intent on talking about Nathan and Shauna, and I quickly got irritated with the line of questioning.

'Excuse me, but what has this got to do with anything?' I snapped.

'Mr Galsworthy,' a male officer began. 'We have to know everything there is to know about the family in order to investigate fully.'

I suddenly lost my rag. I was feeling exhausted and drained, and I felt that they were wasting time by interrogating me about things that didn't even matter.

'Becky left the house and didn't return. The rest of my family have been at home with me, helping police and taking part in the searches,' I thundered. 'Nathan is my son and Shauna is like a daughter to me.

'My family have nothing to do with this. We know nothing, and we have all told you as much. Your questions are pointless. Please stop focusing on our family and get out there, do your jobs and find my daughter.'

I wasn't proud of my outburst. I knew the police were trying their hardest to find Becky, but in that moment I couldn't help but feel defensive of my family. In my opinion, we were suffering enough without being made to feel like criminals at the same time.

CHAPTER 9

THE ARRESTS

Anjie and I stayed in three different hotels and an apartment while the search for Becky continued. On 2 March we were moved to a small hotel mainly used for airport passengers, just off the A38. It suited us to be out of Bristol city centre because the attention on Becky's disappearance was huge by this point, and sometimes a bit overwhelming. Her face was still plastered over every local and national paper, and we couldn't go for a drink at the hotel bar without seeing the story flash up on television. People recognised our faces in the city, and even though most didn't approach us, I could tell they were staring. I preferred to hide away as much as possible.

Being away from the house was hard, though. I struggled to sleep in a bed that wasn't my own – not that I was sleeping much anyway. Every day that passed made me feel more empty and desperate. Anjie was finding it difficult too. Some days, she could hardly get out of bed, she was so weak and exhausted, and she spoke very slowly, her brain feeling foggy, which was frightening for both of us. Our daily routine was pretty much: get up, try to force down some breakfast (something I never managed) then wait for updates from Jo and Russ, with daytime TV on in the background.

On Saturday, 28 February, we were informed that the police were questioning Nathan and Shauna over Becky's disappearance. We weren't told much more than that and, to be honest, I was instantly dismissive of it. I knew the police had to follow every line of enquiry, including speaking to all the family members, so I didn't think it amounted to anything more. I was sure that they wouldn't get much out of Nathan and Shauna. The pair didn't seem to know anything about what had happened, and they were too wrapped up in themselves to care very much anyway.

On the morning of Tuesday, 3 March, everything changed. We were in our hotel room when Anjie's mobile phone rang. She mouthed to me that it was Russ. I rolled my eyes, thinking that he was calling to give us the usual update – that Becky was still missing and the police were no closer to finding out where she was. I was wrong.

'What's going on?' asked Anjie. There was something different in her voice, urgency – worry. 'Is there any news?'

She listened intently, looking across at me. After she hung up, Anjie stared at me in shock and confusion.

'What's the matter, love? What's happening?' I asked.

She gazed at the phone in her hand for a few seconds then looked up at me, tears in her eyes.

'They've arrested Nathan and Shauna,' she said.

I stared at her in disbelief, then a wave of irritation washed over me. 'What the hell?' I said. 'That's got to be a mistake.

Why on earth go after the family instead of doing their fucking jobs properly and finding Becky?'

'It doesn't make any sense,' she replied, shaking her head. 'What on earth do they think they've done? Nathan wouldn't do anything.'

'It's bullshit, Anj,' I said. 'Absolute bullshit. It's so typical to go after the family instead of actually doing what they need to do. They're completely in the wrong. Those two are just an easy target.'

As we waited for them to arrive, my mind was doing somersaults. Russ hadn't said on the phone *why* they had arrested Nathan and Shauna. A thousand thoughts popped into my head, but the outstanding one was that it must be some kind of mistake.

Russ and Jo came straight to the room and knocked on the door. I answered and waved them in, before sitting back down on the bed. I noticed that they both looked even more solemn than usual.

Russ nodded towards the television, which was on in the background.

'Do you mind turning that off for a minute?' he asked, and I grabbed the remote and did as I was told.

There was an uneasy silence in the room as Anjie and I waited for them to speak. It was unbearable.

'So, why have you arrested those two?' I blurted out.

Russ took a deep breath before speaking. 'Nathan is being very uncooperative with us at the moment,' he said.

I laughed a bit too loudly.

'Well, he's going to be, isn't he?' I muttered. 'This is ridiculous.'

Jo and Russ looked at each other, and I could tell there was something they weren't telling me.

'There's no easy way to tell you this,' Russ said, 'but the situation has escalated. The investigation is now a murder inquiry.'

The room went blurry as I tried to take in what he was saying. It felt as if someone had punched me hard in the chest. I could feel my heart pounding, could hear my blood rushing, and I felt dizzy and sick. The word *murder* had caught me completely off guard. I looked at him, dazed, and instinctively I reached out and put my arm around Anjie to comfort her. Neither of us had started to cry yet – the shock was too great. Every breath felt like a tremendous effort.

'We discovered body parts at an address in Barton Hill last night,' he added. 'I'm so sorry, Darren.'

My whole world crumbled around me in that moment.

'How do you know it's even her?' I asked slowly. My mind was struggling to understand the full gravity of what he was saying.

Russ looked at me sympathetically. 'I'm sorry. It's definitely her,' he said quietly.

He began explaining that they had identified the body using DNA, from the sample they had taken from Becky's toothbrush, but his voice faded out. All I could think was that my little girl was dead. She had been found only a mile away from our home. The way he worded it – *body parts* – made my stomach lurch, and I ran to the bathroom to be sick. However, I had been surviving on cans of cola for days, so nothing came out. I looked into the toilet bowl, shaking with shock and anger, with beads of cold sweat prickling my neck. I had horrendous images of my daughter cut into pieces. How many? Did the police even have all of her, or was some still missing? It was unbearable.

I slowly walked back into the room, and that was when I felt a bomb explode inside me. My daughter was dead. I no longer had any hope of ever seeing her again. It all became too much to bear. I let out a huge roar and completely lost the plot. I couldn't see anything clearly – everything around me went blurry and fuzzy, and time slowed right down. I felt furious with every-thing and everyone as I punched the floor and the wall, and grabbed the nearest thing I could reach – one of my shoes – and threw it hard across the room. It bounced off the wall.

Russ, Jo and Anjie just watched me in silence. Anjie finally broke down then, letting out a massive, heart-breaking wail and gripping her head in her hands. I felt as if the ground was giving way beneath me, so I let myself slump down the bed and tried to catch my breath.

Russ gave us some time to pull ourselves together a bit, then slowly, gently, he began to explain that Becky's remains had been found in a man's house at number 9 Barton Court, in the Barton Hill area of Bristol. The man was called Karl Deme-trius. Apparently Nathan knew him. Anjie and I looked at each other.

'I've never heard of him,' I said. 'We weren't even aware that Nathan had many friends. He usually only hangs out with his girlfriend. Do you know this guy, Anj?'

Anjie shook her head, still sobbing quietly. She looked so small and confused, sitting there in her wheelchair, that I reached across and gave her hand a squeeze.

'What evidence is there that Nathan had anything to do with this?' I asked.

'Becky's blood was detected on the doorframe outside her bedroom,' Russ said. 'And Nathan's fingerprints were also there. When we arrested him, he told us where the body parts were. We searched the property and they were there. He admitted being responsible for her death, Darren. We have charged him with Becky's murder, and Shauna with perverting the course of justice.'

I stared at him in shock, followed by what I can only describe as revulsion and contempt. In a flash, every loving feeling I'd ever had for my stepson disappeared, and in its place red-hot hatred ran through my veins.

'That fucking bastard,' I muttered, and Anjie cried even harder. 'What the fuck was he doing? What the fuck made him do that to her? I'm going to fucking kill him.'

I rocked back and forth in my seat manically, feeling unhinged. The more I thought about it, the more everything started to fall into place. That's why there had been no sightings of Becky after she had supposedly left the house. Nathan and Shauna were there at the time she'd apparently left, and they were the ones who said she had gone out. Nobody else saw Becky leave.

I felt dumbfounded. Nathan might not have been perfect, but I regarded him as my son, and Shauna had become family to us too. It had never occurred to me before that they could be lying, that they could be responsible somehow. I didn't ever consider it. I simply trusted what they were saying because neither of them gave me any reason to believe otherwise. The betrayal took the wind out of me. It was crushing. I felt like the stupidest man on the planet.

How could a member of my own family carry out such a

thing, hurt a young girl like that? I couldn't contemplate how Nathan could callously take her life, without a care in the world. How could he cut her into pieces? She was his stepsister. She had adored him from the day they first met. The first word she ever spoke had been his name. What had Becky done to deserve this? What must he have thought of her to do such a thing?

I couldn't think of a single reason why he would do it. It would have been far easier if a stranger had murdered her. Instead, it was a man I had raised as my own son, who had accompanied us on our many family holidays while Becky was growing up. Someone whom I had supported financially and emotionally for more than a decade. A best man at my wedding. The betrayal stung so badly, it made it ten times worse.

I was lost in my own thoughts for what felt like ages as I tried to come to terms with the utter devastation we had just been dealt. Anjie was inconsolable by this point. She looked as if she could drop dead with shock. I felt terrible for her. Her own son had done this to the teenage girl she had brought up as a daughter. It was unbearable for her knowing that her own flesh and blood had done something so vile. I held her hand tightly, aware that my whole body was shaking violently.

From that moment on, I discarded any feelings of affection I ever had for Nathan. All the happy memories I had of him – taking him for his driving test, enlisting him in the army cadets and taking him out for his first pint – were forced from my mind. All that was left was anger, hurt and hatred. I had never felt a hate so strong in my entire life. As far as I was concerned, Nathan was no longer a member of my family. He was absolute poison.

'I'm going to kill him,' I kept repeating, and Russ and Jo looked at each other uncomfortably. 'In the slowest, most painful way possible. If it's the last thing I ever do, I am going to kill him.'

My feelings for Shauna were similar. In that explosive moment I was reminded of my instinct the first time I saw her. I knew from the moment I set eyes on her that she was bad news. I knew that it made me feel uncomfortable to watch Nathan and her play happy families, but I could never figure out why. Instead, I allowed her into our lives, into our family. Shauna had told Anjie and me that we were the closest thing to a family she had ever known. And this was how she repaid us? I couldn't believe it.

'I knew she was bad news,' I muttered to Anjie, bitterly. 'I never, ever should have allowed her anywhere near this family. I should have told her to fuck off, right from the start. I should have thrown her out of our fucking house.'

Russ held his up hand. 'Please try to calm down, Darren,' he said softly.

I just glared at him. 'How calm would you be if it happened to your daughter?'

I knew it wasn't his fault, but at that moment Russ was the bearer of bad news. I was the most vulnerable and hurt I'd ever been in my entire life.

Jo tried then, with a more sympathetic tone. 'I know it must be incredibly difficult for you both. It's completely understandable that you feel angry. I can't begin to imagine how you feel.'

I nodded, took a deep breath and tried hard to regain my composure. I squeezed Anjie's hand even tighter. She still hadn't said anything.

'When can we see her?' I asked quietly.

'We'll find out for you as soon as we can,' Jo replied.

There were a few more practical details Russ and Jo had to share with us, but I didn't take much in. They said Tanya and Danny would be informed by their own family liaison officers, but it was up to us to tell the rest of the family. As soon as they left, I gave Anjie a massive hug. She felt fragile in my arms. We were both shaking with shock.

'Shall we have a drink, love?' I asked, and she nodded tearfully. We were in such deep shock, hurting so badly that having a drink was the only thing I could think of to numb the pain.

That afternoon, we sat in the bar together and I sank several vodkas. At one point, the latest update on Becky's disappearance appeared on screen. It said that 'body parts' had been discovered at an address in Bristol and that two people had been arrested. A further four people had also been seized on suspicion of assisting an offender. Who were they? We didn't think Nathan had any friends. Why would they have agreed to help him?

I put my drink down and stared at the screen. Something about it being on television brought home to me that it was actually happening. The woman behind the bar noticed the look on my face, and when she asked me if she should switch the channel, I nodded grimly.

I kept trying to think of something to say to Anjie, but every time I opened my mouth the words wouldn't come. For the most part, we sat in silence and stared into space. What do you say to comfort the woman you love when her son has just admitted to killing your daughter? It was too much to take in.

That day, I tried my very best to drink myself into oblivion, until the room was spinning and my words were slurred. More than anything, I wanted the drink to take the edge off the pain I was feeling, but if anything it just intensified it. I went to bed that night a completely broken man.

The following morning, Russ called to say that we were to be questioned further following the discovery of Becky's body parts. We were going to be taken to separate police stations, on opposite sides of Bristol.

'Why do we have to be separated?' I asked, but Russ just said it was to do with where they had space.

He then told us that they knew the cause of death: Becky had been suffocated. He assured us that it would have been quick. I had dozens of questions. How was she suffocated? Where was she? But he said we could only be told a limited amount while they were still putting the legal case together.

The police came to get Anjie first.

'I'll see you later,' I said as I helped her into the car.

I turned to one of the officers. 'My wife relies on me to take care of her, so if she needs something, please make sure she gets it.'

When I got to the station where I was being questioned, I went in with quite a different viewpoint than on the last time I'd been there. I wasn't going to defend Nathan any more. He had already admitted killing Becky. Instead, I told them every-thing I could think of that might help, while still being honest about his personality and his relationships with the different members of our family.

'What is he like as a father?' they asked me.

'I have to admit, he is a good father,' I said. 'He does everything for his child.'

'Does he have a temper?' they pressed.

'Yes, he does, occasionally,' I answered. 'He can sometimes have a bit of a short fuse. But I never would have thought that he would be able to do what he has, not in a million years. I never knew he was a monster, otherwise he would not have been welcome in my home. He was always a good enough kid.'

I had mentioned in previous police interviews how young Shauna was when he first got involved with her, and I had already told them about the incident when he brought home those twelve-year-old girls in his car. At the time, I had thought it was a wind-up, but now, after everything he had done, I believed he was capable of anything. This time I made sure I mentioned it again. It seemed to take on new significance, somehow.

My mind was turning over every memory I'd ever had of Nathan. I remembered those times when he kept jumping out on Becky to scare her. I had dismissed that as just an older brother trying to wind up his younger sister, distressing as it was, but now it felt much more sinister and evil.

There were so many things that kept circling around in my mind. When I looked back, Nathan and Shauna had seemed to be getting on better with Becky in the few months before her death, and I had been pleased. Was that all part of the plan? Was he trying to get Becky to trust him so that he could attack her?

I spoke to the police for hours that day. Talking about Nathan for such a long time made me feel incredibly angry and bitter. My mind started to fill with some disturbing images as I fantasised about what I would do if I ever got my hands on him. I thought about killing him, about chopping him up – just as he did to my precious little girl. Thinking such awful, sick things made me feel disgusted with myself, but I couldn't help it. I found myself in some dark places, and began to worry that maybe I was somehow as twisted as him. It was an uncomfortable feeling, but I now think that most fathers would feel the same way. I kept reminding myself that I only felt that way because of what he had chosen to do to my daughter.

I was mentally and physically exhausted by the time I was driven back to the hotel. I had no doubt that Anjie was feeling the same too. When I got back to our room, she was already there, waiting for me. She looked completely worn out.

'You all right, love?' I asked as I walked in.

She simply nodded.

'How the fuck are we ever going to get through this, after what he's done?' I suddenly blurted out. 'I'm going to kill him, that's for sure. If I ever get close to him again, I will end him. He won't get away with this.'

Anjie got upset then. She stifled a sob before speaking. 'Dar, I can't listen to you go on about him like that,' she whispered. 'He's still my son, whatever he's done. How do you think I feel, knowing he's done this to our family?'

I tried to rein it in a bit more after that. I was so caught up in my own anguish that I was forgetting about the woman who had always been there for me, my rock. Whatever I was going through, it had to be ten times worse for her, knowing that her own son was the monster who had done all of this.

'I'm sorry, my love,' I said, wrapping my arms around her. 'Anj, I'm sorry. I'm just falling apart. I've lost my girl.'

'I have too,' she said, meeting my gaze. 'Becky was my daughter too. I feel just as betrayed as you by all of this. I'm devastated. I just can't understand why he did this to us.'

Over the next few days, our family gathered around us and gave us the strength we needed to cope. I could only take one day at a time. Thinking about a future without Becky in it was too painful.

Meanwhile, Anjie became worried about the effect Becky's murder would have on our marriage. It had never entered my head that Anjie could be held responsible for Nathan's actions, but she grew scared that I was going to leave her. She relied on me for so much more than love and emotional support – throughout her illness I had been the main person who took care of her.

'Are we all right, you and I?' she blurted out one evening when we were watching television. 'Are you going to leave me, Darren? Because of him?'

My heart stung when I heard those words. I sat down next to her and looked into her eyes. 'Of course not,' I told her firmly. 'I would never blame you for what he has done. I love you. You're my soulmate, and I'm not going anywhere. I can't be without you, you silly thing.'

Anjie smiled weakly, then started to sob into my shoulder.

That night, I comforted her. It seemed like one of us was always falling apart during those days, while the other one would try desperately to put them back together again.

CHAPTER 10

SAYING GOODBYE

It was always the same dream that tortured me during the nights. Becky being attacked by Nathan, and her terrified screaming as she realised that this time he wasn't just fooling around. Shauna holding her hand tightly over my girl's mouth to shut her up. The fear on her face and my desperate frustration at not being able to save her.

It always ended with me waking up drenched in sweat, with tears stinging my eyes and my mind filled with terrible images of what Becky might look like after her brutal murder.

An agonising two days passed from the day Russ and Jo first told us the terrible news to when we were allowed to see Becky. Two days of trying to come to terms with the fact that she had been killed, and that my stepson and his girlfriend had been arrested on suspicion of her murder. I can count on the fingers of one hand the hours of sleep I managed to get in that period.

When Anjie and I had a call from the police to tell us we could see Becky, we arranged to drive to the morgue the following day, 5 March. To be honest, even though I had been told my beautiful girl was gone, there was a part of me that needed to see her body to accept that it was true. I guess I was still holding onto a tiny shred of hope – maybe that poor girl was somebody else's daughter, not my Becky.

I woke up that morning feeling numb, and Anjie and I got ourselves dressed without saying much. What was there to say? I didn't dare eat any breakfast.

The drive to the mortuary in Flax Bourton, North Somerset, was also spent in silence. I was trying my hardest to focus on the roads to stop myself conjuring up images of what we were about to see.

I knew that the police had found the body severed into several pieces, but we weren't warned as to what to expect when we saw her. All Russ and Jo had said beforehand was 'Becky is all there.'

The idea of seeing her in that state horrified me, but I knew I had to do it. If it was Becky in there, I had to say my goodbyes. I owed her that much.

We pulled into the car park and I squeezed my Land Rover into one of the spaces. I helped Anjie out and into her wheelchair, and I pushed her slowly to the front of the old building, where Russ and Jo were waiting for us.

It was a grey day, typical British weather for March. The building was set in rural grounds, and I couldn't help but think how much Becky would have enjoyed exploring the countryside nearby. She never much cared what the weather was like – she just loved any excuse to pull her wellies on. Some of our happiest times were spent outside together.

As we approached Russ and Jo, I nodded grimly before we all walked inside. The officers went into the room where the body was kept first, to check everything was OK. Five minutes later, they returned.

'She's ready for you now,' Russ said. 'You don't need to rush. Take your time.'

I looked at Anjie, who was shaking, and I nodded again. Words were beyond me at that point.

'We'll be just out here if you need us,' Jo added as she opened the door for us. I took a deep breath and pushed Anjie through. My heart was hammering so hard in my chest that I wondered if I was having a heart attack.

'Are you sure you want to look at this?' I asked Anjie. 'This is what your son has done.'

She looked me in the eyes, and nodded. 'She was my daughter too,' she said. 'I'm her mum.'

As soon as I lifted my head, I could see a stone-slab table at the far end of the room. It was small and dingy in there, and it was so cold that I could see my own breath in front of me. On the slab was the body, covered in a red blanket. Only the head was visible, but there was a clear outline of the rest underneath.

Despite the room being quite dark, I recognised Becky straight away. My heart stopped hammering then – it just stopped dead in my chest. Time slowed down, and I willed my legs to move forward. It was as if I was watching myself push Anjie into that dark and unwelcoming room. Anjie let out a loud sob as she caught her first glimpse of our beautiful girl. Somehow, I managed to push her close to where Becky was laid. I was vaguely aware of the door closing behind us.

It took all of my strength not to collapse with grief when I was close enough to see Becky's face. Her appearance knocked all the wind out of me, as if my chest had been hit with a sledgehammer. She looked small and fragile, and unbearably young – no older than twelve years old. Her skin was pale and her little mouth was slightly open. Her lips were blue, her eyes were closed and her hair was pushed behind her head, matted and untidy. In the midst of all my despair, I couldn't help thinking that Becky would have hated her hair being untidy like that. She took great pride in her long hair, and she was a complete clean freak, like her dad. She would often have two or three showers a day.

I wondered how her body shape could still look intact under the blanket, and then I realised that she had been carefully pieced together, like a human jigsaw puzzle. They must have assumed it was the best way for us to see her – the way we remembered her – rather than the horrific reality.

I gazed at her face, taking in the purple bruises on her forehead, and as my eyes travelled down I could see that her hands were sticking out from beneath the blanket. Her knuckles were covered in dark bruises too, and I instinctively knew that those bruises showed she had tried to fight back. I had taught Becky to box, and I'd always encouraged her to defend herself if she ever needed to. I could tell that my daughter had fought for her life. I later learned that Becky had suffered forty injuries in the struggle. Her little body was completely battered.

Anjie's sobs were getting louder, and she was struggling to catch her breath. I broke down in floods of tears myself then – everything just seemed too much to bear. The bottom had fallen out of my whole life. Tears were rolling down my cheeks as I wrapped my arms around Anjie. I still couldn't bring myself to utter a word. I felt an overwhelming sense of being crushed, as if an elephant was sitting on my chest.

After a few minutes I reached forward and gently pulled the blanket down slightly, just past Becky's shoulder. I had to see for myself what they had done to her, but I made sure that Anjie couldn't see. Becky's neck was covered in white crêpe bandages, but on the right-hand side the bandage had slipped down, revealing an ugly, gaping wound where her head had been removed from the rest of her body. Her wrists had the same bandaging around them. My little girl was so damaged that she had to be bound up like a mummy. I felt sick to my stomach and didn't pull the blanket down any further. I knew the rest of her body was likely to look the same.

Swallowing hard, I wondered how anyone could possibly do this to a young girl, to take her life and simply discard her body in such a brutal and horrific way. It was inhuman. To make matters worse, the two people responsible for this brutality were family members, whom I had spent years taking care of and helping financially. My stomach twisted into a horrible knot.

'What the fuck have we done to deserve this?' I muttered.

I reached out again and slowly stroked Becky's hair, then I leaned forward and gently kissed her forehead and her lips. She was as cold as ice.

'I promise you, Becky, I will get those bastards,' I said, sobbing. 'I will get them for what they've done to you, even if it's the last thing I do on this planet.'

Anjie reached for Becky's hand and kissed it. She was still sobbing uncontrollably. I couldn't help but wonder how she felt, knowing her son had done this. She looked in so much pain that Nathan might as well have stuck a knife in her as well.

'I love you,' I whispered to Becky. 'You'll always be my little girl. Why didn't you come to me and let me know what was going on? Why didn't you tell me you were scared? I would have protected you. I was always the one who protected you. I would have given up my life trying.'

I wished I could trade places with my daughter right then. I wanted so much for her to be alive. I wished it were me on that table. It would have been kinder to kill all of us rather than leave us behind with this pain.

We stayed there for about half an hour, until it became apparent that Anjie couldn't take it any more. To be honest, I didn't know how much more I could take either. I felt so weak and lightheaded, I thought I might fall down.

'Have you seen enough?' I asked her, squeezing her hand. She nodded. Her face was blotchy from all the crying.

'Come on, love,' I said. 'Let's get you out of here.'

I turned back towards Becky one last time, and bent down to give her one more kiss on the forehead.

'I'll see you again, my beautiful little Bex,' I whispered, trying hard not to break down again.

As I started to push Anjie out of the room, I felt surrounded by blackness. My little girl was dead. My world had caved in around me. When we emerged into the corridor outside, I could hardly see for my tears. Jo held the door for us and pressed something into my hand. It was a small transparent bag, with a lock of Becky's hair inside. I was deeply touched by the gesture, and very grateful.

I could see Tanya, her aunt Lyn and her mother, Pat, standing in the hallway, waiting to go in. They were clearly nervous. As we walked past, I looked at Tanya and could see that she was going through the same hell as us.

'I need a fag,' I said to her. 'Don't pull the blanket back.'

I pushed Anjie out of the door, and with shaking hands I lit a cigarette for each of us and inhaled deeply. We were closely followed by Russ and Jo. Suddenly, my grief was replaced by a tidal wave of anger. I turned to Anjie and spat out the most hurtful thing I could think of.

'You gave birth to a monster,' I screamed. 'Your fucking son is gonna die. When I get my hands on him I'm going to fucking kill him.'

I knew that I would never get close enough to Nathan to touch him, but at that moment I wanted to cause him as much pain and suffering as he had to Becky.

Anjie stayed silent, apart from the sounds of her sobs. I knew it was unfair of me to lash out at her, and I felt dreadful afterwards, but I was consumed with red-hot rage. It seared through my body, and I ended up punching the spare tyre on my Land Rover over and over again.

If I had ever had the slightest inclination about what Nathan and Shauna were going to do to my little girl, I would have killed the pair of them and happily spent the rest of my life in prison. I would have done anything to keep Becky safe. But I knew it wasn't Anjie's fault, and I instantly regretted what I had said to her. I knew that I couldn't have found a better mother figure for Becky. Anjie loved her as her own child, and she would have done anything to bring her back to us.

'I'm sorry,' I whispered.

After another fag I calmed down enough to get back in the car, and we began the drive back to the hotel. We hadn't been allowed back to the house because they were still collecting forensic evidence. We remained silent in the car, but I reached across for Anjie's hand. We were both stunned. I found it hard to comprehend what we had been through that day. I just wanted all the emotions – fury, despair, unbelievable sadness – to stop, just for a moment.

When we pulled into the hotel car park, I noticed that we were surrounded by bright yellow daffodils, which had opened during the past few days. Once again, my thoughts flashed back to Becky, and I thought about how much she would have delighted in seeing them. She was such an outdoorsy girl.

I swallowed the lump in my throat, and Anjie and I went straight to the bar, where I asked for a double vodka and coke and Anjie ordered a double Malibu. For twelve years I hadn't had a drink that often except at Christmas and on family birthdays. But from the moment I learned that Becky was dead, I drank every single day. I just wanted to shut out the world, to feel numb again. I longed to feel absolutely nothing, rather than the gut-wrenching devastation I had grown so used to. I was an empty husk of a man without my daughter in my life. Drinking was the only escape I had.

We sat down at a table in front of the bar, and as the drink started to kick in, we relaxed a bit. But I couldn't help feeling distant from Anjie that day. I loved her, but the truth of the matter was that her son had brutally killed my precious daughter. That's enough to tear any man in two.

We drank at least six doubles before we felt ready to talk.

'I don't know if you can accept this or not, but I'm going to kill your fucking son, and that girl he's with,' I said to her.

Anjie met my gaze. Her eyes were heavy with sadness, and she looked completely wiped out. 'Do what you have to do, but don't tell me about it,' she replied.

She didn't attempt to defend Nathan, which surprised me. It

was clear that she was just as angry as I was about what had happened.

We sat there in silence for a while longer, each trapped in our own hell, both trying to work out where to go from there, and how we could possibly survive.

Even though we weren't allowed to go home yet, people started leaving flowers, sympathy cards and teddy bears at the gate to our driveway. A lot of them didn't know our family, hadn't known Becky, and it touched me deeply that strangers could be so kind and thoughtful. Becky soon gained the nickname of 'Bristol's Angel', which I rather liked. She looked angelic and so young in all the photos used in the media, and it was a reflection of how well the people of Bristol had supported us during our horrific ordeal. The city's two football clubs, Bristol Rovers and Bristol City, each paid their own tribute to Becky. Bristol Rovers held a minute's silence before their game against Eastleigh in the Vanarama Conference, and Bristol City organised a minute's applause during their match against Walsall at Wembley in the Johnstone's Paint Trophy final.

On Sunday, 8 March, almost a week after Becky's death was announced, my family organised a balloon-release memorial for her in St George's Park, one of her favourite places. It was a way of bringing together all the people who had helped us with the search, as well as providing us with an opportunity for some sort of acceptance of what had happened. Not everyone had been able to see Becky to say goodbye properly, so this seemed like the next best thing.

My whole family came out for it – even Anjie. She was determined to be there. As I pushed her wheelchair across the field, I was amazed to see that around 400 people had gathered together, all clutching a variety of colourful balloons. Becky's boyfriend, Luke, was there, and I nodded when he caught my eye. I greeted a few of my friends and family, then we all stayed silent as we lifted our balloons up into the air and let them go. It felt as if I was letting go of Becky in that moment. The crowd gave a small cheer, but I couldn't help bursting into tears as I watched the balloons float away. The sky was filled with different colours and shapes, and it was beautiful. I knew Becky would have been delighted by it and I hoped that somehow she could see them.

It was a really moving day, and I was overwhelmed by the great kindness shown towards us. After the release of the balloons, I shook hands with almost everyone there. I wanted to personally thank as many people as I could for making the effort to support my family during the hardest time of our lives.

One person especially sticks in my mind: he was a huge mountain of a man, but he was sobbing like a baby as he came over, clasped my hand and gave me a great big hug. And that response was typical in Bristol. I'll never forget the way the people of the city rallied to our side.

On 26 March, Nathan and Shauna, along with four other defendants, appeared at Bristol Crown Court for a preliminary hearing. Nathan was charged with Becky's murder, and Shauna was initially charged with perverting the course of justice, but in June she was also charged with murder. Both of them appeared via videolink. I attended the hearing with Anjie, my dad, Denise, Sam, Joe and Sarah. A lot of supporters also turned up and sat in the public gallery wearing badges with Becky's face on them. I started to shake with anger when I saw Nathan and Shauna's faces appear on the screen, but I had to stay because I wanted to be there for Becky. Looking at Nathan, I felt immense rage, but also sadness. I had loved him as a son and this was where it had got me.

Jaydene Parsons, who was charged with assisting an offender, also appeared via videolink, while James Ireland, who faced the same charge, appeared in person. Also facing charges of assisting an offender were Karl Demetrius – whose house Becky's body parts were discovered in – and his twin brother, Donovan. I didn't know any of them. How could they live with themselves? What kind of people were they to help cover up the murder of a teenage girl?

We had to wait for justice to be done. The trial would not take place until October. In the meantime, we had seven months to come to terms with the fact that my beautiful daughter Becky was gone, and that no matter what we did, she wasn't ever coming back.

CHAPTER 11

THE FUNERAL

The pain I felt after saying goodbye to my beautiful daughter knocked me for six, leaving me cold and emotionless for weeks afterwards. As soon as we were allowed back in our house after six weeks of staying in hotels and an apartment the police had found for us, I locked myself away. In my mind's eye I kept seeing Becky's lifeless body lying in the mortuary. I couldn't bring myself to discuss the practical things we needed to do, such as arrange her funeral. I'd lost four stone and the clothes were hanging off me because I was still struggling to eat. Everything seemed pointless. I'd never felt so empty in my whole life. It's not that I didn't think that Becky deserved a special send-off – it was just that organising the event seemed far too real. I preferred to spend my days in denial, staring into space.

My family were constantly coming over, making sure Anjie and I were all right. Without their support, I would simply have given up. I didn't see the point in doing anything any more, but they repeatedly provided a source of positivity, as

159

well as taking care of little jobs around the house for us. We had so many visitors every day that we could have put a turnstile on the front door. Meanwhile, strangers were still leaving flowers and heartfelt tributes for us outside the front gate. Their handwritten notes were touching but heartbreaking at the same time.

My sister Sarah was one of those who came most frequently, and a few days after we'd said goodbye to Becky in the mortuary, she raised the issue of a funeral.

'Come on, Dar,' she said, plonking herself down on the sofa next to me. 'It's time to organise the funeral now. She needs a proper send-off.'

I nodded.

'Do you want me to sort everything out for you?' she offered kindly, and I nodded again.

'Yes, please,' I replied. 'But it has to be at St Ambrose Church.'

I wanted to lay Becky to rest in the same church where Anjie and I had got married just eighteen months earlier. Becky had been so happy that day that the smile never left her face. It seemed like the right place to say goodbye.

Sarah is one of those people who is at her best when she has a project to focus on, so she started researching funeral directors and options for the day. Our supporters had been raising money online so we could afford a special funeral for Becky. I was so wrapped up in my grief that I couldn't even think about money – and our lack of it – so I was truly appreciative of the effort they made. In the end, they raised more than £11,000 to provide a 'send-off for a princess', and we decided that was exactly what Becky was going to get.

Sarah and I sat down and drew up a list of ideas for the day – including a white carriage pulled by four white horses. I knew Becky would have loved something like that for her prom or her wedding – all those life events that tragically she would never get to experience – so I felt it was only right to do it for her funeral. We already knew that we wanted her favourite colours, baby blue and baby pink, to feature prominently, so I decided to buy matching baby-blue shirts for myself, Danny, Lee, Sam, Joe and Asa. Anjie, Sarah and Denise also planned to wear baby blue.

Sarah was brilliant at taking care of the details, so all I had to do was write a reading in tribute to my daughter. I also planned to carry Becky's coffin into the church, and I had to come up with a list of people to help me. I knew that I wanted Danny and my brothers Sam and Joe to be pallbearers, but I also asked Luke, Adam and my brother Lee to help as well. Luke and Adam in particular were very touched that I asked them. They had both been so important to Becky, I couldn't think of anyone I would rather have helping my girl to her final resting place. We agreed that Danny, Sam, Joe and I would carry her into the church for the service, and then Lee, Adam and Luke would help me carry her out. None of us had realised how difficult carrying a coffin actually was. We had to practise for a few days beforehand, making sure our steps were all in time so the coffin could be kept as still and level as possible. We all took it incredibly seriously. This was our opportunity to pay our last respects to Becky, and we didn't want anything to go wrong.

I sat down one evening to write my reading, and as I stared at the blank sheet of paper in front of me, I started to choke up.

I never would have thought in a million years I would be doing this for my daughter's funeral. It just wasn't right. My funeral should have been decades before hers. At first, I struggled to write anything that didn't sound ridiculous, but after a while I started to think of all the things that made Becky wonderful and the words came to me. In fact, it was hard to stop myself from saying too much.

Sarah managed to organise the whole thing in just a few weeks, thanks to all the donations from the public, and it was planned for Friday, 17 April. That was the day we had to say our final goodbye.

Around the same time, we had been informed that the post-mortem results had come back, confirming that Becky had died because she was suffocated. Whatever else had happened, that was how she had been killed. It made me feel sick to my stomach to know that her final few moments were spent gasping for air while fighting for her life, but I tried to push that out of my mind as much as I could.

I barely slept a wink the night before the funeral. My mind was full of all the things we needed to do the next day, all the things to remember. I was terrified of something going wrong. Most of all, my thoughts were dominated by memories of Becky. I still couldn't quite believe that I was going to be burying her the next morning.

As soon as dawn broke, my family started pouring through our front door to get everything ready. It was hard to keep the tears at bay as I put my suit on. When I was dressed, I looked at myself in the mirror and drew a huge breath. It was the smartest I had looked in a while, and I knew that Becky, who was always immaculate, would approve if she could see me. I could clearly imagine her smiling at me and telling me that I 'scrubbed up well'.

I came downstairs to where Anjie was sitting in her wheel-chair, dressed in a baby-blue top with black trousers and a black coat. She had a white rose pinned to her coat with a blue ribbon. I sat opposite her and she smiled weakly at me.

'You look lovely,' I said, smiling back. 'Are you sure you're going to be able to do this, love?'

I was worried that the day might be too tough on her. Her mobility was decreasing by the day as her MS worsened, and she often experienced a scary mental fog that made it hard to think or speak.

'I want to be there for you,' she replied. 'And I have to say goodbye to Bex.'

I reached across and gave her hand a squeeze. Anjie had always been my rock. Even when times were difficult for her, she always supported me.

It was a beautiful sunny day, and as my family and I waited outside for the hearse carrying Becky's coffin, I was a bag of nerves and emotion. I looked across at Danny, and the poor boy seemed to be struggling with the situation even more than I was.

'You all right, boy?' I asked, putting my hand on his shoulder. He nodded, but he shifted uneasily on his feet.

I could tell he was nervous. Danny hadn't even set foot inside our house since Becky's death. He was completely shaken up after losing his sister. The whole thing had been as traumatic for him as it had been for us all. Nathan had been a friend of his, and Becky had been his baby sister. He must have been struggling to understand what on earth had happened, and why – the questions none of us had proper answers to yet.

The hearse pulled up outside the house. The coffin was to be lifted into the horse-drawn carriage waiting at the top of the street. Seeing the coffin hit me like a ton of bricks, causing my heart to thump rapidly in my chest. It was almost as bad as when I saw her on that slab in the morgue. It broke my heart knowing my little girl was in that box.

It affected Danny too, because he suddenly turned to me, pale as a sheet and trembling.

'Dad, I can't do it,' he said. 'I can't carry it in.' He was still so young, only just twenty. To be honest, I don't think I could have done it at his age.

'That's OK, son,' I said. 'I understand. Don't worry, I've got a back-up plan.'

I had told everyone who had agreed to be a pallbearer that if any of them suddenly had a change of heart, I wouldn't be offended. I didn't want anyone doing something they found too difficult, so Dan Broom, Sarah's husband, quickly stepped in to take Danny's place.

When I first set eyes on the horse-drawn carriage, I was bowled over. The horses were magnificent creatures, wearing pink feather headdresses. Becky would have absolutely adored them. It all looked amazing, like a princess carriage from a fairytale.

'Only the best for our Bex,' Sarah said, smiling, having clocked my reaction.

'You've done her proud, Sarah,' I replied, genuinely touched by the thought she had clearly put into organising her niece's funeral.

'It was the least I could do, Dar,' she said.

The cars to take the family, following behind the carriage,

pulled up, and we all looked at each other, our faces etched with emotion.

'Let's go and say goodbye to Bex,' I said quietly, before opening a car door.

I got into a car with Anjie, Becky's friends Courtney, Adam and Teela, and her boyfriend, Luke. I had to take a few deep breaths to steady my nerves as the driver started the engine and we moved off slowly behind the carriage.

Because of the huge public interest, the police had agreed to close some of the roads temporarily as the cortège made its way from our house to the church. We had decided that everyone in Bristol should have the opportunity to be a part of the funeral if they wished. We made sure that everyone knew they were more than welcome by putting up the funeral plans on Facebook and publishing them in the local paper.

I was amazed when I saw how many people lined the streets to watch Becky's last journey. There must have been at least 500 of them, many carrying beautiful pink roses, which they threw onto the carriage as it passed. I was moved when I realised that all my work colleagues had come out in force to support us, alongside countless friends and hundreds of strangers. People who didn't even know us came to say their own goodbyes to the girl who was now known as Bristol's Angel. Gazing at the sea of faces, I felt humbled.

Some people waved at us through the car windows, while others simply nodded to show their solidarity. A few folks were bawling their eyes out; some were consoling each other and dabbing at their eyes with handkerchiefs. The scene really touched me.

Despite being timid and shy, Becky had become famous. Even though it was tragic that her death had been what made her so well-known, I couldn't help smiling a little. I knew that she would have absolutely hated being the centre of attention like this, with everyone looking at her, but it was a moving demonstration of Bristol's community spirit. It made me feel very proud of my city.

As we got close to the church, I saw a line of supporters – the people who had helped with the searches and raised the money for the funeral – wearing white T-shirts with Becky's photograph on the front. As we passed they turned around to reveal the words 'Shoulder 2 Shoulder' on their backs. Their show of sympathy really got to me and I started to choke back tears.

'Come on, you have to do this,' I told myself as I tried to regain composure. 'Get it together – don't crumble now.'

Anjie squeezed my hand. I think she was too stunned by the view out of the car window to say anything.

As we rounded the corner and came to a halt at the gates, the people gathered outside the church remained respectfully silent and still. It was a stark contrast to the anger that had been shown by both the public and my family following Becky's death. Now, there was only grief. Only the sounds of quiet crying and distant traffic broke the silence.

I got out of the car, my legs shaky beneath me, and Dan, Joe, Sam and I carefully lifted the coffin out of the carriage then started walking towards the church entrance, one foot in front of the other, just the way we had practised.

As we slowly made our way into the church and set down the coffin, 'Footprints in the Sand' by Leona Lewis was playing. Sam had been the one to pick it, not just because he thought

Becky would have liked it, but also because the lyrics seemed right for the occasion, particularly the chorus: 'I promise you, I'm always there. When your heart is filled with sorrow and despair. I'll carry you, when you need a friend. You'll find my footprints in the sand.'

I felt a stabbing pain in my heart as I listened to the song. The last time Becky had been in that church, she was beaming at me while I was saying my vows to Anjie – the woman she had loved like a mum. Now, I was staring at her coffin, overcome by grief. It felt unreal. No parent should ever have to go through this, and I still couldn't begin to get my head around why it had happened to us. All I knew was that somehow I had to hold it together and get through the day.

The church was packed for the half-hour service, with around 350 people inside and another 150 outside watching on screens. Reverend David James – the same man who married Anjie and me – led the service, which included the hymn 'Lord of the Dance'.

'This is for a young girl who loved dance, and was often encouraged to turn down her music,' said Reverend James, smiling at me.

Then it was time for my tribute to Becky, which focused on her school days and how she always looked after others. I was too distraught to read it out myself – I didn't think I could get through it without breaking down – so I asked Reverend James if he would do the honours. Thankfully, he obliged.

When Becky started school she was so shy that she wouldn't let Anjie leave her there on her own, so Anjie ended up being an unpaid teaching assistant for four years. We remember her coming home one afternoon, when she had just started first year at the juniors, and she was crying. When we asked her what was wrong Becky told us that no one would play with her because she had the wrong doll. So we went out and made sure she had the right doll for the next day, and on that day she returned home all smiles and excitement, and told us about a new friend she had made. This friendship lasted all the way through junior school.

She soon became a mentor for younger children joining the school. Although still very shy herself, she would watch out for any child stood in the playground on their own, looking lost and scared. She would encourage them to join her little mentor group. That was Becky all over. She couldn't make friends herself, but she didn't want younger children to feel like she did. We received letters from the parents of these children, thanking us for all that our big-hearted girl did for theirs.

Secondary school was when our family went through very dark times. Becky was bullied about her weight and consequently we almost lost her to anorexia, but with a lot of care from us and the Bristol Hospital Education Service we were able to get our Becky back. Once in hospital education, she made two new friends, Courtney and Adam, and became inseparable from them. She was the happiest we had seen her in a very long time. We used to call them 'The Three Amigos'.

Gradually building up her confidence, she started to go out more and more, and she became really fashion-conscious, developing her own style and always looking immaculate.

Becky has left a huge void in our lives and touched the hearts of the nation. We all loved you so much, and as you look down from heaven, just look at what your short life has achieved – not bad for a shy girl. You will forever be in our hearts and thoughts. Rest in peace, angel of Bristol.

Thank you to all the people of Bristol, all the fundraisers and all the support we have received from the entire country.

Hearing my own words being read back to me was the strangest thing. It didn't feel real. I burst into tears when he had finished. I couldn't stop myself – I just couldn't stay strong any more. I put my head in my hands and let out a giant wail. Next to me, Anjie was sobbing her heart out, Danny was crying on my other side, and around us I could hear the distress of the rest of the family.

Reverend James said that Becky's death had brought the community closer together.

He said, 'We might not have seen how particularly close our community is, until now. But when events such as this happen to one of our own, someone who went to school in our area, who sat down here somewhere singing carols, who went about being a normal teenager, it unlocks a depth of compassion and care, which has been such an inspiration.

'And so, despite her tender years and her death, which seems deeply sacrificial, she has made a substantial contribution to the neighbourhood.'

I nodded in agreement. Becky's death had shown me just how much kindness there was in my community.

Denise got up and did a reading, and then 'Dream Catch Me' by Newton Faulkner – one of Becky's favourite songs – was played as candles were lit for her. The service ended with the Lord's Prayer. I stumbled over my words towards the end of the service, dread growing within me that I would soon have to carry her out to be buried. My hands started shaking so violently that I was scared I would drop the coffin.

In desperation, I turned to Joe. 'I can't carry her out,' I said, showing him my hands.

'I've got it, Dar,' Joe replied. 'You walk with Anjie. It's all right.'

So Luke, Joe, Lee and Adam carried Becky's coffin out of the church, and I followed behind them, pushing Anjie in her chair. We walked out to a song my dad, John, had recorded especially for the funeral. It was 'Somewhere' from the musical *West Side Story*, and he thought Becky would have liked it. He sang it beautifully, and I sobbed a little harder as I listened. I was in such a state, it was just as well that Joe had taken over for me.

As we left, we noticed a teenage boy a few years younger than Becky standing on his own, sobbing his heart out. Sam went over to give him a big hug, and the boy explained that he knew Becky from school. He had struggled to make friends, just as she had, and Becky had befriended him so that he didn't have to feel alone. My heart was bursting with pride when Sam told me this later on.

After the coffin was placed back in the carriage, it was time for me to release a single dove to mark our final goodbye to Becky. We all thought that this would be a nice touch, but I couldn't stop my hands from trembling as I opened the cage to lift the bird out. I fought back my tears as I raised it as high in the air as I could.

'Bye, Bex,' I said quietly, and I let it go. It flew out of my hands and disappeared behind the back of the church, providing a fitting tribute to our beautiful angel. As I watched it fly away, I dissolved into tears once more. I was comforted by Sarah, who threw her arms around me while sobbing quietly herself. As I cried, I could hear the crowd around us clapping and crying with us. It was both an extraordinary and heartbreaking moment.

We all got back into the waiting cars and drove to Avonview Cemetery for a private burial for family only. There were still around sixty people there because our family was so big. Tanya hadn't come to the church, but she did attend the burial. In a newspaper interview published in the *Daily Mail* the day before, she had said that she felt nervous about seeing Anjie, the mother of her daughter's killer, at the funeral.

She greeted us with warmth when she arrived with her mother, Pat. She put an arm around Anjie and asked how she was coping. Despite Tanya's difficult relationship with me, and the way she must have felt knowing that Anjie's son had been charged with Becky's murder, she put all that aside to say good-bye to her daughter. It was clear that this was a day for peace, not war, and I was grateful to her for that.

As we lowered Becky's coffin into the grave, the pain in my heart grew worse than ever before. I kept thinking, I shouldn't be doing this. It felt completely unnatural and wrong to put my beautiful Becky into the earth.

'I should be in that hole, not her,' I whispered to Anjie. She gasped out a sob in reply.

A few of us, including Sarah, my dad and Denise, threw some soil into the grave. There was a funny, bittersweet moment when Sam's brand-new sunglasses fell off and into the hole, never to be seen again.

'That's quite fitting actually, because Becky was forever stealing my sunglasses,' I commented, and everyone smiled through their tears.

Afterwards, we held a wake at Arnos Court Hotel for friends and family to celebrate Becky's life. Once again, I was amazed by the amount of people who wanted to offer their support and raise a toast to my beautiful daughter – about 200 altogether.

We had some food and a few drinks while remembering Becky, and then I got up on stage and sang 'Ain't No Sunshine' by Bill Withers, closely followed by my dad, who sang 'Somewhere', the song he had recorded for the funeral. It was even better live.

After he had finished, I got up on stage and made an announcement.

'Right, everyone,' I began. 'Becky was not a miserable child, so let's celebrate her life in the way she would have wanted.'

With that, we kicked off a disco, and everyone started to clap and cheer. It wasn't long before we were hitting the dance floor, and the mood lifted.

Looking around the room, I could see so many faces I knew: friends of Anjie's and mine, both past and present, my work colleagues, Becky's friends and our family, all mixing together. It was a surreal moment for me. We were all there for one reason – we loved Becky. More than anything, it made me realise how much joy and friendship her short life had brought to these people. I was a proud father for that fact alone.

Everyone got on the dance floor that night, even me. Becky loved to dance, and I knew that she would have been up there with us if she could.

'I bet she's looking down on you now and laughing her head off,' Anjie said as I came back from busting some dance moves.

'She always did go out of her way to make fun of her dad,' I replied, chuckling at the memory.

People were even having dance-offs to find the best dancer – a bit of a Galsworthy tradition. It felt so good to have a few laughs after the intensity of the past few hours.

While we were celebrating my daughter's life, Nathan and Shauna were still in custody, awaiting trial in October 2015. As for the rest of us, we were prisoners in our grief. Becky had been taken from us far too early, and we had been forced to say goodbye and bury her in the ground. I still wasn't sure how I was going to cope with each passing day, or even if I wanted to cope without Becky in my life. All I knew for sure was that we needed the truth – and we needed justice.

CHAPTER 12

LIMBO

The next few months were a waiting game for us. We knew there wouldn't be any major developments before the trial. Frustratingly, the police weren't able to give us any details about what had happened on the day Becky died, or about what had been done to her body after her death. We knew from the post-mortem that she had died from suffocation, but we were completely in the dark about the rest of the details. We were still in close contact with our family liaison officer Jo, but Russ was retiring from the force, so he was replaced by another officer, Detective Constable Ziggy Bennett.

Ziggy had originally joined the investigation as a detective, and she switched to a liaison role when Russ stepped down. We knew that she was arriving with a deep knowledge of the case, but she explained to us that her hands were tied in terms of giving us information. She told us that in order to protect the investigation, some details needed to be kept confidential. I understood that she was doing her best to make sure the trial wasn't jeopardised, but it was frustrating for us not to know exactly how and why Becky had lost her life. It made me feel very anxious about the forthcoming trial, as we had no idea what we were going to find out. We were in limbo, and would continue to be for several more months.

We knew that Nathan had admitted to killing Becky. He hadn't entered a plea in court, but he had told the police that he was responsible for her death. The big question was why.

After he was charged with murder back on 4 March, Anjie had asked if she could see him. She wanted him to look her in the eye and explain why he had done such a despicable thing. Nathan was always honest with his mum, or at least he found it difficult to lie to her, so she thought she could get an explanation out of him – but his solicitor refused to let her see him. Neither of us could think of anything that would give him the motivation to do something so horrific and life-shattering.

We didn't have much contact with Nathan and Shauna's child after their arrests. It broke our hearts all over again, but it was difficult to see the little one, for various reasons. The time that we could spend together we cherished. Seeing our grandchild reminded us of a time when everything was normal – when we were a family who loved each other, cared for one another. Before our family had been completely torn to shreds.

The morning after the funeral, I opened my eyes and instantly felt an immense sense of emptiness wash over me. There was nothing immediate to arrange or to keep myself busy with, so for about five days, I just stayed indoors with Anjie. I told my family and friends that we needed some time alone, and we refused to answer the front door. Of course, they all respected that and didn't try to push us, but everyone said that if we needed them, they would be there. Strangers still kept leaving flowers and teddies at our gate, which was lovely, but I didn't even have the energy to go outside and collect them. I felt wiped out, a completely battered man. After two months of being in the media spotlight, I just wanted to hide away.

During that period, Anjie spent a lot of time in front of the television, watching her soaps and trying to forget about reality. Meanwhile, I battled my demons and hit the bottle almost every single night, sinking vodka after vodka and drinking myself into a stupor. It seemed to be the only way to numb the pain and blot out the bitter reality.

Eventually, we decided that enough was enough. We couldn't go on living like that, holed up inside the house. We planned to go away for a few days, just the two of us. We thought it would be good to escape from the press and to leave Bristol for a bit, and we started looking for somewhere to escape to.

'What about Butlin's?' I suggested. 'It was always Becky's favourite place to go when she was younger. We have so many happy memories there. It might be good for us to revisit them.'

Anjie nodded in reply, and we booked a last-minute four-day break. When we set off the next day on the journey to Minehead, it felt good just to be driving out of our street. I hoped that taking a holiday in a place that Becky loved would be therapeutic for us, and I looked forward to seeing our old haunts. Instead, it soon proved to be just the opposite.

When we pulled up in the car park, I looked at the entrance to the resort and felt grief slam me hard in the chest. It was almost as if Becky was there with us. Everywhere I looked, I could see memories of her, things I had done with her, quality time we had spent together as a family. We had been on loads of family holidays to Butlin's, and every time Becky had been beside herself with excitement on the drive down. I could picture her splashing around in the pool, larking about in the play area with a huge smile on her face, and shrieking with delight on the funfair rides. It was always a happy time for all of us. Now I felt guilty for being there without her. It wasn't right.

I tried to shrug off the sadness as we checked in and made our way to our apartment. It was nice, the weather was dry and sunny, the place was as welcoming as ever, but I couldn't shift my mood. After a few hours, we decided to grab a bite to eat, and then, following our meal, we went for a few drinks. Once the alcohol started to kick in, that's when everything started to unravel.

'She should be with us,' I blurted out as we sat in a beer garden under the last of the April sunshine.

'I know,' Anjie said, reaching across the table for my hand, but I snatched it away from her. She looked surprised.

'This is all due to your bastard son,' I said, seething, looking her straight in the eye. When she blinked back at me, her eyes were filling with tears.

'Darren …' she began, but I shook my head, a fire burning in my throat as I tried not to cry.

'If it wasn't for him, Becky would still be here. She would be on holiday with us right now,' I spat.

'I know. But Darren, please stop. He's my son. I can't help still loving him for that reason alone,' she said, sobbing.

I shot her an incredulous look. 'That boy – or should I say monster – you still love, says he killed my girl,' I said, snarling.

'How can you say you still love him after what he's done to us? I wish your son was dead, not my Becky.'

Anjie broke down in tears then, and I instantly felt terrible for the way I had behaved. I looked at the drink in my hand and slowly put it down on the table.

'Come on, let's get out of here,' I said, and I got up to leave. I shakily pushed Anjie back to our apartment, and as soon as we got through the door I knelt down in front of her.

'I'm so very sorry, my love,' I croaked, tears freely rolling down my face now. 'I didn't mean to take it out on you. I'm disgusted with myself. I'm so sorry for saying those things. I'm just finding it all so difficult, Anj. I think I'm losing my mind. It doesn't get any easier, ever. I just miss her so much.'

Anjie put her arms around me and hugged me tightly.

'She should be here with us, Dar. I know that,' she replied softly. 'I miss her too.'

We spent that night as we would spend hundreds more – holding each other and trying to make sense of our obliterated lives.

When we came home from our break, I felt even more exhausted than before. I knew just moping around the house wasn't going to get me anywhere, so I decided to start putting Becky's bedroom back together.

The police had left it in a bit of a mess after their thorough search, so at first it was quite upsetting being in there. I knew that Becky would have hated it being in that state – she was one of the few teenagers I knew who actually kept her bedroom tidy – so I spent days tidying it up and putting things back where they belonged. I could clearly remember her showing me a sketch of the way she wanted her bedroom to look. She had thought through every last detail, and I decided to redecorate and keep it as true to her design as I possibly could. I went out and bought a new bedspread in fuchsia pink, as per her sketch, and I put up a stencil on the wall that read 'The best thing about memories is making them'. She had chosen that before her death, but I had never got around to putting it up for her.

I know it sounds silly, but as I cleaned and redecorated her room, I started talking to Becky.

'I'm going to put this just here, Bex,' I whispered. 'If you don't like it, let me know – give me a kick. I won't mind.' I was disappointed when nothing happened, but I could imagine her laughing at me from the other side.

Once I'd started, talking to Becky proved cathartic for me. Whenever I struggled to sleep, I'd go and sit on her bed. I'd tell her all about my day, and how I was feeling.

'Bex, I'm missing you loads,' I confessed one night, in a whisper so I didn't wake Anj. 'Sometimes I'm not sure if I can face the next day, or the days after that, but I'm looking after Anjie – don't worry. And your room is taking shape. You'll love it when it's all done. It's going to look lovely.

'Your granddad, your brother Danny, your uncles and auntie miss you very much. They have been a great support to your dad. I hope you're out there somewhere, my beautiful girl. I've got to go to bed now. Will you help me to sleep? I love you, Becky.'

The new things I bought for her room went perfectly with her own possessions, like the full-length glittery mirror we had made together years before. We had lots of gifts and tributes from the people of Bristol, ranging from beautiful bibles with the pages cut out to form the word 'Becky' to touching memorial plaques and candles, so I decided to put several of those in there for her. I also framed all the notes and 'rest in peace' messages we'd received and put them in her room for safekeeping. I found her boxing gloves and placed them on a shelf. I hoped that somehow Becky could see her room and know how loved she was, and how her death had touched everyone.

After I arranged her bedroom exactly as she had wanted it to be, it felt quite serene. I would go in there whenever I wanted to feel calm and reflect on things. When Sarah stayed over, she slept in Becky's room, and she claimed that it was so peaceful in there she always got a good night's sleep. However, Marley, Becky's cat, will not go into the room any more. He sleeps on the landing outside. He's grown so big that he scares every dog in the area, and he's killed three foxes so it's not that he's scared of anything, but it's as if he knows about the horrific events that unfolded in there.

At the end of April, I decided to go back to work full-time. The bills were mounting up and, with me as the only earner, they weren't going to get paid unless I starting making some money. I thought that if I adopted a tunnel-vision approach and just tried to focus on work, it would help me get over the devastating two months we'd endured. My employers were more than happy to welcome me back, but they told me to let them know if I needed any extra support. I felt very lucky to have such understanding bosses.

However, I soon learned that getting up every day and going to work was a lot harder than it used to be. During the day I tried my best to bottle everything up, but as soon as I returned home in the evenings, emotions would erupt out of me like lava from a volcano. Something simple, like seeing a programme on TV that Becky had liked, or hearing a song that reminded me of her, would trigger a memory, and suddenly I would break down. My reactions ranged from dissolving into fits of uncontrollable sobbing through to throwing objects across the room in anger. Some days, I was reduced to lying on the bed in the foetal position, clutching the pain in my chest and crying for hours. My heart hurt so much that I thought it might stop beating. Sometimes I wished it would just stop, as I could see no end to the pain I was feeling. Every day, I wondered if I was losing my mind. I had never felt so out of control in my whole life. My emotions were in charge and I was powerless against them.

Eventually, I started snapping at people at work. The human resources manager, Jo, called me to her office, but instead of giving me the warning I'd expected, she offered something entirely different.

'Everyone can understand why you're a bit volatile at the moment,' she started. I nodded awkwardly, and then she asked, 'Would you like to try contacting Becky? To try to get some closure?'

I looked at her, confused about what she meant.

She smiled. 'I go to a spiritualist church and, if you like, I could come to your house and we can try to get in touch with Becky,' she explained.

I'll admit to being sceptical at first, but I was so desperate for some kind of comfort, no matter how slight, that I agreed to give it a try.

'Are you free tonight?' I asked.

Jo came over to the house that evening, and I invited Lee and his wife, Joanne, to join us, as they were interested in that sort of thing. I was a bag of nerves. I wasn't sure if it would work but, if it did, I had a million questions to ask. My biggest fear was Becky being mad at me for not protecting her that day, so I wanted to ask about that.

We sat in a circle in the living room, and Jo asked us to empty our minds and close our eyes. After she said a prayer of safety, we opened our eyes and Jo began to speak.

'Becky is in a healing circle,' she said softly. 'When a spirit is taken suddenly, it gets damaged. Her spirit is being healed by others. She's with someone called Charlie.'

Anjie's eyes bulged out of her head in shock. 'Charlie is my grandfather,' she exclaimed, clearly surprised.

'She's also with a lady called May,' Jo announced, and then it was my turn to be surprised. May was my grandmother, the woman who had been so special to me when I was a child.

'She can't make a lot of contact, I'm afraid, but she wants me to do something.' Jo was about to have a knee operation, so she used a walking stick to help her struggle to her feet then limp over to Anjie, and she put both her arms around her neck affectionately, just as Becky used to do.

Anjie burst into huge sobs, and I grasped her hand tightly. Jo then turned to me and punched me hard in the arm.

'I'm sorry, Darren,' she said, chuckling, 'but apparently you'll know what that means.'

I was stunned! It was a clear reference to the boxing sessions Becky and I used to do together. At the end of every session she'd always tell me that she was getting stronger, and she'd try to punch me in the arm to prove it.

'It's going to take a while before she'll be able to contact you again,' Jo told me. 'I've been told that she has a bell in the house somewhere and you'll hear it ring when she wants to get in touch. When that happens, call me and I'll come straight over.'

I was stumped. Becky didn't have a bell. I would have known if she did, mainly because she would probably have rung it jokingly to order me about.

A few hours later, I was putting some things in her room when I opened a drawer and gasped. Inside, there was a little purple bell with a handle. She must have bought it on one of our seaside holidays years ago. I put it on our living-room shelf, and for months afterwards I would stare at it, willing it to ring.

That night, I slept soundly for the first time in months. I know some people may scoff at the idea of speaking to those on the other side, but what Jo did for us that night gave Anjie and me some much-needed comfort during a period of acute despair.

June soon arrived, and with it came Becky's seventeenth birthday. I woke up on Wednesday, 3 June, with a heavy heart. We didn't do anything special that day, but I took some time to think about Becky's previous birthdays and remember how much she had enjoyed celebrating them with us.

'Happy birthday, Bex,' I said softly as I walked past her room.

She would have had so much to celebrate that year. She was becoming a young woman, starting to come out of her shell and live life independently of her family. She would have taken her GCSE exams by then, and she would have had her whole future to look forward to. I tried hard to be positive and not to dwell on how her flame had been cruelly snuffed out, but it was particularly hard that day.

Later, I went to visit her grave and leave some flowers for her. Other members of my family had done the same thing. It was a short but sweet visit to the cemetery. I didn't really like going there, to be honest. It felt wrong that she was there and not at home with us.

While Anjie and I were having a cuddle on the sofa that evening, we raised a glass to her and spoke about the good times we had shared together. I was sure that's what Becky would have wanted us to do.

We had already organised a birthday party for Becky the following Saturday. A few weeks before her death, we had booked the St George Labour Club for the event, and we were planning on it being a surprise for her. We decided to have it anyway, even though our guest of honour was missing. I thought it would be nice to have a celebratory bash with her friends and family, instead of locking ourselves in the house and feeling depressed about the fact that she wasn't with us.

I bought Becky's favourite chocolate cake, covered in Maltesers and chocolate stars, and invited about a hundred people. We laid on a buffet and organised a disco. All of Becky's friends – Adam, Courtney, Teela and Luke – came wearing something of hers. After I had sorted out her room, I told her friends that they could each take something to remember her by. Adam took a half-chewed cross necklace that had, quite frankly, seen better days, but I don't think I've ever seen him without it. Courtney picked a T-shirt that everyone at school had signed, and Luke and Teela both took small pieces of jewellery.

All the family came, and a few supporters, including two women called Joanne and Michelle, whose help had been very important to us. It was a fantastic evening, as we toasted Becky and shared fond memories of her. It wasn't a sad occasion – in fact, the laughter was deafening.

'Good party,' Danny commented as we looked around the room at these people who loved Becky, all of them with big smiles on their faces.

'Becky would have absolutely loved it, Dar,' said Sarah, as she chased after one of her six kids. 'You've done a great job.'

Her words meant a lot to me, because I was thinking the same thing. If Becky was there she would have been delighted to see how many people came to her party, and I know she would have had a great time. We kept any mention of the party out of the press, because we wanted something just for us, and it was perfect.

At the end of June, Ziggy got back in touch, calling me at work to say that she had some news. She asked if she and Jo could pop over that evening.

When they arrived, I eyed them warily. I was so used to getting bad news, I was worried they would tell us that the charges had been dropped. That was my worst fear.

'What do you need to tell us, then?' I asked as they sat down.

'We just wanted to give you an update on Shauna,' Ziggy answered. 'As you know, she was originally charged with perverting the course of justice, but she's now been charged with murder as well. She'll stand trial with Nathan on the same charge.'

I breathed a huge sigh of relief.

'It's about time,' I said, looking across at Anjie. She looked relieved too. We both suspected that Shauna had a lot to do with what happened. It didn't seem likely to us that Nathan had managed it all on his own. Shauna seemed more ruthless than him, and I'd long thought she was the smarter of the two.

Ziggy explained that they both faced further charges in relation to Becky's death: perverting the course of justice, conspiracy to commit false imprisonment, possession of a prohibited weapon, and preventing her lawful burial.

'What was the weapon?' I asked, but Ziggy shook her head.

'I'm sorry, I can't tell you.'

Although we now knew the charges, we still didn't know much about what they meant and what had actually happened on the day Becky died. I wasn't happy about the lack of information because I'd thought we would know a lot more by this point. I wanted to feel prepared for the trial, but the police still weren't allowed to give us many details.

Anjie and I remained very nervous about the court case. To be honest, I didn't have much faith in the legal system. I was also worried that the truth about Becky's death, and the knowledge of what Nathan and Shauna had done to her, would destroy me.

I lay awake night after night worrying that they might be found not guilty for some reason or another, even though Nathan had admitted it. I knew that my family would be on hand to support me throughout, but there was no doubt that it was going to be incredibly difficult. I promised myself that, whatever happened, I wouldn't get too emotional inside the courtroom. I wanted to remain composed. Most of all, I didn't want Nathan to see me crumble.

Meanwhile, I was saving money for Becky to have a nice headstone. She just had a wooden cross, a little picket fence and flowers covering her grave at first. It looked pretty, but I was keen to get her a proper headstone, and the one I'd chosen didn't come cheap. It was really special, though: black speckled marble with baby-blue chippings on the top. It came complete with little plant pots and a polished biblical figurine attached. The figurine was what grabbed me, because the child was clinging onto the woman by wrapping her arms around her shoulders and neck, just as Becky used to do with Anjie. I was sure that she would have liked it.

I also bought the plot next to her grave, so that Anjie or I – whoever died first – could be buried next to her. Sarah bought the plot one along from that.

While Anjie and I rattled around in our empty house and tried to prepare ourselves for the trial, our supporters were putting together a plan to set up a foundation in Becky's name. The aim was to provide emotional and financial support for the loved ones of missing children. I liked the idea of launching a charity to help people through those dark, desperate times. We wouldn't have survived without the unparalleled support from our community. I thought it was a good opportunity to keep Becky's name alive. It would be one small positive thing to come from her death.

Our supporters had always used the slogan 'Shoulder 2 Shoulder' when helping us search for her and while fundraising for the funeral. We decided that this message would be at the very core of any charity set up in Becky's name.

There were other touching acts of kindness too, which we appreciated. They provided some small comfort amid the grim torment.

People raised money to pay for a lamppost in St George's Park in memory of Becky. She had walked through that park many times, and it was lovely to think of her light helping to keep other people safe as they passed through after dark.

Others planted an apple tree in Becky's honour. It was one of five planted by Meadow Vale Community Association in tribute to Becky and four other teenagers – Shevon Wilson, Daniel Cockram, Jacob Seaman Ind and Zoe Smith – who had died in tragic circumstances in Bristol. Anjie and I felt humbled as we attended the ceremony in the park behind the Meadow Vale Community Centre in the Speedwell area of the city. We were able to find a certain peace and give mutual support by coming together with other grieving families.

After the planting ceremony, Reverend David James individually blessed the trees and said a prayer for each family. He had become a big part of our lives over the past few months, a source of strength and comfort, and his words will stay with me forever. Although the emotions were still very raw, it was a touching occasion for Anjie and me. As time passes, no doubt we'll go back to that tree many times to think about Becky and all that she achieved in her young life.

I worked full-time until the end of September, when I fell ill with a bad dose of flu. My body completely packed in, so my family rallied around us once again, helping to look after both Anjie and me. Soon after I recovered, it was time for Nathan and Shauna's trial to begin, so my bosses told me to take as much time off as I needed. I really appreciated their continuing support. I was incredibly lucky to have such understanding employers at that time.

Though despair and grief had left me feeling weaker than ever, the hope of some kind of justice was enough to shake me from my numb lethargy. I reached inside myself for whatever strength remained, picked myself back up and did my best to prepare for the horrors that I knew lay ahead in the courtroom.

CHAPTER 13

THE TRIAL BEGINS

The night before the first day of the trial was a restless one. I tried to get to bed early in order to prepare myself mentally, but it was no use – I had too many things circling my mind to sleep. By the time the sun came up on 6 October 2015, I was feeling sick with nerves. I got dressed, looked intently at my reflection in the mirror and took a deep breath. I promised myself again that, however hard it got, I wouldn't show any emotion in front of Nathan. I wasn't going to let him see me crumble, even though I knew it would be difficult setting eyes on him again.

'Are you going to be all right today, my love?' I asked Anjie as I helped her get dressed. 'It's going to be hard seeing Nathan and Shauna. You don't have to come if it's too much for you.'

Anjie nodded determinedly. 'I'm going,' she replied.

I know Anjie wanted to see Nathan; after all, she had been denied the opportunity after he was charged. She wanted to see if he would have the courage to look her in the eyes after admitting to killing Becky. I knew that, like me, she needed to know exactly what had happened.

I felt drained as Ziggy and Jo came to collect Anjie and me. They decided to drive us in the back way, as journalists and photographers were already gathered at the entrance of Bristol Crown Court, hoping to catch a glimpse of us. Tanya and Pat would also enter the court through the back entrance, while Sarah, Sam and the rest of the family walked in through the front.

I had never been to a trial before, so I wasn't sure how everything would work or how long it would last. We had originally been told that it could take up to eleven weeks, and I didn't think I could last that long to find out if justice was going to be served. Luckily, the estimate was shortened to five to six weeks.

In the car, Ziggy explained that we would be briefed each morning by the prosecutor, William Mousely, on the agenda for the day.

'You'll be given a short outline of what will be said,' she told us. 'But it won't be all the information. Be aware that things will often come out in court that you won't expect and may find hard to listen to. If that happens, try not to attract any attention to yourself or to interrupt proceedings. You can leave the courtroom at any time if you feel that you need a break.'

I swallowed hard. Although I was desperate to know what had happened to Becky, I knew that it was going to be agonising to sit there listening. I was determined not to let my anger get the better of me and shout out; whatever happened, I would maintain my dignity.

The whole family decided before the trial to wear something to show that we were a united front, so we all pinned baby-blue ribbons to our lapels. It was also a mark of respect for Becky, choosing her favourite colour once more.

We met everyone in the witness-protection area of the court, and as soon as Sarah clocked me she rushed over, Sam by her side.

'How are you feeling?' she asked, putting her hand on my arm.

'On edge, Sar, I must admit,' I croaked. It all seemed much more real and serious now that we were actually in the court. She nodded and looked at Anjie, who was sitting in her wheelchair, staring straight ahead. Her face gave away how nervous she was, so I put a reassuring arm around her.

'It's the fear of the unknown, isn't it?' Sarah said, squeezing my arm. 'We'll get through this as a family, Dar, I promise.' She gave me a hug, and soon we were being called to our first briefing.

That day turned out to be a bit of an anti-climax, as it was dominated by legal arguments. Pretty much all I really remember is meeting William Mousely for the first time and thinking to myself that he was the man who was going to get justice for my Becky and put away those two evil pieces of filth. First impressions were good: he looked and sounded like a man who knew what he was doing. I felt a brief surge of confidence, although it soon gave way to the usual nerves, doubts and apprehension.

We were told that the following day would be the official start of the trial, the day the jury would be sworn in. We were also told that when the prosecution opened its case at the beginning of the trial, they would give a brief summary of the crime. All the information would be explored in detail as the trial progressed, but some of it would be new to us. We knew very little about the actual circumstances of Becky's death, probably because we were deemed to be too close to the man who admitted he had ended her life. What unsettled me was that the only people who really knew what happened to Becky that day were Nathan and Shauna. They held all the cards.

Every day I attended, I sat in the family gallery, which was big enough to accommodate eight people. On the first day, Anjie and I were joined by Tanya and Pat, Ziggy and Jo, and Sarah. Tanya and I were civil to each other, each asking the other how they were doing; we were united now in our desire to get justice for Becky. Danny came often during the course of the trial, and I was impressed by his strength in listening to the evidence. Like me, he was determined not to let Nathan see him break down. Anjie only came to court a handful of times; her MS meant that just a day away from home would exhaust her, and the stress of listening to the information we were due to hear was likely to have a huge impact on her condition.

Other family members joined us when there was space, but otherwise they sat in the public gallery, which was also full of people who had supported us throughout the search and funeral – people who wanted justice for Becky. As well as Sam and Sarah, my dad and Denise were often there, my brothers Joe and Asa, and my stepbrother Ben. The media interest in the trial was so great that a video link was being streamed to a separate annex inside the building to accommodate the scores of journalists reporting on the case.

On the second day of the trial, 7 October, Anjie was too exhausted to come, so Sarah, Sam, Joe and my dad came to support me. Once the jury – eleven women and one man – were sworn in, the four defendants due to face trial were led to the dock. Nathan and Shauna were joined by Donovan Demetrius and James Ireland, who were both charged with assisting an offender.

We were told that Donovan's twin brother, Karl Demetrius, and his girlfriend, Jaydene Parsons, had already pleaded guilty to the same charge at an earlier hearing. They admitted assisting Nathan by storing Becky's remains in their shed, but claimed that they didn't know what the packages contained. It was alleged that Karl Demetrius and James Ireland had driven Becky's body parts to Karl's house after Nathan promised them money to help him move some packages. Donovan Demetrius was staying with Karl at the time, but he claimed to know nothing of the criminal activity.

I craned my neck to get a good view of Nathan and Shauna, but it was difficult. The defendants had a huge screen protecting them, and they were sitting behind James Ireland and Donovan Demetrius. The dock was also full of security guards who blocked my view. It was probably just as well; I didn't trust myself not to explode with rage the second I set eyes on them.

There was a hushed silence as William Mousely opened the case for the prosecution. I closed my eyes tightly and held my breath. I knew that what we were about to hear would not be easy.

He started: 'Rebecca Watts, known to all as Becky, aged sixteen, was killed in her bedroom. She was suffocated, despite fighting for her life. There followed a deliberate, carefully planned and grotesquely executed plan to cover up her killing.

'Following her removal from her home, her body was cut up with a knife and a power saw, the parts carefully packaged and then moved to another address to prevent them being found, and to prevent them being lawfully buried.'

As William addressed the courtroom, I was vaguely aware of Tanya getting up from her seat behind me and walking out. She obviously found it too upsetting to listen to the gory details. I tried to remain composed. Even though I couldn't see Nathan, I wasn't entirely sure he couldn't see me, and I was determined not to break down with him watching.

'Nathan Matthews and Shauna Hoare were responsible for her death,' William added sharply. 'And that cover-up was assisted by four others, including James Ireland and Donovan Demetrius, all acting together and who, to varying degrees, helped in the hiding of her by-now disguised remains, in the knowledge that she had been killed or that some other significant offence had been committed by Nathan Matthews.'

He paused for a moment, and looked around the room before refocusing on the jury members.

'Becky's death was the result of a plan by Matthews and Hoare to kidnap her, and it seems that items may have been taken to Becky's home by them to carry out that plan,' he said. 'In addition to their apparent dislike of Rebecca Watts, there is good reason to believe there was also a sexual motive behind the scheme, arising from a shared unnatural interest in attractive teenage females, and that a foreseeable conclusion to that plan being carried out would be either Becky's death or serious injury.'

My stomach lurched as I took in the words 'sexual motive'. What possible sexual motive could Nathan have for attacking Becky? He had known her since she was a toddler. It made me feel sick to my stomach. Had he been sexually abusing her? Surely she would have told us if that were the case?

Continuing with the evidence, William said: 'Becky went home in the early morning of 19 February to Crown Hill, St George, Bristol. Her last phone contact was during the morning, when she sent a text message to a friend from her home, where she was alone.

'Nathan Matthews and Shauna Hoare had visited 18 Crown Hill on the morning of 19 February. When asked by the police, they both lied by saying they had heard but not seen Becky at the address on their visit and had heard the front door slam, as if Becky had gone out, and that her whereabouts were as unknown to them as to anyone else. As a result of Becky's blood being found on doorframes outside her bedroom, some of which contained Nathan Matthews' fingerprints, Matthews and Hoare were arrested for kidnap. These arrests later became arrests for murder.'

He added that the police investigation had uncovered two stun guns at their home, which may have been intended for use in the planned kidnap. They had been ordered in the name of Shauna Phillips, as Hoare had once been known, in January 2015.

My stomach knotted tightly and I felt Sarah's hand reaching for mine. I glanced at her and saw that she was as white as a sheet. Shauna had ordered those stun guns a month before Becky was murdered. It was beginning to sound as though the pair of them had been carefully planning her murder all that time.

The court heard that, on the morning of Becky's death, Nathan and Shauna had driven to our home, stopping off at a

Tesco Express on the way to buy some batteries, which Mr Mousley suggested were for a stun gun.

He said that Becky had died at some point between 11 a.m. and the early afternoon (Anjie had returned from her hospital appointment at 12.45 p.m.), and her body was put in the boot of Nathan's car. CCTV footage showed Nathan and Shauna driving to their home shortly before 7 p.m.

I felt a wave of nausea as I realised that I had walked past Nathan's car when I got home from work that day. Without knowing it, I had walked past the dead body of my little girl. I started shaking violently, and Sarah squeezed my hand in an attempt to calm me down.

When they arrived home, Nathan and Shauna ordered a Chinese takeaway before settling down to watch television for the night.

'All normal behaviour, other than having a dead body on their hands,' William said, looking at the dock accusingly. I hoped that he had a better view of them than I did.

William then explained how Becky's body parts were discovered at a house in Barton Hill, where Karl Demetrius and Jaydene Parsons lived. He said that Karl and another man, James Ireland, had helped to transport her body parts and items used in her dismemberment – four days after she was killed. Donovan Demetrius was staying with his brother, Karl, at the time, and was present when they arrived.

William then said something that made rage surge through my body.

'Nathan Matthews finally admitted to the killing, stating that he had tried to kidnap and imprison Becky and that he had strangled her,' he told the court. 'He said that he had acted alone in the killing, the removal of her body from Becky's house to his home, the subsequent dismemberment, and in arranging the removal of her body parts.'

William explained to the court that, after his arrest, Nathan had told the police that he wanted to kidnap Becky 'to scare her and teach her a lesson because she was selfish and treated his mother badly'.

I started to tremble with fury at that point, and I felt Ziggy's hand on my shoulder as a gentle warning that I had to behave myself. It was the most ridiculous thing I'd ever heard. Becky was just a normal teenager. She was sometimes stroppy, but she wasn't by any means the worst kid in the world. Even if she had been, why on earth did Nathan think it was his right to 'teach her a lesson'? His arrogance infuriated me, and I had to take a deep breath to calm down.

Nathan's account was that he had taken a large bag, a stun gun, handcuffs and tape to attack Becky. He'd been wearing a mask, but it slipped and she saw him, so he put her in the bag and strangled her. He said that he put Becky's phone, laptop and some bedding and clothing into the bag and placed it in his car.

'He said that he waited until Shauna had gone to bed before putting the bags in the house,' William added. 'He moved the bag containing Becky's body and put it in the bath. He said that he cut up her body with the circular saw, wrapping up the body parts and carrying them downstairs and hiding them. He stated that Shauna Hoare didn't know anything about what he had done, because if she had known he believed that she would have called the police.'

Nathan had made sure to cover his tracks. When the police searched Nathan and Shauna's house, they noticed that it was a cluttered mess apart from the bathroom, which was spotlessly clean.

The court heard that although Nathan denied murder and conspiracy to kidnap, he had pleaded guilty to hiding and cutting up Becky's body, being in possession of two stun guns and preventing her lawful burial. Shauna pleaded not guilty to all five charges she faced – murder, conspiracy to kidnap, perverting the course of justice, preventing a lawful burial and possessing the stun guns.

Shauna completely denied any knowledge of or involvement in Becky's death, but the court later heard that, on the evening Becky was killed, her mobile phone was used to search YouTube for a video called 'Do You Want to Hide a Body?' – a parody of 'Do You Want to Build a Snowman?' from the Disney film *Frozen*. To me, that was pretty damning evidence and also shed further light on her twisted mind. Her DNA was found on a facemask, which police discovered in the shed along with Becky's remains. I stared hard at the floor, trying to keep my anger in check. Surely all that could not be coincidental? It baffled me how she could expect us to believe that she was innocent.

William told the court that the day after Becky was killed, Nathan purchased two bottles of one-shot drain cleaner before heading to a B&Q store. There, he was captured on CCTV buying a circular power saw, gloves, a facemask and goggles. He had queried the price, as if it was an ordinary purchase. How could he be so calm, knowing what he had done? Did he have no emotions at all? Nathan and Shauna were also captured on CCTV buying black bags, rubble sacks, rubber gloves and three rolls of cling film.

My stomach churned as the jury were told that Becky was stabbed fifteen times in the abdomen after she died. According to Nathan, he did it to drain her body fluids, something he had seen on *CSI* on the television. It was sick. They were depraved.

William continued: 'The body was dismembered with a circular power saw in eight different locations. Experts said it would have been easier to carry out that exercise if more than one person was involved.' He glanced up at the dock as he spoke. I hoped Nathan and Shauna were cowering in fear. I hoped they realised that they sounded like the scum of the earth, the lowest of the low.

He went on to describe how Becky's remains had been carefully packaged and covered in cling film, plastic bags and tape, and concealed within a blue plastic box, two black suitcases and a rucksack.

Sarah stifled a huge sob, then suddenly got up and left. I rose to go after her, but Ziggy quickly left the room to console her instead.

William paused for a moment as he watched Sarah leave. He turned back to the jury, and informed them that two years previously Becky had told a friend that Nathan had described in graphic detail how he planned to kill her.

I sat bolt upright in my chair. This was news to me. 'That absolute bastard,' I muttered under my breath. My heart started thumping hard in my chest when it dawned on me that perhaps Nathan had been planning this for a long time. What hurt the most is that Becky hadn't felt she could tell me about the dreadful things he was saying to her. If she had, I would have sorted him out. Instead, she had confided in a friend. I wondered who it was. Becky and I were so close, it wasn't like her to hide anything from me. I wondered how much Nathan had managed to get inside her head. Maybe she'd believed that I couldn't protect her from him; I remembered her saying one day that I was 'too old'. Is that something Nathan had told her? The thought was almost too much to bear.

William concluded the evidence for that day by telling us that Becky was wearing a green jumper and a blue onesie when she was killed. I realised that they were the clothes I'd last seen her alive in when I looked in on her as she lay sleeping, so peaceful and innocent.

The courtroom began to empty. I felt unsteady as I rose to my feet. I walked out with Sam and my dad beside me, and caught sight of Sarah and Ziggy in the hallway. Sarah's face was blotchy from crying. She threw her arms around me when she saw me and hugged me hard.

Hearing that my daughter had been killed in her own bedroom as part of a bungled kidnap attempt by my stepson was devastating. I was left angry, confused and deeply disturbed by the evidence we heard that day. More than anything, Nathan's motive for the attack – his claim that Becky treated his mother badly – left me bewildered. First of all, it wasn't true; and secondly, I couldn't understand why he thought that was enough of a reason to end someone's life. He was obviously a complete headcase.

We went for a few drinks afterwards, before heading home to let Anjie know what had been revealed in court. I dreaded telling her that her son had plotted such a sick and disturbing attack on Becky, and that he had used *her* as his excuse for doing so.

Predictably, she was left crushed and bewildered by the information. Watching the light in Anjie's eyes dim after she heard what an evil monster her son had turned out to be was heartbreaking.

Another sleepless night followed. I tossed and turned as everything I had heard that day came back to haunt me. I prayed that my memories of my daughter wouldn't be tainted by the knowledge of what he did to her. I tried hard not to think about it, but images of Nathan butchering her swam around my mind. The bath. The powersaw. The blood. It was agonising. All I could do was put my faith in the jury and hope that they would make the right decision. I hoped that they were as sickened and appalled by it as I was.

At the beginning of the following day's proceedings, Nathan admitted manslaughter as opposed to murder, and the jury were told that they would need to consider this option through-out the trial. I thought it was a complete joke, of course. It was laughable that Nathan was denying the murder charge when he had already admitted to killing Becky. If what he did to Becky wasn't murder then I'm not sure what is. Shauna remained adamant that she had nothing to do with the whole thing – something William labelled 'ridiculous'. I couldn't have agreed more.

On day three of the trial, 8 October, Shauna's mother, Lisa Donovan, gave evidence to say that she hadn't seen her daugh-ter for four years. They used to live in an annex of her house but then fell out after an argument, and she hadn't seen them again until they suddenly turned up a few days after Becky went missing. From the witness stand, she explained that

Nathan and Shauna visited her and her husband, Shauna's stepfather, Kevin Stone, on 23 February. They then visited her three more times in quick succession that week. Lisa was so surprised by their visits that she asked them if something was wrong, or if they needed money. She had heard that Becky was missing, and even made a joke about Shauna and Nathan having something to do with her disappearance.

'I know why you're at my house all the time – it's because you kidnapped her,' she said, but Shauna had been quick to dismiss it, replying, 'No.'

Lisa commented that Nathan seemed very controlling of Shauna, and that Shauna 'did whatever he wanted'. The couple were later arrested while at her house on 3 March.

The court was then told that Shauna giggled as she was questioned by police seven days after Becky died. She told them that she had been playing Simpsons Monopoly with Nathan during the evening of the day Becky was murdered. William pointed out that Becky's body would have either been just yards away in the boot of Nathan's car, or in the bathroom of their home while they played the game. The thought made me boil over with fury, but I kept my cool. Yelling across the courtroom at Nathan and Shauna would only make things worse. I needed to keep my composure and dignity for Becky.

Shauna also mentioned during police interviews that she thought Becky was 'disrespectful' to Anjie, and that she used her struggle with anorexia to manipulate people. She said it seemed like it was more of an 'attention thing' rather than a true eating disorder. She also said that Becky and I argued all the time, and that Becky thought her life would have been much better if she had gone into foster care.

I was furious – I knew she was lying. While it was true that Becky and I argued, like all fathers and their teenage daughters, I didn't for one minute believe that Becky had ever said she would have preferred to be in foster care. She knew how hard Anjie and I had fought to get her and Danny out of care, and I know she appreciated it and was, for the most part, happy at home. Shauna was weaving a huge web of lies to distract the police from the role she had played in the murder of my little girl. I shouldn't have let it get to me, but some of the rubbish that came out of that girl's mouth really wound me up. I suppose part of the problem was not being able to have it out with her and set her straight on a few things.

Day six, 12 October, marked the start of the second week of proceedings. It was set to be a gruelling and unforgiving day as the prosecution geared up to present more evidence. We were warned by William beforehand that this would be the day when a forensic pathologist would read out all the horrific injuries Becky had sustained during the attack. We would also learn how her body parts were discovered. Once again, Anjie stayed at home. It was for the best, as we knew we would be learning some truly terrible things.

I was a bag of nerves before entering the courtroom, but I was determined to hear all the evidence. Sarah sat next to me and we linked arms, steeling ourselves to listen to the gruesome truth about how Becky had been found. I couldn't stop myself from shaking with nerves. Ziggy and Jo sat behind us, in case we needed them. Once again, Nathan and Shauna were seated at the back of the dock, so it was impossible for me to see their faces.

Detective Sergeant John Dowding was asked to stand, and

he described to the jury how he and another officer searched the shed in Barton Court.

He spoke carefully as he gave his evidence, remembering every detail.

'The shed was full,' he said. 'Just to the right of the door was a blue plastic bag with a rucksack on top of it and a number of suitcases. The officer and I then opened the large case nearest the door and found a number of items inside. They appeared to be parcels of cling film with plastic bags, and the bags had numerous parcels inside.

'I pulled out one of the smaller parcels, about the size of a rugby ball, to see what the item was. I examined the parcel by feeling it; I tried squeezing and manipulating it to see what was inside. It was squashy, but there was something harder within the squashy material. We tried unwrapping the parcel to confirm what the contents were.

'After two to three layers of cling film, it was apparent that it was a right hand, and the fist was clenched and severed at the wrist.'

My mouth dropped open in horror and Sarah gripped my hand, her nails digging in. She looked pale.

'She fought for her life,' I whispered, and she nodded, staring straight ahead.

I struggled to suppress my rage as I pictured my little girl clenching her fists and trying to fend Nathan off. I had taught her how to defend herself in our boxing sessions, but I never imagined she'd have to use those skills against her own stepbrother. She must have been petrified.

William then called forensic pathologist Dr Deborah Cook to give her evidence. She walked calmly to the stand before explaining to the jury that she had conducted Becky's post mortem.

Dr Cook said that she had looked first in a black-and-grey suitcase, which had been removed from the garden shed in Barton Court. She found four parcels inside.

She briefly looked across at where we were sitting before continuing to describe one particular package. It was as if she was apologising to us for what she was about to say.

'The outside packaging was an Asda carrier bag, inside that was cling film and then inside that was duct tape and further wraps of cling film and thick blue plastic, wrapped in silver duct tape,' she said carefully. 'The head was inside that plastic bag, and there was clear tape over the face. The head was covered with damp white crystals.'

Sarah suddenly stood up and bolted from the courtroom, her hands covering her mouth.

Here is Sarah's recollection of that horrendous moment:

I made sure that I went to every single day of the trial because I wanted to be there for Darren. I wanted justice for my niece and that thought kept me going. But as the days passed, I found it harder and harder to cope with what I was hearing. Like the rest of the family, nothing could have prepared me for what I heard in court that day. I knew Becky had been dismembered, but I had no idea that her head had been taken off her body. I guessed that Darren must have known after seeing her body in the morgue, but I had no idea. The moment the pathologist said that her head was found inside a plastic bag, vomit rose in my throat and I just had to get out of there. I rushed to the door and kicked off my shoes because I knew I needed to get to the toilet fast. As I ran down the corridor, I tried to stop myself throwing up in my hands. Once inside, I hurled myself down on my knees and threw up in the toilet bowl, my body shaking from the shock and disgust at what I had just heard. I started to cry, but it wasn't an ordinary cry, it was an agonising cry from the pit of my stomach. I probably sounded like a wounded animal. Ziggy followed me in, and I turned and looked at her before retching again.

'Why did they do this to her?' I screamed, tears running down my face. 'Why did they do this?'

'I know, Sarah,' Ziggy replied gently. 'It's awful. That's why we couldn't tell you some of these things before today. We didn't want these images to be in your head for all those months. That's why we had to do it this way.'

'I don't understand why they needed to do that to her,' I said weakly, still staring into the bowl. I was too scared to get up in case I needed to be sick again. I curled my legs around the toilet and started to shiver on the cold floor. My stomach cramped up, and I gasped from the pain. My heart was pounding so hard that it hurt with every beat.

'They've taken everything from my family,' I sobbed.

Ziggy stayed silent. I suppose there wasn't much she could say. I couldn't rid myself of the thought of Nathan sitting there, carefully packaging up Becky's body parts. He had packed them up so meticulously, it was sickening. I couldn't believe he could just discard someone else's body like that. I wouldn't be able to do that to a stranger, let alone somebody I grew up with.

It took me a while to calm myself down before I could face going back into the court. I knew they were talking about the *way Becky's other body parts had been found, and I wasn't sure if I could face hearing more of that. But, eventually, I sat up, wiped my face and pulled myself together. A member of the court staff brought me my shoes and Ziggy stayed with me until I was ready.*

'Are you sure you want to go back in?' Ziggy checked as I stood up. 'You don't have to if you don't want to.'

'No,' I said, taking a deep breath. 'I have to go back. For Darren.'

When I sat back down, Darren was white with shock. I grabbed his hand and tried to steady myself to hear the rest of what the pathologist had to say.

While Sarah was out of the courtroom, my eyes were fixed on the jury while the pathologist explained the way Becky had been chopped into pieces and wrapped up, as if she was nothing more than a slab of meat. I wanted to gauge their reaction to the horrific things Dr Cook was telling them. A few looked as if they might be sick, and I knew that they must have been wondering what sort of a person could do something like that. I was certain that if anything was going to convince them that Nathan was a true monster, this was it.

I always thought I would struggle to contain my rage when I heard all the gory details about how Becky was found, but instead I just felt weak. I was doing everything I could not to bolt out of the room behind Sarah. I had to be there, for Becky.

Dr Cook took almost an hour to list all the different injuries Becky sustained, including fourteen cuts and bruises to her face, which were consistent with a hand being placed over her face to suffocate her. There were also the fifteen horrifying stab wounds, inflicted after she died. I tried to put myself in a calmer place as Dr Cook described how Becky's left arm, right hand and right leg had been stored with her head in the suitcase.

The pathologist said that she then examined the contents of a blue plastic box. She said that underneath several layers of clothes, plastic bags and cling film, she made a harrowing discovery.

'There was a plastic sack saying "It's my birthday – Wacky Warehouse",' she said. 'Then a white shower curtain, and underneath that, a human torso.'

I held my head in my hands and I could hear Tanya weeping behind me. It was almost too much to bear. I couldn't believe they were talking about my beautiful little girl. I shifted in my seat, trying to catch a glimpse of Nathan and Shauna, but there were too many people in the way.

Dr Cook explained that Becky would have had a 'fight or flight' reaction as she was being suffocated, a survival mechanism causing her to struggle and fight back. She also described the way that some of her body parts had been packed with cat litter and table salt, which act as a preservative. I supposed that they must have found that out on the Internet. It's not the kind of thing you get to know otherwise.

On the same day, the court was played a recording of a police interview with Nathan eight days after Becky was killed, which was before his arrest. He labelled her as 'self-centred' and 'demanding'. He said that he 'didn't particularly like her', and added that he didn't truly believe that Becky had ever suffered from anorexia.

I couldn't believe his ignorance. Becky's struggle with anorexia was taken incredibly seriously by the health professionals who treated her. What made him more of an expert than them?

Did he really have the arrogance to believe that because he didn't really like his stepsister, he had the right to attack her and take her young life? I hated him more with every second that I listened to his pathetic little voice on that recording. He also told police that he hadn't helped us during the search for Becky because nobody had notified him that it was happening. Another lie. It was all over the news and, of course, we had been talking about nothing else.

The following day, 13 October, we were shown the green jumper belonging to Anjie and the blue onesie Becky had been wearing when she was killed. Both were stained with Becky's blood and had been cut up the back. We were also shown the suitcases that were used to hide the body, and the court heard how blood-stained goggles, a knife and handcuffs were recovered, among other things. One important piece of evidence was the circular saw used to cut up the body, which was found in the black suitcase. Sarah once again left the room at this point, but I stayed, my eyes glued to the defendants' dock. I couldn't wait until it was time for Nathan and Shauna to stand and answer questions. I wanted to see them clearly, and I wanted to watch them squirm.

As we left that day, I had to stop myself telling the TV cameramen waiting outside exactly what I thought about the monster I used to call my son. I knew it wasn't the right time for that yet, however fiercely the anger burned inside me.

Dealing with the media was a daily issue. While we were trying to get our heads around what we were hearing in court, we also had to contend with the huge press interest in the case.

Anjie and I had received countless letters from magazines, newspapers and television programmes, all asking if we would be interested in giving them an interview after the verdict was delivered. It was difficult to comprehend the sheer number of journalists all falling over themselves to speak to us. While we were grateful for the media's role during the search, and for all they had done to try to find Becky, it was a little overwhelming, to say the least. We knew that we would probably want to have our say after the court case had finished, in order to pay a proper tribute to Becky and let the world know what she had really been like, but legally we had to stay silent until then for the sake of a fair trial.

As the trial progressed, the media interest just seemed to grow and grow. Every day, there would be a scrum of photographers waiting outside the court, trying to get a snap of my family and me to use alongside their reports. In most of the pictures I look completely broken, clinging on to Sarah. I know they were only doing their jobs, but it did feel very invasive at times.

On day eight, the trial delved deeper into Nathan and Shauna's apparent interest in teenage girls. Shaun Groves, a police criminal intelligence officer, took to the stand and read out a series of texts and Facebook messages that he had retrieved during his investigation. Disturbingly, the pair had texted each other about kidnapping a sixteen-year-old girl from a supermarket. The messages began in November, three months before Becky was killed. The thought of it sent a shiver down my spine.

In a conversation on 5 December, Nathan texted Shauna, telling her to bring him back 'two pretty schoolgirls'.

She replied: 'LOL yeh I'll just kidnap them from school.'

Later that day, Shauna texted Nathan again. She wrote: 'Just went into Costcutter and saw a pretty petite girl. Almost knocked her out to bring home lol xoxo'

A reply from Nathan twenty seconds later read: 'Don't you 'almost' me … Now DO IT bitch!! xxxxx'

She replied: 'Yeah I'll just go back in time to when I saw her then time travel her to our attic LOL xoxo'

Hearing the messages being read out made me feel sick to my stomach. Just a few months before they attacked Becky, they were texting each other, joking about kidnapping another sixteen-year-old girl. My overriding feeling was profound shock. I had thought these people were my family, but I realised that I didn't know them at all, and possibly never had.

I went home that night and spent the weekend trying to take in all the things I had heard in court, but it was difficult. I spent most of the time in my own world, detached from reality, as I tried to come to terms with who Nathan and Shauna really were. Anjie shook her head in disbelief when we relayed the information to her.

'Who the hell are they?' she muttered when I told her about the messages. 'Who have we been letting in our house?'

My heart went out to her. Becky was a typical teenager and may not have been perfect, but she rarely hid anything from us and we knew her character well. As far as Anjie was concerned, Nathan, the boy she had brought up, was like a stranger.

The following week, from 19 October, was equally hard, as we listened to a forensic scientist explain how Becky's blood was discovered on the upstairs doorframes in our home. Claire Morse also told the jury that there was a match for Shauna's

DNA on one of two facemasks found in one of the suitcases, as well as traces of make-up. Nathan's DNA was found on both masks. Shauna's DNA was also discovered on a bin bag and on a T-shirt found at the same time.

William then called a friend of Shauna and Nathan's to the stand, who was not named in court. She said that she thought Nathan was controlling of Shauna and didn't like her going out without him. She said that he could be a paranoid person, who got jealous of Shauna speaking to other men. She added that he had told her that he 'hated Becky', labelling her as spoilt and selfish.

Another difficult moment came when the jury were shown a replica of the saw that was used to cut up my beautiful daughter. My heart was in my throat and Sarah squeezed my arm as the saw was plugged into the wall. Everyone in the entire courtroom jolted in fright as it was switched on. The noise was deafening, and I felt sick to my stomach as my mind filled with terrible images of Nathan using it on Becky. I held my head in my hands, and I heard Sarah sob as she pulled away from me to leave the court in order to compose herself.

The following day, the jury was shown a recording of a police interview with Becky's best friend, Courtney. She also gave evidence via video link. Obviously emotional, Courtney told the officer that Nathan had repeatedly told Becky he would kill her in the years before her death. My jaw dropped and my blood started to boil at that point. Why had Becky decided not to tell me? Had Nathan really managed to persuade her that I couldn't protect her from him? I was her dad. I would have done anything – anything at all – to keep her safe if I had known.

During the interview, Courtney said to a police officer: 'Becky's told me a few times, like this has happened on a number of occasions, that Nathan would graphically describe – this is her exact words – how he would kill her. He'd describe it in detail, and she mentioned it a few times, like it was troubling her, the fact that he said it. She did seem a bit scared of him.'

I was proud of the way Becky's friends were willing to play their part in the trial. Giving evidence as part of a police investigation or trial is nerve-racking enough for an adult, let alone a teenager. Adam also gave evidence to the court, and Luke gave a written statement, which stated that Becky had texted him saying 'I love you so much' at 3.52 a.m., just hours before she was murdered. My heart went out to him. He had obviously been besotted with her and had been suffering badly since her death. He also wrote that when he came around to the house later on the day Becky was killed, Shauna had answered the door and acted as though nothing had happened.

Anjie's mum, Margaret, came to testify on the same day as the jury heard Courtney's evidence. She said that she believed Nathan's mental health had deteriorated noticeably in the two years before Becky's death. Margaret also said that Nathan's dislike of Becky had started about a year or eighteen months before and was at its worst during the period before Becky was killed. She claimed it began around the same time that he started getting more paranoid and hoarding junk he found in the street, so that their house was full from floor to ceiling of broken fridges, washing machines and all kinds of stuff. He planned to fix it up then sell it, but never got around to it. She finished by saying that she had never seen Nathan act violently towards Shauna, and that in many ways she was the dominant one in the couple.

'She very often told him what to do,' she said, looking across at the jury. 'She seemed quite dominant in the way she spoke to him.'

I hoped that the jury would believe her. She knew Nathan as well as anyone, since he had lived with her during the week as a child, and she had often seen Nathan and Shauna together.

Before we left, we were told that, the following day, the court was going to hear Nathan's prepared statement in which he would admit to killing Becky. Although we had heard his account through the prosecution, we had never heard his statement in full. I dreaded hearing what he had to say for himself, but at the same time I couldn't wait, because I had to know. I only hoped I would be able to keep my anger in check.

CHAPTER 14

THE TRIAL CONTINUES

On 20 October, in the third week of the trial, I tried to prepare myself for hearing Nathan and Shauna's side of the story. I arrived at the court with Sam and Sarah, and we were once again briefed by William Mousely on what we were about to hear.

'Today, we'll be reading out Nathan's prepared statement in full,' he told us before we went into the courtroom. 'That's where he makes his confession.'

My stomach twisted into a tight knot and I swallowed hard. Although I knew the gist of what Nathan had said in his confession, I couldn't help feeling nervous about what we were about to hear, and how I would react. We decided that Sam would sit near me on the days when Nathan was in the dock, or when we were going to hear any of his statements or recorded interviews. I knew that hearing him try to justify why he killed my daughter would make my head spin, and I needed somebody strong next to me to keep me under control. Sarah sat on my other side as usual, holding my hand.

A detective who interviewed Nathan when he was first arrested told the court that he had described himself as being 'emotionally unstable' and 'psychologically disturbed'. Two days later, after the police had found his bloody fingerprint on Becky's doorframe, a pre-prepared statement was read out to officers by his solicitor, confessing to the crime in full.

It read:

I, Nathan Charles Matthews, accept that I am responsible for the death of Rebecca Watts. On 19 February 2015 I attended 18 Crown Hill, St George, Bristol, with my girlfriend Shauna Hoare. Eighteen Crown Hill is where my mother lives with Darren Galsworthy; Rebecca Watts also lived there.

Shauna is my mother's registered carer so we regularly go to the house to help with housework and other help my mother needs. Although we usually went there on Mondays, Wednesdays and Fridays, we did also go there on other days.

On Thursday, 19 February, part of the reason for going round was to return a tin to my grandmother. My grandmother was due to take my mother to a medical appointment and bring her back.

In my car I had a large bag, a stun device, handcuffs, tape and a mask. I had developed an idea to scare Rebecca by kidnapping her. I wanted to kidnap her to scare her and teach her a lesson. I believe that she was selfish and her behaviour towards my mother was a risk to her health.

When we got to 18 Crown Hill we let ourselves in with a key my mother had left in the recycling box. Upon entering the property we all went to the front room. A few minutes after arriving, Shauna said she wanted a cigarette and went into the garden.

When she was in the garden I went to the boot of my car and took out a bag which contained the other items. I took everything upstairs to the landing. I think I then took the items out of the bag before knocking on Rebecca's door.

She replied: 'What?' or 'Hello', and I said, 'Can I see you a minute?' or similar words.

Rebecca then opened the door. I am wearing the mask. I cannot be sure in which order things happened immediately after she came to the door, but I used the items I had to subdue Rebecca.

During a short struggle my mask slipped and Rebecca was able to see my face. This caused me to panic, and I strangled her while she was partially in the bag.

I collected the items I had used, put them and Rebecca into the bag and zipped up the bag. I also took her phone, tablet and laptop, together with shoes, some clothes and a duvet cover from the spare room in a separate bag. I took everything downstairs and put it into the boot of my car.

Back in the house, I waited to hear Shauna then slammed the front door shut. Before going into the front room I checked that Shauna was not in that room.

The rest of the day at the house goes as it would normally, if we were there. We leave about 7 p.m., probably a little after 7 p.m. We returned to 14 Cotton Mill Lane. I go and lie on our bed, which is what I would normally do. The rest of the evening passed as usual but I cannot remember exactly what we did. After Shauna went to bed and to sleep, I waited a while and went out to the car and brought the bags into the house.

The following day we went back round to 18 Crown Hill, and I tried to behave as normal as I could. When we returned back to 14 Cotton Mill Lane, I again waited for Shauna to go to sleep, and this time I collected the bag with Rebecca's body and took it to the bathroom.

I took the body out of the bag and placed it in the bath. In order to stop Shauna using the bathroom the following morning, I poured drain cleaner down the toilet so I could tell Shauna it was blocked again. The toilet would often get blocked, and when that happened I knew Shauna would not go into the bathroom. I also locked the door.

My memory of the days that followed is not perfect so I'm not sure which day I returned to 14 Cotton Mill Lane, having left Shauna at my mother's, but I think it was the Saturday.

When I got back to 14 Cotton Mill Lane I tried to dispose of the body by cutting it up with a circular saw. Initially, I wrapped up the body parts and took them back downstairs and hid them, I'm not sure how many days later, but on another day I took the body, the saw, and other items to 9 Barton Court, Barton Hill, and placed them in the garden shed.

I took them to this address with two other people. I did not tell them what was in the bags and the box, and said I would collect them in a few days. Both of the people are men, but I do not want to name them.

I have chosen to give my account by means of a written statement because I believe I have mental health and learning difficulties that make it difficult for me to say it out loud. Also, I

*find it difficult to express the detail in this account in spoken
words.*

    *I would like to add that my denials to date have been
motivated in part by a wish to avoid the pain and
disappointment these admissions would cause to my partner
and family.*

    *Shauna did not know anything about my causing the death
of Rebecca or my attempt to dispose of and hide the body.
Had she known, she would have reported me to the police.*

    Apart from this statement, I will exercise my right to silence.

In a sick twist, Nathan told officers during the interview that
he had hatched the plan in order to make Becky 'more appreciative of life'. I couldn't figure out if he was trying to be ironic
or whether he was just really stupid.

William then read out extracts from Nathan's interviews
with police.

'I came up with the plan to scare her,' William read out
slowly, his eyes fixed on Nathan, who was sitting in the dock.
'She would leave things out for my mum to trip over on the
floor and talk to her like dirt. I thought if I was able to scare
her, and she would not be harmed when she got back, she
would have been scared and more appreciative of things.

'I would have stuck her in a suitcase. I would have put tape
around her mouth so she would not make a noise. Then I was
thinking of a wooded area or whatever to take her back out –
obviously I'd still have the mask on – scare her and say something along the lines of, "You have got to start treating people
better, not being a bitch and self-centered," and make a threat
that this could happen again, or worse.'

William paused for a second after reading the extracts, and he looked over at the jury.

'That's all the prosecution has prepared for today,' he finished, and the court was adjourned.

As we got up to leave, I was shaking with anger. Sarah held my hand tightly as we made our way out, and when I looked over at Sam he was staring straight ahead, stony-faced.

'He's a complete coward,' I spat out, the second we spilled onto the pavement outside. 'He's a psychopathic monster, and a coward. He knew I'd come for him if he ever kidnapped or did anything to her. He was always going to kill her, it's absolute bullshit.'

Sarah nodded as she lit a cigarette. I noticed that her hands were shaking too.

We went for a drink in a nearby pub before heading home. Once I got in, I cooked tea and sorted myself out for the following day. As I went through my usual routine, I felt empty inside. My movements were slow and my whole body felt heavy as lead. The court case was starting to take its toll on me, and Anjie noticed.

'I'll come with you tomorrow,' she volunteered.

'You don't have to do that, love,' I replied, squeezing her hand. 'I know how difficult all this is for you.'

'It's difficult for you too,' she pointed out. 'I want to come.'

I didn't argue with her. When Anjie decided she wanted to do something, usually there was nothing you could do to change her mind. I just hoped she would be able to cope with a day listening to the garbage that spouted from her son's mouth as he tried to explain why he took away the girl Anjie had loved as her own daughter.

The proceedings didn't resume until midday the next day, so it meant that Anjie and I could take our time getting ready. I was pleased it wasn't an early start, as sitting in court for just half a day would be easier for her to cope with.

It started with a bang, though, as the first thing the jury was shown was a video of Nathan's interview with the police, after his account of killing Becky had been handed over. Scruffily dressed in a navy T-shirt, Nathan was crying loudly and had his head in his hands. He begged the police not to read the confession out loud, or to use Shauna's name during questioning.

I hoped that the jury wouldn't feel any sort of empathy with him. He looked and sounded like a complete maniac, angrily wiping away tears and saying that he might have got the kidnap idea from television or from a couple of dreams he'd had. I reached across and grabbed Anjie's hand as the video was playing, and she stared straight ahead. It was hard to guess what was going through her mind as she watched Nathan admit to killing Becky. She just looked desperately sad.

We were also shown early police interviews with Shauna, in which she said that Nathan had been violent and controlling to her in the past. After hearing what Nathan had admitted to doing, Shauna claimed that she was always slightly scared of him. I shook my head with disbelief. Although I knew Nathan had shown signs of jealousy and paranoia around her, I highly doubted that Shauna was ever actually frightened of him. Like Nathan's nan, Margaret, had said, Shauna often gave the impression that she was the dominant one in the relationship. Anjie and I both thought that she was the smarter of the two, and if anyone was a bully in the relationship, it was her.

When quizzed about the noise that must have been coming from the bathroom as Nathan cut up Becky's body, Shauna said that she had believed Nathan when he told her that the toilet was blocked and that he was fixing a pipe. In all further interviews with Shauna, she continued to deny having anything to do with Becky's death.

The following Monday, 26 October, Detective Constable Claire Langley read a transcript to the court of an interview carried out the day after Becky's dismembered body was discovered.

The police officer asked Shauna what she knew about Becky's body being taken into the house she shared with Nathan.

She replied, 'Nothing. No idea whatsoever.'

The officer then asked, 'What was the plan when Becky's body was put in your house?'

Shauna said, 'I have no idea. I'm feeling sick to know she was there. Appalled, disgusted, outrageously angry. I think I'm feeling that I'm going to wake up and it's not actually happening. I'm really confused why he thought he could get away with it. I felt sick looking at him, knowing what he had done. She was a nice enough girl, so young. I don't understand how he could have done it.'

The police officer then told Shauna that she was in the house when Becky was killed, in the car used to carry Becky's body in the boot, and at the house she shared with Nathan, which was used to cut up the teenager's body.

'You can see the picture I'm painting,' said the officer.

'Yes, I know it looks bad,' Shauna replied.

She cried throughout the recording, adding that she was not trying to cover up for Nathan. 'There is still a part of me that cares for him, but it is more anger and disgust that has taken over. He is just sick, literally physically sick,' she sobbed. 'If that was his intent to just scare her like that it is just so twisted and wrong. I don't understand his logic, his theory, his justification. I couldn't live in a house knowing he had just viciously killed somebody who in my mind – in everyone's mind – didn't deserve it.

'You can imagine the suffering she went through – how scared she was – and to know I was right there. She deserved to live her life. She didn't do anything wrong. She was not always the nicest person, but she didn't do anything bad.'

We then listened as Shauna was asked about searching the Internet for the 'Do You Want to Hide a Body?' video. She told officers that she had searched for it as a joke to cheer Nathan up, claiming at that point she didn't know what had happened to Becky. It took everything in me not to shout out across the court that she was a complete liar. I hoped that the jury were thinking the same as I was, the same as Anjie was. We'd have to wait and see.

On Tuesday, 27 October, Anjie and I woke up and looked at each other wearily. It was the first day of Nathan's defence, meaning that he would be in the witness box. Anjie was more determined than ever to come to court that day, even though we were all worried about the effect it would have on her health, both mentally and physically. She had been worn out after the previous time, finding it dreadfully upsetting and that was only half a day. Sam and Sarah came to support us again, along with my dad and Denise. Tanya, Pat and Danny were there too. I worried about poor Danny, still only twenty years old, hearing all the gruesome details about his little sister's murder, but he insisted that he had to try to understand what was going through Nathan's head. He had to try to make sense of it.

As I pushed Anjie into the courtroom, I was buzzing with nervous energy. It was day fourteen of the trial, and it was going to be the first day I would be able to get a clear view of Nathan. Until then, he had been sitting at the back of the dock, where we couldn't see him or Shauna clearly. Now, I would be able to look the murderer who took my little girl away from me in the eye, and see what he had to say for himself. It was a strange feeling, because even though I couldn't wait to see Nathan on the stand, I had to think of Anjie's feelings too. It was her son being tried for murder. Sometimes I forgot that.

Before Nathan was called to the stand, the prosecution closed its case by telling the jury that police had discovered a porn film of a teenager being raped on a laptop belonging to Nathan. I was horrified when we heard that the film had a scene in which a man tied the rape victim's hands together, covered her mouth with his hand and slapped her face. I glanced at Anjie, who looked distraught as the similarities to the attack on Becky dawned on her. I gave her hand a squeeze.

After a short break, Nathan was called up. My heart was hammering in my chest as he slowly made his way to the witness box. He looked smaller than he used to. Hunched over, with his eyes fixed on the floor, he was a complete shell of himself. He was wearing a white jumper with a light-blue shirt underneath, and had dark circles under his eyes, looking as if he hadn't slept for weeks. I wondered if he would glance in our direction as my eyes bored into him, but he didn't dare.

His barrister, Adam Vaitilingam, asked him to confirm his name and age, and his voice faltered as he answered. One by one, Adam took him through the charges he faced. Nathan pleaded guilty to manslaughter, but when Adam asked him if, while carrying out his plan to kidnap Becky, he had intended to murder her or cause her serious harm, he suddenly started sobbing.

'No, I didn't,' he cried. He rested his head on his arms as he gave his answer.

Rage consumed me as I watched Anjie start to cry. I hated him with all my soul for what he had done to our family – to Anjie, to me, to Danny, and to all our extended family.

During questioning, Nathan said he suffered from fibromyalgia, which left him in constant pain. He claimed he suffered to such an extent that he would collapse in pain from sneezing. I couldn't help rolling my eyes. If he was in that much pain, how the hell did he manage to kill and dismember a sixteen-year-old girl?

'What about your relationship with your stepsister, Becky?' Adam asked. 'What was that like?'

'It was good when we were younger. It was civil when she got older,' Nathan replied.

When Adam asked him about Anjie being diagnosed with MS, Nathan starting crying again. He sipped some water before replying, 'I was really worried. She is nice and kind and would do anything for anyone and not expect anything back in return.'

I narrowed my eyes and shook my head slowly. It stuck in my throat that Nathan was pretending to care about his mother after everything he had put her through. She gripped my hand tightly as he denied ever threatening Becky but added that his kidnap plan was motivated by the way he had seen Becky treat Anjie.

'The main problem was that Becky would leave things on the stairs or in the kitchen in places where my mum would walk,' he said quietly. 'My mum could have fallen over and been seriously injured. She talked to my mum like dirt. She used to swear at her.'

Anjie shook her head at this.

Adam then asked Nathan to explain to the court what happened on the day Becky died. I could feel Anjie shaking beside me, and I squeezed her hand again to comfort her. It must have been unbearable for her to hear Nathan using her as an excuse for murder.

'I was going to scare Becky,' Nathan said, as he twisted a tissue around his fingers. 'I had the thought for a couple of months. I knew my mum was going out for the appointment. It was an opportunity.

'My plan was to get her in the suitcase and get her in the car and drive off. I hadn't decided exactly which of the locations I had thought of. Basically, to tell her you have to treat people better – you have to change the way you are with people.

'I knocked on the door. The door was opened and straight away I used the Sellotape around Becky's mouth,' he said. 'She turned around and I think I said something along the lines of: "As long as you do as you're told you are going to be fine." She got down on to her knees and I got the handcuffs. I put the handcuffs on her hands, from behind. I was getting her into the suitcase when my mask slipped and my hands went over her eyes. I took the mask off and Sellotaped over her eyes.'

I was barely breathing as I listened, picturing the terror my little Bex must have experienced. She would have been petrified. I came out in goosebumps imagining what she must have been thinking, especially after Nathan had threatened to kill her so many times before. Nathan said that he was using a deeper voice so she wouldn't know it was him, but I was sure she must have realised. Who else could it be?

He sniffed as he explained that Becky didn't resist until he attempted to put her into the suitcase.

'That's when she started wriggling and resisting,' he said. 'I got my fingers on her nose to restrict her breathing, so that she would pass out. Then I tried getting her back into the suitcase, saying, "Don't struggle, you will be released unharmed," and she was still refusing to get into the suitcase.'

Nathan paused for a second before continuing. I willed him to look over at us and see Anjie sobbing uncontrollably. The selfish bastard had broken her heart. He claimed that he attacked Becky because he was trying to protect his mum, but I wanted him to see what he had actually done to her. No matter how long she lived, she would never recover from this.

'I thought to knock her out,' Nathan said slowly. 'I remember punching her just once.

'I didn't feel comfortable trying to do it that way because there would be a lot of pain.'

Beside me, Sam was shaking violently on the edge of his seat. His eyes were blazing with anger, and he looked as though he was ready to fly across the court and go for Nathan. I felt the same, but this was unusual for Sam, who was otherwise quiet and gentle.

'The last thing I did was try to make her pass out, which is something we did at school – it's like strangling but it doesn't completely restrict the air. People at school would pass out. Some would take a minute, some would take fifteen or twenty seconds, at a guess. After that, she stopped kicking. I moved her head and her legs and tried to position her in the suitcase. Then I picked up all the other bits. Something didn't seem right with her breathing. I checked for a pulse and she didn't have one.'

I clutched my face in my hands. Had my poor darling Bex's life been snuffed out just like that? I was sure there had been more of a struggle than he was letting on, and I was pretty sure Shauna had been involved too. I shot a look of pure hatred across the room at Nathan, but he was still far too cowardly to glance in our direction.

Anjie let out a huge, choked-up sob, which echoed across the courtroom. On hearing his mother cry, Nathan broke down in tears, hunching over and laying his head on the stand. I didn't believe he truly cared: Nathan was crying for himself, nobody else. To me, he was the lowest of the low.

I tried to comfort Anjie as best I could while struggling to keep my anger in check. The court was adjourned for a short break, Nathan was led out of the room, and I turned and gave Anjie a huge hug. She was crying loudly now, and the sound was awful. I almost broke down as well, but I was afraid that if I started, I wouldn't be able to stop. The only way I could get through this whole trial was by keeping my emotions under control as much as possible.

When the court resumed, Nathan was led back in, and he sat down and put his hands out in front of him, lacing his fingers.

He was asked why, if Becky's death was an accident, he didn't go straight to the police.

He said, 'I didn't want anybody to know what actually happened. It was the panic of everybody finding out and being hurt. I went in the bedroom and got her phone, laptop and tablet thing, and make-up and clothes, and chucked them in the black bag to make it look like she had just gone off somewhere.'

Courtney and I hadn't noticed any of Becky's things missing when we searched her room the day after she disappeared, but maybe he hadn't taken clothes or make-up she normally used.

Nathan said that he used the stun gun on Becky, but it didn't work. He took the handcuffs off her and threw them in the suitcase, which he put straight into the boot of his car.

'Everything happened really quickly,' he said. He then told the court how he put Becky's body in the boot and tried to act normally in front of Shauna and, later on, Anjie.

He claimed, 'I didn't tell Shauna. I wanted to hide it from her. The suitcase stayed in the car. Some time that night or in the early hours of the morning, I decided to dismember Becky's body. I bought drain cleaner to dissolve the body but that didn't work.'

Anjie started crying again, and I clenched my jaw to stop myself shouting out across the court how sick he was.

'You vile piece of shit,' I muttered under my breath. It was obscene to be talking about her in this way, just disgusting. She was my daughter, not a 'body'. She was a loving, fun, gorgeous girl, and he'd treated her like you wouldn't treat an animal.

Nathan was then asked about his state of mind at the time he cut up Becky's body.

'I just did it. I tried not to look. I did it, like, and it was just surreal. That's the only way I can explain it,' he said slowly. 'I was just doing what I had to do to protect everybody else, stop them finding out that she's gone.'

He then explained that he offered Karl Demetrius £10,000 from money he and Shauna had in their ISA accounts in exchange for his help moving items and storing them. He chose him because he couldn't think of anyone else. He said that he watched as Demetrius and James Ireland put them into the shed, and he told them not to look in the boxes. The court had heard earlier that Ireland believed the boxes were something to do with a robbery.

We were all relieved when the proceedings ended that day, as we were badly shaken up. Anjie had slumped right down in her wheelchair and didn't have the strength to sit upright any more. She looked frail and exhausted. The day had obviously been harrowing for her, as it had been for me. We already knew Nathan's story, of course, but hearing it come out of his mouth was incredibly difficult. Ziggy and Jo tried their best to look after us, but we were engulfed by anger and grief, imagining the horror of Becky's last moments of life.

Nathan was to be cross-examined by the prosecution on 29 October, which we knew was going to be stressful. When I opened my eyes that morning, I felt an overwhelming sense of dread, but I knew I had to go. Anjie said that she was deter-mined to make it to court too. I think she wanted to see if Nathan would ever actually look her in the eye, but I was sure he wouldn't. He was far too much of a coward.

The jury first heard that Nathan accessed porn almost every day, downloading and streaming multiple videos, including a lot of teen porn in which actresses who were over eighteen would dress like schoolgirls. He denied that he was sexually attracted to Becky, but admitted that he had always been attracted to teenage girls. The court heard how Nathan had tried to contact a sixteen-year-old girl on Facebook because he fancied her. I wondered if that girl now realised what a narrow escape she'd had.

William Mousley began his cross-examination of Nathan by accusing him of peddling lies to Anjie and me for days on end after Becky's death.

I fixed my eyes on Nathan, and he slumped slightly before giving his answer.

'I had no choice; I couldn't tell them,' he said.

The jury then heard that when Luke had visited the house looking for Becky on the day of her murder, her body was lying a few feet away in the boot of Nathan's car.

William looked at him hard for a moment before speaking.

'You repeatedly lied about what happened to Becky, didn't you?' he said.

'Yes,' Nathan said, sobbing.

'And when you were arrested you lied for as long as you could in interviews with the police? What was it that made you come up with your prepared statement?' he quizzed.

'My emotions all came out. I broke down in front of the solicitor. I basically admitted it, not in so many words. He saw that I was struggling,' Nathan answered.

Rage built up inside me as I watched him sitting there, feeling sorry for himself. William's eyes were still fixed on

Nathan as he accused him of changing his story and only admitting things he couldn't avoid in order to keep Shauna out of it.

'Shauna had nothing to do with it,' Nathan said firmly. 'The reason I told the lies in the beginning was because of everybody else I wanted to protect.'

Breaking down in tears, he added, 'I couldn't think of a way of being able to actually, effectively protect them, as in them believing she was off somewhere, getting messages from her saying she was fine, she was happy, that kind of thing. Obviously, because I couldn't do that they deserved to know the truth, have a burial, be able to say goodbye.'

The courtroom was silent apart from the sound of Anjie and Sarah sobbing. It made my skin crawl that he was pretending to care about whether we had a burial or not. If he cared one iota about that, he wouldn't have chopped up her body.

Mr Mousley narrowed his eyes and asked, 'Do you agree it sounds ridiculous that Shauna had no idea what was going on?'

Nathan replied, 'I wouldn't say ridiculous, no. I can understand suspicion of things but what happened, happened.'

Nathan said that he had planned to tie Becky to a tree and scare her after he had kidnapped her.

William looked at him incredulously. 'And what was going to happen after you finished terrifying her?' he asked.

'I would have let her go, after warning her to behave,' Nathan replied.

'She had been bound, gagged, handcuffed, tied to a tree and terrorised – and you thought she would have just walked off and lived her life? Did you live in a fantasy world in February this year?'

Nathan looked up at him before he replied, 'I didn't live in a fantasy world.'

Then William began to really grill Nathan, asking, 'Did your attitude towards Becky change after you killed her?'

'I didn't have an attitude to her,' Nathan replied.

'What about how you treated her after she died?' William asked.

'That's got nothing to do with how I felt about her,' Nathan muttered.

William glared at him. 'What about stabbing her fifteen times with a knife?'

Nathan looked at the floor. 'That's nothing to do with how I felt about her.'

'What about cutting her up into pieces?' William demanded.

Beside me, Anjie started to tremble.

Nathan simply replied, 'Like I said, I did what I had to do.'

William paused before quietly asking, 'Did you take pleasure in what you did?'

Tearfully, Nathan answered, 'No.'

The next day in court, Nathan continued his evidence. William started to ramp up his questioning, the disdain dripping from his voice as he addressed him.

He asked if he was lying about having a mask on, to help his story that this was a prank that went wrong. Nathan shook his head.

'No, because then there would have been a massive struggle. The whole point was for her not to know it was me,' he replied.

'You didn't have a disguise, she clearly knew who you were … It was all rather pathetic what you were doing – and you killed her,' William accused.

Matthews sniffed as he replied, 'No, it was doing a drastic thing to have a good end result.'

My stomach knotted at the words 'good end result'. I had no idea that my stepson had such a twisted mind. I stared at him, feeling nothing but contempt and bitterness towards him.

Nathan began crying in the witness box, with his head on the table, as William continued to question him sharply.

'She was putting up too much of a fight for your liking, wasn't she?' he asked.

Nathan shook his head again. 'There was no liking in it – it wasn't like the way you are trying to paint it. There wasn't a massive struggle.'

William went on, not giving any ground. 'Was she fighting for her life?'

'Not for her life, no,' Nathan replied.

William then asked if Nathan was prepared to look at the computer-generated images of injuries to Becky's head and face.

Nathan said no.

'I didn't think you would be,' William snapped. He then looked up to where we were sitting, his expression softening slightly.

'Have you ever expressed any remorse or sorrow to Becky or her family about what you did to her?' he asked. Nathan shifted uncomfortably.

'Not directly, no,' he said, 'I haven't tried to contact any of them.'

'Or do you feel sorry for yourself?' William suggested.

'I feel sorry for myself,' Nathan replied. 'But I feel sorry for everybody.'

Nathan said that he wasn't entirely surprised when he was arrested, and he just kept saying how his plan had gone 'horribly wrong'. William continued to press him on Shauna's involvement in the crime, but Nathan was adamant that she'd had nothing to do with it. He even claimed that he managed to cut up Becky's body with just one hand, which was obviously absurd. He then explained how he carefully packaged up the body parts, even storing some of them in the freezer. I felt a huge wave of nausea, and I looked up to see Sarah leaving the court. I couldn't believe I had allowed Nathan to be a part of my family. I didn't recognise him any more. Maybe I had never truly known him at all.

Shauna's questioning began the next day, Friday 30 October. Anjie stayed at home while Sarah came with me. She was gunning for Shauna in particular. She was determined that just because the emphasis had been on Nathan so far, Shauna should not get off scot-free.

She looked a lot more confident than Nathan as she made her way over to the witness box. She was wearing a peach blouse, black jacket and some smart black trousers. I hoped that the jury wouldn't be fooled by her act. The court was told that Shauna had grown up in care, only moving to Bristol to be with her mum when she was thirteen. Once again, she played the innocent card, claiming that Nathan controlled everything she did. She said that he once tried to strangle her, and once stabbed himself in the face with a fork during a row. When asked about Anjie, Shauna's face softened.

'She is amazing, very kind – cares for everybody,' she said quietly. 'As her health declined she still did what she could for anybody – that was the way she was. I was always taken on family holidays, invited over for Christmas and to celebrate my birthday.'

'And you paid us back by helping to kill my daughter,' I muttered to myself as Sarah reached for my hand. Shauna was nasty and scheming, as far as I was concerned. I prayed that the jury would see through her and that she wasn't going to be able to wriggle out of the charges against her.

Her defence barrister, Andrew Langdon, asked her about the multiple 'kidnap' messages exchanged between her and Nathan, and she admitted that, initially, she had lied to the police about them.

'I knew what Nathan had been charged with, I knew what had happened, I knew how bad it looked,' she said. 'It was meant sarcastically. I have a very sarcastic nature. It wasn't an actual idea. I regret it massively.'

Andrew then started asking Shauna about the day Becky was killed. Shauna explained that she arrived at the house and went into the kitchen to find one of Anjie's cigarettes, then she went for a smoke outside in the back garden. She could hear Becky's music playing upstairs, and when she came back into the kitchen she thought she heard Becky leave the house. She said that later that evening, they went home and ate pizza and watched films before they went to bed.

The next day, the couple drove back to our home. She mentioned that Nathan had left at some point during the day, saying that he had to go and help a friend. Anjie started to become worried about Becky being missing, so Shauna put a post on Facebook to help locate her. She later noticed that Nathan had a scratch on his wrist, but she did not ask him about it. That night, Nathan told her that she couldn't use the bathroom because the toilet was blocked and he needed to fix it. She didn't quiz him when she heard the power saw because she thought it was just a boring job that he needed to get on with. When asked why they were caught on CCTV buying cleaning products, she said that she thought Nathan wanted to clean up their cluttered home. She said that she did not help Nathan with the packing and bagging of Becky's body or with cleaning up the bathroom, and she had never touched the two facemasks found in her house.

I went home that night ranting at what, to me, was an obvious pack of lies from start to finish. How could she possibly have ignored the sounds coming from the bathroom? There was no way Nathan could have dismembered Becky all on his own. I just didn't believe it. I wondered if Nathan had any more injuries than just a scratch on his wrist. I hoped that some of Becky's frantic punches as she fought for her life had connected. I hoped that she had hurt him, and not just got those bruises I'd seen on her fists from hitting out wildly and striking the doorframe or the wall. I kept going over all I'd heard about her final struggle, and the more I thought about it, the more I was convinced that Shauna must have helped to subdue Becky. My daughter was only little, but she knew how to punch properly.

On the next day of the trial, 2 November, Shauna was cross-examined by William Mousely. He asked her if she just happened to be in the wrong place at the wrong time.

She answered clearly and confidently, saying, 'I didn't believe I was in the wrong place. I was in my house, which is the normal place to be.'

'Is it just an unhappy coincidence that you and Nathan were talking about kidnapping a teenage girl?' William asked.

Shauna nodded. 'It is just extremely unfortunate.'

'You were in blissful ignorance of everything that had taken place?' William asked, raising an eyebrow.

'Yes,' she said.

Shauna also said that it was a coincidence she had made an Internet search for 'Do You Want to Hide a Body?' on the day Becky died, claiming she only played Nathan the video to make him laugh.

'It was just a coincidence that Becky was lying dead in the bath a few feet away?' William said incredulously.

'Yes,' she replied.

Sarah was leaning forward in her seat now, her knees shaking with the anger that filled her whole body. Her eyes were locked on Shauna, and she looked as though she was going to pounce and attack her. Our roles were suddenly reversed: now it was me trying to calm her down. She half stood up, and I had to pull her back onto her seat as Ziggy and Jo looked over anxiously.

Shauna kept insisting her version of events was true. She seemed very composed compared to the blubbering mess Nathan had been. I didn't believe a second of it. I knew in my heart that she had been involved. She was cleverer and much more calculating than Nathan, although she was seven years his junior. I prayed that the jury would be able to see that.

'It might seem slightly unlikely to people but it is completely plausible,' she told the court.

William started to fire questions at her then: 'Isn't it the case that you and Nathan were in this together from start to finish?'

'No,' she replied instantly.

'That you went there together with the clear intention of taking her away to use for your purposes, in which you were both so interested?'

'No,' she said.

'You thought you could get away with it, didn't you?' William demanded.

Shauna frowned a little. 'I didn't have anything to get away with,' she said.

'But in the end there were just too many bits of evidence against you?' William asked.

Shauna once again said no.

'Are you just very unlucky?' William asked sarcastically.

'Yes,' she replied.

Sarah gripped the barrier in front of us so hard her knuckles turned white. Luckily, the court then adjourned for the day so she could calm down. None of us believed Shauna's story, but she hadn't slipped once in answering William's questions. She was cool and collected, as if something like this happened to her every day. There was no remorse. She didn't once say she felt sorry that Becky was dead, and I wanted to kill her for that alone. Why should she have a life when my beautiful daughter had been robbed of hers?

Over the next two days, James Ireland and Donovan Demetrius were called to the witness box. James maintained that he did not know what was in the cases when he was asked by Karl Demetrius to help move them. He said that if he had known the vile truth, he would never have agreed to help. Donovan claimed that he was not involved at all. He said that he had simply been staying at his brother Karl's house at the time Karl agreed to store the boxes for Nathan. In an emotional speech, he denied playing any part in hiding Becky's body and said he was 'horrified' by what his brother had done.

'Why would he put himself in that position?' he asked, looking across at us. 'Who in their right mind would do something so animalistic? My heart goes out to her family. I couldn't believe that man, Nathan Matthews, could do such a horrible thing. Who in their right mind would dismember their own stepsister? It is sickening.'

His words drew cheers and claps from people in the court, as they summed up what so many of us were thinking.

William delivered his closing speech for the prosecution on Thursday, 5 November. I sat down with my family around me once more, but Anjie stayed at home. She needed to build up all the strength she could muster, so she could be in court for the verdict.

My heart was beating about a thousand times a minute when William turned to face the jury. I willed them to listen hard and hear the truth in his words.

'This is a case where you have heard about two worlds: the fantasy world lived in by the defendants, and the real world where you and I live,' he said. 'Our world of good sense, and logic, where obvious and safe conclusions can be drawn from the evidence. Their world where people ignore the natural consequences of their actions. That world where complicated theories and suggestions that fly in the face of everything which is sensible take precedence. That world where when lies are told, they are all innocent lies; and that fantasy world where nobody tells anyone else what they have done, and nobody displays any emotions.

He then spoke about Becky, calling her a 'not untypical teenage girl, putting the problems of the past behind her, with a long life to look forward to'. He looked over at me and added: 'Clashing sometimes with her dad and her stepmother, a girl whose life was cruelly, and we submit callously, taken away from her at the hands of Nathan Matthews and Shauna Hoare. Because they didn't like her, and because they thought she could be their sexual plaything. Not satisfied with that, the contempt they have for her extended to the grotesque way in which her body was treated after her death.'

He described Shauna as a cool customer, who had undoubtedly played a part in Becky's murder. 'Did she strike you as the downtrodden girl in fear of Nathan Matthews, or was she a confident, calculating woman who appeared older than her twenty-one years? She was hardly the little girl lost – and not a flicker of emotion the whole time she was in the witness box. A very cool, very cold individual. Hardly, if any, indication of remorse.

'Becky was not going to go quietly – why on earth would she? She would fight, she would struggle, she would resist. It would take a lot of force to take her away. How do you improve your chances of doing that quickly and effectively? I suppose if it is two against one, it is easier, isn't it?

'And I suppose if you are both involved you have not got to hide from each other. Of course, in the fantasy world of Shauna Hoare she did not see or hear anything – she was in blissful ignorance.

'It is quite clear that Shauna Hoare was complicit in the murder of Becky Watts.'

William then described Shauna as Lady Macbeth, quoting the famous play and telling the jury, 'Be like an innocent flower, but a serpent beneath it.'

Turning his attention to Nathan, William pointed out that he had lied and lied again to cover up what happened to Becky. He questioned whether his manslaughter plea had been an attempt by him to exonerate Shauna out of loyalty and affection.

He asked the jury, 'What has been his purpose in this trial? Has it been to tell you what really happened? Or has it been to try to get away with murder?

'If it is possible to see that scene in your mind's eye, might it not see the determination that it would have taken so far as Nathan Matthews is concerned, and the sort of hatred required to do it. When you suffocate someone you have only one intention, and that is to kill.

'If this was a terrible accident, what would you have expected him to do? Might he have raised the alarm? Might he have himself made an attempt or an effort to save Becky? Might he have made some attempt to resuscitate or something like that, to call 999, to call for help?'

William shook his head before glancing at the defendants' dock.

'No. What he did, and what he thought of, was having put his hands around her neck and having stopped her moving, he then took her pulse and that confirmed she was dead. That suggests someone who is making sure he has achieved what he wanted to.

'He is racked with self-pity for the situation he finds himself in. There is a complete absence of sorrow for what he did to her, not a whiff of it. All he can bring himself to say is that he was worried how it might affect Anjie and Darren, worried for them, upset for them, and that he wanted to protect them.'

I felt like my heart might burst out of my chest at that moment, and I realised that I had been holding my breath. Although it was hard to bear, I was deeply impressed by how well William had put it. Surely anyone in their right mind would believe his version of events?

In his closing speech, Nathan's barrister, Adam Vaitilingam, urged the jury to put their emotions to one side when considering a verdict. It was obvious that he was clutching at straws. He said the plot to kidnap Becky was boneheaded, extreme and absurd. He reminded the jury that Nathan was highly upset when he attacked Becky, and that she had fought back, causing the plan to go wrong. He said that Nathan had no intention of killing Becky, but recognised that he had treated her body with a lack of compassion and humanity.

'I do not ask for sympathy for Nathan Matthews,' he said. 'He deserves none.'

Despite being a bag of nerves, I couldn't help but laugh when Andrew Langdon's closing speech described Shauna as a 'survivor' who'd had to learn how to deal with Nathan. He reminded the jury that there was a lack of DNA evidence against her. (Her DNA had been found on a facemask and two of the bin bags, but the defence claimed that it could have been transferred there by innocent means.)

He said that if they did not find Shauna guilty of conspiracy to kidnap, then they could not find her guilty of murder. He then added, 'I'm not asking you to feel sorry for her, although if she's innocent, she has, in any view, had a wretched few months.

No intelligent person listening to this case can make their minds up on half the evidence. I leave my client in your hands. She's at your mercy now, as they say.'

As I walked out of the courtroom that day, my head spun and I felt sick. The fates of Nathan, Shauna, James Ireland and Donovan Demetrius were now in the hands of the jury. What if they got away with murder? What if we failed to get justice for my Bex?

Sarah squeezed my arm as we walked.

'This is it,' she said. 'Now we wait.'

CHAPTER 15

VERDICT AND SENTENCING

As soon as I opened my eyes on Wednesday, 11 November 2015, a sense of trepidation washed over me. I heaved myself out of bed and went downstairs to put the kettle on, my mind already focused on the day ahead. As I waited for it to boil, I couldn't stop thinking about how vital it was to my family that the jury made the right decision. I was pretty certain that Nathan was going to be found guilty of murder, but I wasn't so sure about Shauna. Her lawyer had done a pretty good job of portraying her as a helpless victim – something I was sure was false. In fact, I found the whole charade of her defence to be despicable and infuriating.

I mulled things over, growing more and more anxious, until it was time to get Anjie out of bed and ready for court. As I carefully pinned my pale-blue bow to my jacket, my hands were shaking, and I told myself to get it together.

Sarah arrived shortly before Ziggy came to pick us up. She wanted to travel to court with us, as she knew how nervous we were.

When we pulled up outside, there was a sudden burst of flashing lights from the photographers' cameras. I was used to being snapped from afar as we went in and out of the court, but this time the sheer number of reporters, photographers and television crews outside the building was overwhelming. As we walked in, I kept my head down and refused to comment.

In the court, we met up with Sam, my dad and Denise, and Danny and his girlfriend, Sarah. Courtney also came to hear the verdict, as well as Tanya and Pat. Our faces were masks of apprehension.

Danny had the same worry as me – that Shauna would go unpunished.

'I really hope she doesn't get away with it, Dad,' he said.

'I know, son,' I replied, putting my arm around his shoulder. 'Me too.'

The judge, Mr Justice Dingemans, gave his final instructions to the jury to help them make a decision, and he told them that there was no time pressure. At around 10.30 a.m., they retired to consider their verdict.

'How long do you think they'll be?' I asked Ziggy as we walked out.

'Could be anything from a few hours to a few days,' she replied. 'We'll just have to wait.'

While we waited for the verdicts to come back, Anjie and I were interviewed by Mike Ridley, a reporter from the *Sun*, because we had agreed to talk to the paper exclusively about what we had been through. We were aware that if the jury returned guilty verdicts we would also be required to give a statement on the court steps. Sarah and Sam volunteered to write ours for us, and my dad also wanted to say something.

At around 2 p.m., Ziggy came to tell us that the jury were ready to give their verdicts. Nobody had expected them to be so quick in reaching their decision, and we had to rush back to the courtroom. We arrived just as the jurors were filing in, and, as I sat down with Anjie on my right-hand side and Sarah on my left, I was trembling with nerves. Sam sat in front of us and reached back so he could place his hand on top of Anjie's and mine. Sarah also held my left hand tightly. I felt a little better with my family sitting so close around me, and I took a deep breath and tried to calm myself as I watched the judge speak to the jurors.

Nathan and Shauna were both in the dock, standing very still.

'Have you reached a verdict?' the judge asked the jury foreman.

'Yes,' the foreman replied, rising from his seat. He passed an envelope to the judge, who opened it, read its contents and nodded.

Then the court clerk asked the foreman for the jury's verdict on both Nathan and Shauna on the first charge, conspiracy to kidnap. His answer was a clear 'guilty'. I let out a sigh of relief. They hadn't been taken in by Shauna's claims to know nothing about it.

'In relation to charge two, the murder of Becky Watts, how do you find the defendant Nathan Matthews?' the clerk asked.

'Guilty,' the foreman replied.

'Yes!' I shouted, at the same time as Sam and Sarah. There were cheers and clapping in the public gallery, where our supporters were sitting, and the judge had to call for order. I was so relieved the scumbag was being sent to prison that it took me a moment to notice Anjie sobbing quietly. I squeezed her hand and reminded myself to rein it in a bit for her sake. Nathan bowed his head in the dock, staring straight at the floor.

'In relation to the same charge, the murder of Becky Watts, how do you find the defendant Shauna Hoare?' the clerk then asked.

'Not guilty,' the juror replied. 'Guilty of manslaughter.'

A low murmur echoed around the court as everyone tried to work out what this meant. We knew that Shauna would still be going to prison, but she wouldn't get the same sort of sentence that Nathan could expect. However, at that point I was just grateful that she wasn't being let off the hook completely. Tears started filling my eyes, and I willed them not to fall.

The jury also found Shauna guilty of perverting the course of justice, preventing a lawful burial, and possession of a stun gun. Nathan had already pleaded guilty to those charges. Donovan Demetrius and James Ireland were both found not guilty of assisting an offender.

After all the verdicts were delivered, Shauna dabbed at her eye with a tissue, but otherwise appeared emotionless.

The next few minutes were a blur as we hugged each other, trying hard not to cry. When I looked around I could see relief etched across Jo and Ziggy's faces too. Our family liaison officers had had to be strong for us all over these months, and it was easy to forget the strain they had been under. Jo had even postponed her retirement from the force so she could get us through the trial, and I was incredibly grateful to her for that.

The judge announced that he would sentence Nathan and Shauna two days later, on Friday 13 November. After everyone had left the courtroom, there was a flurry of hugs and hand-shakes. One person whose hand I was keen to shake was Detective Superintendent Mike Courtiour, the senior investigating officer on Becky's case. Time stood still as we thanked countless people for their help and determination to get the right verdict.

Soon, it was time to give our statements on the court steps. As we shuffled slowly outside, the press formed a crescent shape in front of the court so that every photographer and reporter could get a good view of us. I suddenly felt a rush of adrenaline and a wave of nausea at the same time.

Mike Courtiour stepped forward to address the press first.

He said, 'I would like to take this opportunity to pay tribute to Becky's family and friends, who have shown the utmost composure and dignity during what has undoubtedly been the worst period of their lives.

'Becky Watts was a typical teenager who was well loved and, like most teenagers, had many plans and hopes for the future. Tragically, Nathan Matthews and Shauna Hoare have made sure these hopes and dreams will never be realised.

'Matthews and Hoare concocted a heinous plan to kidnap his stepsister Becky for reasons they have failed to fully disclose, other than that she occasionally left items on the floor which could have tripped up Matthews's mother. The body of evidence, however, has suggested a more sinister motive relating to their deep-seated hatred for Becky and their twisted sexual desires.

'On 19 February this year, the pair carried out their macabre plan, which resulted in the murder of Becky at her home in Crown Hill, Bristol. They then took her body back to their home in Cotton Mill Lane and began the horrific and grotesque task of dismembering her over a matter of days. It's virtually impossible to comprehend this level of depravity.

'In the following days, Matthews lied and misled the police then recruited a number of associates in a bid to conceal Becky's body and prevent us from discovering what happened to her. Karl Demetrius and Jaydene Parsons were involved in assisting Matthews with his attempt to hide Becky's body parts in a shed in Barton Court in a number of bags, cases and a box.

'After we arrested Matthews, he quickly realised it was only a matter of time until we found Becky and had sufficient evidence to charge him. This led to him admitting to killing her and telling us where he had hidden her body. By this time, our search teams were already in close proximity to the Barton Hill address, and I believe it was only a matter of hours until we would have searched the shed.

'Although he admitted manslaughter, Matthews has never taken full responsibility for his actions, and he has forced Becky's family and friends to endure the additional trauma of a lengthy and extremely distressing trial. Hoare has never admitted her role in any capacity, demonstrating her cold-blooded and calculating nature.

'This investigation was one of the largest in the force's history, with over 500 officers utilised throughout its entirety. Our primary aim was always to find Becky safe and well – but Matthews and Hoare had already made sure this was never going to happen.

'Nothing will ever fill the void in the lives of Becky's family and friends, but we hope that these verdicts can finally bring them some much-deserved comfort.'

Then Barry Hughes, the chief crown prosecutor for the South West, stepped forward.

'As we reviewed the evidence they gathered, it became clear not only that Nathan Matthews and Shauna Hoare had conspired to kidnap Becky Watts, but that their actions were motivated by their own sexual interests,' he said.

'Throughout the trial, Matthews maintained that he had killed Becky by accident during a bungled "prank" to kidnap her. Having heard details of Becky's injuries, as well as the cold and calculated way in which he attempted to dispose of her body, the jury has today found him guilty of murder. Shauna Hoare claimed that she knew nothing of Matthews's plans or actions, that she had no involvement in Becky's death or the concealment of her body. Again, the jury found the evidence did not support these claims, and she has been found guilty of manslaughter.

'Unable to complete the task at hand without additional help, Matthews and Hoare recruited Karl Demetrius and Jaydene Parsons, both of whom will now be sentenced for assisting an offender, for their unwitting part in concealing Becky's body.

'Matthews and Hoare have never expressed any remorse for Becky's death, demonstrative of the callous way they took a young woman's life just as she was starting to plan her future.'

Then it was time to give the family statements. I felt light-headed, and I reached down to squeeze Anjie's hand as Tanya's family liaison officer, Detective Constable Liz Cousins, gave a statement on behalf of Tanya, Pat and Danny.

'We wish that Becky was still alive,' Liz read. 'Instead, we have spent the last five weeks hearing evidence about how she came to be killed by someone who she regarded as her own family.

'We loved Becky and knew her better than most. We can tell you that she was a beautiful, happy, funny, feisty, caring, loyal and witty girl. She was like a tornado, hurricane and sunbeam all at once. She came into your life and made you feel alive.'

Their statement finished with a message to other parents, urging them to cherish the time they have with their children.

Then my dad stepped forward to speak to the cameras. I draped my arms around Anjie, who was in front of me in her wheelchair. She still looked completely stunned by the whole thing.

My dad thanked the police, the jury and everyone who had supported us, before he said, 'We know collectively you have cried for us, remembered us and prayed for us. When we have weakened, you have been our strength. When the weight of this evil has wounded us so much, you have helped us to stand strong and tall again. What an incredible force for good you have all been.

'Now the formalities have been concluded, we can start the process of rebuilding our lives – lives which will never, ever be the same, but that have been defined for all of us. And that has, of course, and will forever include our Becky.'

I almost cried at my dad's words. They conveyed exactly how grateful I was to everyone who had supported us.

Finally, it was Sam's turn to speak, and he stepped forward nervously. Sarah stood next to him, linking his arm. We stood behind them as the photographers snapped away.

He said, 'Justice has been done for our beautiful Becky. We would like to record our enormous gratitude to Avon and

Somerset Police, in particular the major crime investigation team, whose professionalism and perseverance secured this outcome.

'We would also like to thank our family liaison officers, who have been amazing throughout this whole process. From the day Becky died, the kindness shown to us by the people of Bristol and wider has been immeasurable. For this, we will always thank you from the bottom of our hearts.

'For us, as a family, today is not the final chapter in this tragedy, but now we can at least begin the challenge to rebuild our lives. Thank you to everyone who has walked this journey with us.'

The flashbulbs and questions continued long after Sam stopped speaking, but there was nothing more to say to the press for now.

The following day passed in a complete blur as we processed the fact that Nathan and Shauna would be going to prison for Becky's death. Even though it was a victory, it was incredibly bittersweet. Nothing was ever going to bring Becky back to us. Nonetheless, that night and the following night, I slept better than I had for many months.

I woke up bright and early on the morning of Friday, 13 November, anxious to find out how long Nathan and Shauna would serve in prison. We all arrived at the court, knowing that it would be the last time we would set foot in there, and hoping that they were both going to be put away for a very long time. Karl Demetrius and Jaydene Parsons were due to be sentenced at a later date.

Before Mr Justice Dingemans made his decision on the sentence, both Nathan and Shauna's barristers would have one last chance to speak. I had also been asked to write a victim-impact statement to read out. It took me three hours as I struggled to convey how much Becky's murder had affected me. It was almost impossible to put into words how much the pair of them had destroyed our family, but I did my best in the hope that it might influence the judge in his sentencing.

I had geared myself up to stand and read it myself, but at the last minute I decided that I couldn't go through with it, so Sam agreed to read it for me. I didn't want to stand there telling everyone how my world had collapsed, knowing that Nathan was listening to my every word. It was a longer statement than the one read out on the steps of the court, and I had done my best to word it so that the judge would understand how Becky's death had obliterated our lives.

Sam looked at me and nodded before he stood up and started to read out the statement I had written.

'My name is Darren Galsworthy and I am the father of Rebecca Watts, now known as "Bristol's Angel",' Sam began, as the room fell silent. 'Our Bex was a child who, through no fault of her own, needed constant reassurance, love and cuddles in her formative years. She soon clung to my wife, Anjie, who became not only a doting mother, but Becky's best friend. Anjie's love was so immense nobody lost out. It didn't matter that we were a mish-mash of gene pools, we were a strong loving family who shared and supported each other.

'We will never understand why this happened, but we now believe we were just disposable pawns in a plot borne out of hatred, jealousy and greed. The heartless, cold and calculating perpetrators of this despicable act of evil can never be forgotten or forgiven. This act of violence sent shockwaves through not only our family, but the whole country.

'When the news came that two people had been arrested and it was now a murder inquiry, our entire world collapsed. Police informed us that body parts had been found, and then we were told who did it. I simply don't have the vocabulary to describe accurately the searing pain and anguish Anjie and I felt at that time. The only way I can describe it is like being cast off a cliff into a bottomless depth of despair and non-belief. These family members sat in our home knowing what they had done, and watched my very public descent into madness and despair. They said nothing and carried on with the pretence of helping us, showing no emotion at all.

'We would not have got this far if not for medication and unyielding support from the community of Bristol. The betrayal we feel is insurmountable. It would have been much kinder to have killed us all, than to have to cope with the after-math of this crime. I've had to watch my loving wife's daily decline in her ability to function or to do the easiest of tasks. She is now solely reliant on me to get through each day.

'We both feel we are just marking time until our demise. Everything beautiful in our lives has been ripped from us in one selfish act of violence. We can't go outside the house with-out people pointing at us or making comments they believe we can't hear. Not only did they cruelly rob Becky of her life, they also took her dignity in death, and did all this on Danny's birthday.

'When I close my eyes to go to sleep, I see Becky's death over and over again. I see what they did to my child. I hear her cry out: "What are you doing?" Then I feel her terror as she realises they are not going to stop and she is about to die. I feel her heart racing. I see all this, and I am powerless to help her. All too frequently, I awake drenched in sweat and physically shaking. Becky was so small and fragile, she never stood a chance.

'These nightmares consume my every thought, like advanced cancer. They haunt my days and terrorise my nights. This is the reality of what transpired that day – a legacy I cannot escape.

'At this time, I pray that the law and justice will go hand in hand, and the sentence will fit this evil act of murder and butchery.'

I bowed my head as I listened to Sam. My words did little to convey how dark and desperate the last year had been for me, but Tanya, Sarah, Anjie and even some of the jury members were in tears.

Then it was time for Liz, Tanya's family liaison officer, to read out Tanya's statement on her behalf.

'I am Tanya Watts, the mother of Rebecca Marie Watts, born 3 June 1998. She was known to me and others as Becky,' Liz read. 'Becky's murder has had an impact not only on my life, but also that of my son, Daniel Watts, and my mother, Pat Watts. Becky has always very much been a big part of our lives since the day she was born. Mum was in the hospital with me when I had Becky and was the first person to hold Becky.

'Danny was always a lovely, protective big brother to Becky. Yes, they had their little fallouts as teenage brothers and sisters do, but whether they were with me or their dad, the two of them always lived with each other and were there for one another.

'When I had Becky, it was in hospital and I had to have a caesarean section. It was a little complicated. Becky didn't want to come out – she was happy where she was. So when they finally brought her out, she was screaming the place down. I always said, "The world knew about it when Becky was born. And they will know about it when she is a teenager!" I never thought it would be like this. Now the world knows all about her death too, in every horrific detail.

'People always ask, "How are you?" and I don't know what to say because I am not sure how I am feeling. My beautiful, kind, funny, loving, loyal, feisty, creative daughter has been murdered. Every day has been a living nightmare.

'And if that wasn't bad enough, for some reason that I will never, ever be able to understand, after my daughter was murdered she was mutilated, cut into pieces. It is like the worst of all horror movies – but this is real. This is my child, she was only sixteen. How am I meant to cope with that? What can anyone say or do to help me come to terms with that? It just goes round and round in my mind all the time; it is never-ending. I don't want to remember Becky like this, but the thought of her being dismembered is always at the forefront of my mind.

'The 19th February 2015 is the day that we have been told Becky was killed. That means that Becky was murdered on Danny's twentieth birthday. It should have been a day to celebrate. How is he ever expected to get over that? How is he ever going to celebrate any of his birthdays again? He can't. None of us can celebrate his birthday again. That date will always be etched in our minds as the day that Becky would have been so scared seeing this person that she thought of as a brother attacking and killing her. There is nothing to celebrate any more, not without Becky.

'In March I was told that Becky had been found and that she had been dismembered. I had already been having difficulty sleeping with her disappearance, but this made sleeping impossible. In the end, I had to rely on one of my family liaison officers to contact my GP on my behalf, as I could not function. I could not bring myself to say what had happened to Becky, and how Danny and I needed help.

'I keep thinking about Becky, her situation and how she came to be dead, and I am furious. I have so many questions. I can't rest until I know what has happened, and even then I am sure I still won't ever be able to understand why it happened.'

In her statement, Tanya then wrote about going to see Becky's body in the morgue, and I closed my eyes, remembering all too well the horrors of that day.

Liz continued to read: 'As a family we then suffered further, waiting for Becky to be released in order for her funeral to take place. When the time did come for Becky's funeral, it was a real mixture of different emotions. I will always be grateful that the public made generous donations allowing for a beautiful send-off for Becky, but I couldn't help but be angry, hurt and upset that, actually, Becky's big day should have been her wedding, and not her funeral. Becky has been robbed of her future, and we have been robbed of all of those future milestones we should have been able to share together.

'Becky's death has left a massive hole even in just ordinary, everyday things. I can't believe that I will never have her and Courtney come round my house, going through the cupboards like a pair of locusts! I still have the chicken in the freezer that I was going to do for their Sunday roast. I still have Becky's pocket money in an envelope that she was due to collect around the time she died. The hardest thing is that I can't believe I am never going to see her again.'

She said she was more anxious about Danny now, terrified something might happen to him as well, then it continued: 'Hearing evidence throughout the trial has been incredibly difficult. Becky must have been so scared – thinking she was safely resting in her own bedroom to then be attacked like that, by someone that she regarded as family. Knowing that her last moments were filled with fear and that she would have fought for her life – it is just unbearable for us. I can't get it out of my mind.

'It made sense to me that Becky would have fought for her life. That was the kind of girl she was. Sometimes she had a tough exterior, but those people who really knew her (and only a few people truly knew Becky) knew that, underneath it all, she was a big softie. Yes, she could watch a horror movie without flinching – but equally, when she watched a film like *Marley & Me* she would cry her eyes out.

'The impact of Becky being taken from us, murdered, dismembered and hidden is massive; trying to describe it is difficult. I often hear myself talking about Becky and asking questions about her death, but it is as if I am talking about someone else, not my baby girl. It is surreal. But the actual reality is that those people who were involved in Becky's murder, dismemberment and concealment have left us with a lifetime of emptiness, continuing nightmares of her final moments and a grave to visit.'

Tanya's statement almost reduced me to tears, but I swallowed the lump in my throat and reminded myself that I had vowed not to crumble. We'd had our differences in the past –

far too many of them – but I agreed with everything she said that day. The courtroom remained silent for a few moments after Liz stopped reading, and I noticed that a few of the jury members were still dabbing at their eyes with tissues.

William Mousely then began to speak, telling the court that Nathan should face a mandatory life sentence for Becky's murder. He added that the kidnap involved significant planning, and that the concealment and dismemberment of her body were also aggravating factors in the case.

Nathan's barrister, Adam Vaitilingam, then addressed the court. He pointed out that whole life orders – where prisoners are never released from jail – are only applied to the most horrific and exceptional cases. He added, 'There are only eight people in the country in that category who are not multiple killers.'

I shook my head. In my mind, Nathan deserved to rot in prison for the rest of his life. I didn't think the fact that he hadn't killed before should count for anything.

Andrew Langdon then addressed the court on behalf of Shauna. His argument was that Shauna was a vulnerable child when she met Nathan and, had she not met him, she wouldn't have carried out the offence. He even suggested that Shauna herself could be considered as one of Nathan's victims. I think everyone in the courtroom felt he was clutching at straws with that.

The judge announced that he would pass sentence on Shauna and Nathan at 2 p.m., and the court was adjourned for lunch. We had an hour and a half to wait, so we stepped outside. My stomach fluttered anxiously as the time passed. I couldn't eat, could hardly say a word to anyone because my thoughts were still in the courtroom; I was desperate to hear the sentences.

Finally, the moment we had all been waiting for arrived, and we were summoned to go back in. This was when we would find out how long Nathan and Shauna would each spend behind bars.

Mr Justice Dingemans started his speech by talking about the vile way Nathan had deceived his family after Becky's death. 'Mr Matthews and Miss Hoare lied to the family and to the police, pretending not to know anything about Becky's whereabouts, at a time when they were in the process of dismembering her,' he said gravely. 'Everyone who saw them both, including the first police officers to investigate, were taken in by the apparently concerned couple. Their deceit of the family was particularly cruel and unusual, and the family's sense of betrayal by Nathan Matthews and Shauna Hoare is both understandable and justified. At the same time that they were deceiving the family, Matthews and Hoare were watching a parody of a song from *Frozen*, using the words "Do you want to hide a body?"'

'It is apparent that neither Nathan Matthews nor Shauna Hoare have truthfully said what happened to Becky, and I understand the family's sense of frustration about that fact.'

He continued, 'I am sure, on the evidence that was adduced at the trial, that the planned kidnap of Becky was for a sexual purpose. But in my judgement it does not require a whole life order, in the circumstances where Nathan Matthews had been of previous good character and had directed the police, after a long delay, to Becky's remains.

'This is not in any sense to diminish the loss suffered by Becky's family. In my judgement the behaviour of both Nathan Matthews and Shauna Hoare in feigning concern with the family, as the family desperately searched and looked for Becky, is a further and serious aggravating feature.

'In my judgement, the appropriate sentence for Mr Matthews is a mandatory life sentence with a minimum term of thirty-three years. This means that Mr Matthews, as a twenty-eight-year-old man, will be sixty-one before he might be considered for release, and the reality is that he might never be released.'

I let out a huge sigh of relief, and I was aware of Sarah squeezing my hand. I could just about glimpse Nathan in the dock. He was slumped forward in the chair in his usual position, his head bowed so nobody could see his expression.

Shauna was then jailed for seventeen years, with the judge saying that he believed her involvement in these offences was a product of the nature of her relationship with Nathan. She didn't show a shred of emotion as her sentence was announced.

I wasn't as happy with the length of her prison sentence, but the main thing I focused on was the fact that she was going to prison, and that Nathan might never be released. God only knows what I'd do if I ever set eyes on either one of them again.

The judge concluded his sentencing remarks by paying tribute to us, Becky's family.

In an extraordinary moment, he choked back tears as he spoke. All the way through the court case he had been a strong figure of authority, so it was surprising to see him let his emotions get the better of him.

His voice trembling, he said, 'Finally, I should like to pay public tribute to the family of Becky for the dignified way in which they have conducted themselves throughout these proceedings. Hearing the evidence during the trial has been difficult for anyone, but it is plain that it has been an immense burden for the family.'

With that, he quickly got up and left the court with his head bowed and tears in his eyes. From the shock on everyone's faces, I could tell that his reaction was rare. His compassion really touched me.

I later found out that Mr Justice Dingemans was a father of three himself, and that his kids – two of them girls – were all aged between eighteen and twenty-three. It just went to show that any parent, even a judge who sits through murder trials regularly, would be affected by what happened to Bex. Even though nothing was ever going to make it right, his compassion gave me a tiny shred of comfort that he understood the hell we had gone through.

As we got up, I shot one last look at Nathan and Shauna, who were being taken down to the cells for the final time. Neither of them met my gaze, but they both looked terrified as they contemplated their long prison sentences. It would never be the same level of terror that Becky had faced, but it would have to do. Justice had been served.

CHAPTER 16

AFTERMATH

After the sentencing, Sam and Sarah told me that some members of the jury had approached them to ask if they could meet us to pass on their sympathy. I was keen to speak with them too, so we arranged to meet five of them in a Wetherspoons pub around the corner from Bristol Crown Court. As soon as they introduced themselves, I thanked them for putting those monsters behind bars.

'You have no idea what it means to me and my family,' I told them, shaking hands and hugging every one of them. 'Thank you from the bottom of my heart for seeing through those evil lies. All we've wanted this whole time was to get justice for Becky, and you did that for us. Thank you.'

The family celebrated with a few drinks that night, but it was a bittersweet moment. We were thrilled that Becky's killers were behind bars, but, of course, justice being served was never going to bring her back to us, where she belonged. Every time the story popped up on the pub television that night, we held up our drinks, cheered and proposed a toast to

Becky. But although Nathan and Shauna's convictions were a massive weight off my shoulders, there was still a huge hole in my life.

The sentence Nathan was given seemed like the best possible conclusion to the harrowing five-week trial, but I often wondered if justice had really been done. In prison, Nathan and Shauna would be warm and they'd have three meals a day; they'd be able to listen to music and possibly to make friends. Even though Nathan was having to serve a minimum of thirty-three years, meaning he wouldn't be eligible for parole until he was sixty-one, I couldn't help but wonder if I would rather he had paid for his crime with his own life – something I freely told the press. I didn't want to think of him having any happiness ever again.

As for Shauna's sentence – just seventeen years – I wasn't overly pleased with that. She was twenty-one and if she served half her sentence that would mean she could get out of prison by the age of thirty. She would still have a shot at building a life for herself – something my Becky would never have. Still, I was happy that she was behind bars. There had been times when I worried that the jury would buy her ridiculous story about being completely unaware of Nathan's crime, about not questioning the noise and smell as he dismembered Becky's body in her bathroom.

Wherever we went, newspapers had Becky's name and face plastered all over them, and every time I turned on the television I saw Anjie and myself on the court steps, blinking as cameras flashed all around. Suddenly, the Becky Watts murder trial was absolutely everywhere. It wasn't just a Bristol story any more – all the nationals wanted a piece of us, and it was overwhelming. Not many people murder their stepsister, the girl they've grown up with, so for the media it was a highly unusual case.

We decided to give immediate interviews to the *Sun* newspaper and *BBC Points West*, and we went on *Good Morning Britain* on Thursday, 12 November, the day after the verdicts were announced. Doing interview after interview was draining, and speaking about the devastating effect of Becky's death on my family never got any easier, but I felt that it was important to explain our side of things and bring the focus back onto my beautiful, loving daughter.

It was quite nerve-racking giving our very first live interview on mainstream television. I'd never been on television before, and *Good Morning Britain* was obviously a huge household name. I reminded myself to keep my swearing in check and not let myself get too angry in front of the cameras. Anjie and I had to get up at the crack of dawn for filming, and we both felt fragile after all the tension of the previous day. We were being interviewed by presenters Susanna Reid and Ben Shephard, and when the time came we were led out to sit with them on the famous sofa.

'What were your feelings yesterday, Darren, when those verdicts came in?' Susanna asked, after thanking us for appearing on the show.

'A great deal of relief, I must admit,' I answered truthfully. 'But it's a bittersweet verdict for us.'

Ben then directed his gaze at Anjie. 'Obviously, Nathan was your son,' he said. 'And he committed this appalling crime. How did you feel, sitting there looking at him in court, and hearing that verdict read out, and sitting through the case?'

'Absolutely disgusted,' Anjie replied, shaking her head. 'I couldn't take it all in, what had happened.'

'We've just been stunned all the way through this,' I added.

'As you were sitting there, Anjie, was there any sense that this was the little boy you had brought up and loved as a mother all through his childhood?' Ben asked again.

'No,' she answered adamantly. 'He was a different person. He's not the child I remember bringing up.'

Susanna and Ben then asked us if we'd ever sensed the anger Nathan appeared to be harbouring towards Becky while they were growing up.

'It was just sibling rivalry,' I replied. 'And not even that serious. We never saw any of this coming. Even after Becky disappeared, he was helping me put photos on Facebook, getting the message out there. We were desperate to find her.

'When they arrested them, we still said, "You've got it wrong." We trusted them, and the betrayal hurts so much. We loved them. They were all our kids, even if they had different DNA. It didn't make a difference. We loved them, they were our family.'

When asked how she felt about Nathan now, Anjie simply said, 'I still love him. I just find it hard looking at the monster he's turned into.'

'What happened between you, what one parent's child did to another, is enough to shatter any relationship. How have you managed to stay strong together through this?' Susanna asked, looking at us intently.

'Since we set eyes on each other we knew we were destined to be together,' I said. 'I only blame the people who do things. Anjie isn't guilty of anything – she has no control over what Nathan does. He's a grown man. We've just got to take it day by day –

that's the only way we can do it. Every day is a struggle. Even getting up in the mornings has become almost impossible.'

They asked Anjie whether she would like to visit Nathan in prison, and she hesitated before saying, 'Eventually.' One day, when she is strong enough, she wants to ask him why he did what he did to our family.

'Unfortunately, he got up in the witness box and just lied all the way through it,' I interjected. 'All we want is the truth, and we weren't given it.'

We weren't the only ones who felt that we had not yet heard the truth from Nathan and Shauna. The senior investigating officer, Detective Superintendent Mike Courtiour, told the press that his officers were frustrated that they could not be sure of the sequence of events. He said, 'Nobody actually knows precisely what happened. We have had an account from Nathan Matthews, an explanation of what he said happened. Nobody knows the precise events. It remains a frustration to the police, the prosecution and the family.'

I have loads of questions myself. I think Nathan and Shauna owe it to us to give a full and truthful account of my daughter's final moments of life. It would be incredibly hard to hear, but the facts couldn't be any worse than the images I have in my imagination. One day, perhaps, one or other of them will do us that courtesy.

The morning after the sentencing, I woke up feeling horrendous. It wasn't just a hangover; it was a feeling of overpowering grief. For the past nine months, our sole purpose in life had been to get justice for Becky. Now we had achieved that, all we were left with was our sorrow and heartache.

When I got up I saw Marley standing in the hallway. He looked up at me and meowed loudly. Something about the way he looked at me, and the fact that he was Becky's cat, made everything I had bottled up during the trial suddenly come flooding out, and I completely broke down. I cried for the rest of that day – big, heart-wrenching sobs which made my chest heave and my eyes turn red raw. Absolutely nothing and no one could console me.

All the way through the trial, I had tried my hardest to keep my cool, to remain composed so that Nathan would never see me cry. I had kept my eyes locked on him all the way through the proceedings, but he had never glanced in my direction. That just showed what a coward he was. His absurd story about 'teaching Becky a lesson' hadn't washed with anyone, and I think even he knew it. That's why he didn't dare look across at me and his mother in the courtroom. I think he knows that whatever he was planning to do to Becky that day, it would always have ended with her death. There's no way I would have let him get away with kidnapping my daughter, dragging her to some woods and subjecting her to any sort of torture or terror campaign. I would have been furious, and I would have made his life a misery for hurting my girl. I would have also reported him to the police. He knew that – which is why he had no choice but to kill her.

The days after the sentencing were like the aftershock of a nuclear bomb. The slightest thing would set me off, and it was hard to calm down again. The information we had heard in court circled in my mind over and over again. The images of Nathan suffocating my poor girl, then cutting her up like dog food were too much to bear, but at the same time I couldn't stop thinking about them, wondering what thoughts were in Becky's head during those last moments, hoping she did not suffer for long.

It was then that I reached the lowest point of all. I struggled to leave the house and couldn't talk to Anjie any more because I couldn't put into words the agony I was suffering. Suddenly, Anjie's and my roles were reversed as she began taking care of me, her completely broken man.

The shock of finding out what Nathan and Shauna were really like knocked me for six. I swung manically from feeling complete anguish and despair one moment, to wanting to kill the pair of them the next. I was utterly bewildered about the person Nathan had become. How could he do something so violent and brutal to a member of his own family for no apparent reason at all? What on earth had happened to him?

It crossed my mind that he might have decided to get rid of Becky because he wanted to inherit the house. He had become lazy since getting together with Shauna, acting as if the world owed him a living, but to get the house he would have had to do away with Danny as well. My mind did somersaults, searching for a clear answer that made sense of why he did what he did.

I'd had no idea about his perverse schoolgirl fantasies, and it made me ill to think that Becky could have been caught up in one of his sick, twisted games. My mind flashed back to the time he brought those underage girls to my house in his car. I really believed that he was just joking about, but Shauna had been very young when he first started seeing her too. I knew Nathan didn't fancy Becky – the idea made me shudder – but the judge seemed to think her murder was 'sexually motivated'.

I don't think I'll ever be able to understand what was going through Nathan's head.

Alongside my grief, I also had an awful feeling of guilt, which ate away at me every day. Why wasn't I there to protect my little girl? Why didn't I pick up the signs as to who Nathan really was? I should have trusted my gut instinct before I let Shauna set foot in my house. I truly believe they were a toxic pair, and if they had got away with Becky's death, they would have struck again. In my eyes, they could have been the new Fred and Rose West – the depraved couple who tortured and murdered ten young women together.

When Fred, who was known to have killed at least twelve women, was first arrested in 1994 for the murder of his own daughter, Heather, he confessed to the crime but claimed Rose was not involved. More bodies were then found, dismembered and buried at their home in Cromwell Street, Gloucester. Unlike Fred, Rose never confessed to the killings. She continuously professed ignorance of her husband's murderous activities, but the circumstantial evidence was considered sufficient to prosecute her for ten murders. Fred killed himself in jail before standing trial, but Rose went on trial in October 1995, nine months after her husband's suicide. She was found guilty the following month, and sentenced to life in prison. It was recommended that she never be released. I wish Shauna had got life, I really do.

Sarah tells me there was nothing I could have done, because Nathan and Shauna were always going to carry out a sickening attack like this. She believes that if it wasn't Becky, it would have been some other poor girl. As a family, we take some comfort from the fact that they are now locked away, unable to hurt anyone else.

I'd had nightmares about how Becky was killed before, but they got a lot worse after I heard the gory details during the trial. I went to my doctor, who prescribed some incredibly powerful sleeping tablets, but I still needed a strong drink or two to help me drown out the noise inside my head. All the days started merging into one, and I completely lost track of them. I once tried to phone my boss at the office, only to realise it was a Sunday afternoon.

By gritting my teeth, I had managed to get through the trial, but it hadn't brought me much relief. Even when I knew that Nathan and Shauna were rotting in prison where they belonged, I still felt hopelessly depressed to the extent that I started to have suicidal thoughts. That's when I knew I had to get help. My family were endlessly supportive, but I obviously needed more than that, so our assigned victim support officer, Chrissy, referred me for trauma therapy.

In my first session, the therapist encouraged me to talk about my feelings and to express my anger. I was worried when she asked me to do that; I wasn't sure that she understood just how much anger was inside me – more than I'd ever felt in my life. I'm usually not the type of person to hold a grudge against anyone, but I just couldn't let go of my red-hot, overwhelming fury. Gradually, as time went on, I found that talking to the therapist about my feelings was helpful, and I plan to continue the treatment over the next year. Writing this book also helped, and I'm now planning on returning to work – part-time at first, in order to ease myself back in gently. I'm moving forwards, taking baby steps, trying not to put too much pressure on myself for now.

* * *

On 21 November 2015, Anjie turned fifty. Despite my own torment, I wanted to do something nice for my wife. She had supported me all the way through our devastating year, so I wanted to make her birthday extra special. I enlisted Sarah to help organise a big party, and we decided to ask the guests to wear fancy dress. Anjie loved the idea, and she and I went along dressed as Antony and Cleopatra. We invited the whole family and booked the Labour Club in St George – the place where we'd held Becky's birthday party. It was becoming a bit of a tradition to hold our birthday bashes there.

We hadn't made it clear that we had already organised a cake, so we ended up with five – not that I minded, of course. One cake, brought by our supporters Joanne and Michelle, had a beautiful picture of Becky on top, which Anjie loved. We kept the icing as a special memento.

Becky's friends Courtney, Teela, Adam and, of course, Luke also showed up for Anjie's party, which was a nice surprise. Adam dressed up as a pimp from the 1970s, in a white zoot suit with lots of gold chains, oversized sunglasses and a white hat with a massive feather stuck in it. It was hilarious, and I almost choked on my drink when I saw him. We would have forgiven those four for getting on with their own lives now that Becky was no longer around, but they always made the effort to socialise with my family whenever they could, and we really appreciated that. They are lovely kids, and Becky was lucky to have them as friends.

I was delighted that Anjie had a good time that evening. She deserved to have a smile on her face again after all she had been through. She had put years of her life into caring for me and my family, only to have her own son destroy everything we had created. I spent a lot of time that night gazing at her while she laughed with her friends, thanking my lucky stars that we were still together after all the bad luck we had been dealt.

As Christmas approached, Anjie and I knew that we couldn't face spending it at home. In the past, Christmas would have been one of our annual family highlights. Becky particularly loved Christmas. Even at the age of sixteen, her last Christmas, she still woke Anjie and me at 7 a.m. and insisted we got up to open presents. Nathan and Shauna brought their little one over, and we all spent a lovely day as a family. We still had Danny, of course, but he had moved in with his girlfriend the previous September, just before the trial, and we saw less of him than before. It was likely to be just Anjie and me on our first Christmas Day without Becky, and the idea filled me with dread. Although we had multiple invitations from family and friends, we decided instead to go away for a week, just the two of us. We bought Christmas presents for our nieces and nephews early, and decided to go to Butlin's again. We had never been there for Christmas before, and we hoped that it would be a jollier occasion than the last time we went, just after Becky's funeral. We left on Wednesday, 23 December, and I told my whole family that we would see them at New Year.

All in all, it was a good trip. This time, we dealt with our emotions in a more positive way, choosing to cherish our memories of Becky having fun there rather than be haunted by them. I think it helped that her killers were behind bars and we didn't have an upcoming trial hanging over us. Our only fight now was to try to heal enough so that we could carry on with our lives.

On Christmas Eve, both of us deliberately drank a little too much. Anjie isn't a big drinker, so it was unusual for her. I think we wanted to make sure we slept in late on Christmas Day, rather than opening our eyes at 7 a.m. and wondering why Becky wasn't there to burst into the room. We also missed our grandchild terribly – we'd only seen the little one a few times since everything had happened – and I know there was probably a part of Anjie that missed seeing Nathan over Christmas too, although she didn't admit it. As much as I struggled with it in the early days, I could eventually understand: Nathan was her son, and you can't cut that biological bond, no matter how hard you try.

We had Christmas dinner and watched some live entertainment, and somehow we managed to forget our misery for a few hours. We even managed to reminisce about previous Christmas Days, and we chuckled when we remembered Becky bouncing off the walls with excitement every year.

'No matter what has happened, we can always say that we did everything we could for our children,' Anjie said to me as we sat with a drink. 'That alone is worth celebrating.'

I nodded and smiled. My world had always revolved around my kids; they were the centre of my universe, and it was the same for Anjie. As much as it was tempting to blame ourselves for the way things had turned out, we knew that we couldn't have done more for our family. That consoled me for a while at least.

Sarah also phoned us with some news that made me smile. She had been up to Speedwell to hang Christmas decorations on Becky's memorial tree, and she said that, despite the wintry weather, it had grown quickly and was now the largest of the five planted there a few months earlier.

'That's my girl,' I said grinning.

We returned home in time for New Year's Eve – my birthday. Once again, the Galsworthys decided it was time for a party. If there had ever been a moment to let our hair down and celebrate, it was now, after such a traumatic eleven months. Sarah and Anjie booked the Labour Club again, and we all got together to see in the New Year and to celebrate me turning fifty-two.

I personally couldn't wait to welcome in 2016. I hoped that this year would bring better health to Anjie, and some peace for me and everyone else in my family. I hoped that the pain would gradually ease and that we would be able to move on with our lives, although I knew it wasn't going to be easy. We were over the moon when Danny announced that he and his girlfriend, Sarah, were getting engaged; it seemed like a good omen. As we counted down to midnight, I glanced at all the people around us on whom I had leaned so heavily during 2015. I couldn't have been more grateful for my family's support than I was at that moment, as I got ready to raise my glass to the future. It was a future without Becky, Nathan and Shauna, but it was a future which would hopefully heal our hearts and help us to gain the strength to carry on.

In January 2016, the police told me that I could collect some of the items of ours which Nathan had hoarded at his house over the years. I had never known about this hoarding habit, because Nathan and Shauna always came to our house and, although I gave them many lifts back and forth, I hardly ever set foot in theirs.

I wanted to visit their house to see the bathroom where Nathan had dismembered Becky's body. I know it sounds morbid, but I thought that seeing it for myself would help me come to terms with things. However, I never got the opportunity. Instead, I was told to visit a nearby police station, where I was handed a bag of our possessions, which the police had collected on our behalf. There was some camping stuff Nathan had borrowed, some electric cables, and a television set. I was disappointed, but eventually I decided that it was probably for the best.

Friday, 19 February 2016, marked one year since Becky was cruelly taken from us. Instead of feeling angry and bitter, we chose to spend that day reflecting on all the things we adored about her: her laugh, her wicked sense of humour, her creativity and her sense of style. She may have spent most of her short life as a wallflower as far as the outside world was concerned, but in our world she was a force to be reckoned with. Her love and fierce loyalty towards her friends and family shone out of her, and she made me proud in so many ways. She would have hated all this attention if she was still here, but I'm glad to have the opportunity to tell the world just how amazing my beautiful Bex was. To me, she was everything, and there will always be a huge part of me missing now that she's not with us any more.

The pain is still very raw, but we are trying to pick up the pieces of our broken lives as best we can. Our fantastic family liaison officer Ziggy is still in touch with us regularly, as Jo has now retired. We remain completely bewildered over Nathan's motive for killing Becky, and we still want some answers. As soon as she feels ready, Anjie will request to visit Nathan in prison. She needs to ask him outright why he took Becky away from us. She needs closure. We both do.

I can't face seeing Nathan in person as my anger is far too strong, but I fully support Anjie visiting her son. Despite our confusion about his motives, it's clear to me that as well as his deep hatred for Becky, Nathan must have hated me to take the life of the person who meant the world to me. He must have realised the suffering it would cause me. Maybe his hatred grew over the years because he thought I had stolen the affections of his mother. Perhaps he had long harboured resentment towards me for moving into his life and bringing two kids of my own into the mix.

Everything I did for him, the many times I told him I was proud of him and thought of him as a son, must have meant nothing to Nathan. Sometimes, that is the hardest pill to swallow. The boy I knew, the one who used to enjoy painting his Warhammer fantasy figures and riding about on his moped, is dead to me now. I loved Nathan. It might not have been obvious to him as his mind became more warped and twisted, but it was obvious to everyone else. I gave him everything I could – guidance, financial assistance and, most importantly, love – but he threw it all away for a completely inexplicable reason.

As for what he has done to his own mother, I can never forgive him for that. Nathan always claimed that he adored his mum, but her health has deteriorated drastically due to the stress of the past year. He wouldn't look at her once during the court case, but it was revealed after the trial that he wrote her a letter when he was in custody awaiting trial – shortly after she had asked to see him and been refused. It was a scrawled, barely literate note that didn't contain a word of apology. He wrote:

*Hello Mum, I was told you wanted to ask me a question of
'why' and I know you are going to be very confused amongst
other things. Sorry but I have been advised not to talk about
my case at the moment as what I say can be misinterpreted
but I hope you can find some, even if it is a miniscule [sic]
amount of resolution/help by me explaining to you that what
has happened was not meant to. Love you X*

The letter provided no answers, and Anjie was traumatised by
reading it. When we were finally told about the letter, which
had been kept from us for around eight months, she hoped that
he would at least say sorry in it, but instead she was left bitterly
hurt and angry.

I know we will never fully recover from Becky's murder, but
I feel incredibly proud of the support we have received from
the country, and from Bristol in particular. People rallied
around us in our desperate time of need, and gave us strength,
friendship and love. The masses of people at her funeral showed
how much Becky was loved and how much the city supported
us. It restored my faith in humanity, as I was humbled time and
time again by the kindness we were shown.

I still talk to Becky all the time, and her bedroom remains a
place of solace for me. I know I'll see her again on the other
side. For now, the words my dad sang at her funeral ring true
to me every single day.

AFTERMATH

Somewhere
There's a place for us,
A time and place for us.
Hold my hand and we're halfway there
Hold my hand and I'll take you there,
Somehow, someday, somewhere.

AFTERWORD
BY ANJIE GALSWORTHY

Whenever I am asked how the past year has been for me, I struggle with my answer. How on earth do you convey the devastation, despair and gut-wrenching grief that comes from having your whole family ripped apart? How do you begin to explain that once upon a time your life was filled with love and laughter – and now there is just emptiness?

A lot of people say that they can't believe my husband, Darren, and I are still together after my son, Nathan, brutally murdered his daughter, Becky. This experience has tested us beyond belief – but, to be truthful, the main reason Darren and I are so strong together is because simply we have had to be. We only really have each other, because nobody else could ever understand the hurt, confusion and betrayal we have suffered. The loss we feel, not only at the absence of beautiful Becky, but at losing such a huge part of our precious family, is completely indescribable.

My now-empty home used to be a sanctuary, a place for my children to feel safe and a place for Darren and me to raise the family we both always wanted. There were some difficult times along the way, but we always got through them together. We knew we had something really special.

But now, Darren and I rattle around the house not quite knowing what to do with ourselves. We are lucky still to have Danny in our lives, and to have a loving and supportive wider family, but life will never be the same for any of us after Becky's death.

From the minute I met Becky, I fell for her instantly. With her big hazel eyes and cute smile, she had me hooked. Right from the word go, she adored me and I adored her. She was every inch my daughter. When I think of her now, I try to remember the good times we shared, rather than the tragic way her life came to an end. I have hundreds of happy memories of my time with her, and nobody can ever take them away. As a child, Becky was my sidekick, my mini-me. She was always with me, usually with her little arms around my neck, clinging on for dear life. Far from finding it annoying, I treasured that affectionate side of Becky and felt protective towards her. She was a sweet little girl, and I wanted nothing more than to take good care of her.

When she discovered that I wasn't her biological mother, she cried for hours on end – and so did I. I always felt like she was my daughter, so it broke my heart to see her so upset. I feared we'd never have that same bond again, that, from then on, something would always be missing. How wrong I was, as our relationship grew even stronger from that day.

I miss Becky so much it physically hurts. I can't bear to set foot in her bedroom, the room where I would curl up with her and read to her, the room where she spent so much time as a teenager. The room in which she was murdered. Even the cat doesn't sleep there any more. There is an eerie silence in my house now that she is missing. I would do anything for her to walk through the door one more time: for the door to slam, for her to plonk herself down on the sofa next to me, to be able to chat to her once more – about life, boys, her hopes and dreams. I think Becky would have grown up to be a good, kind and determined young woman. She was just starting to live life, to gain enough confidence to go out into the world and carve out a path for herself. It's a crying shame she never got the chance.

Part of the reason I loved Becky so much was because she was so much like her dad. They both hated to admit it, but they were very similar. They shared the same stubborn streak, the same loyalty to their friends and family, and many of the same mannerisms. I used to find it hilarious when they argued with each other, both of them sounding exactly alike. She was a beautiful girl; I don't think anyone could deny that. She didn't see it, though. She hated her nose and used to blame her father for passing it on to her. She suffered a crisis of confidence for years and was painfully shy, but it was lovely when she finally started coming out of her shell.

People often ask me how I feel about Nathan after what he did. Of course, I still love him – he is my son. When you're a mother, you can't ignore that unconditional love for your children, no matter what they do. But I will never, ever forgive him for what he did to our family. With one brutal and inconceivable act, he destroyed the many years of guidance, support and nourishment we had worked so hard to provide. He revealed a side of himself that I never knew was there. The boy I gave birth to grew up to be a monster, and that is very difficult to come to terms with. I find myself worrying about how he is coping in prison, yet at the same time knowing that he completely deserves to be in there. It is agonising.

The main question I have for Nathan is, Why? Why take another person's life for no good reason other than irritation with her for behaving like any teenager? Becky surely didn't deserve the death penalty for simply backchatting and being a stroppy kid. Nathan was the same at her age, but never once did I think he deserved to die because of it.

My second question for him is whether he ever cared for Darren, the man who brought him up and loved him like a son. Did he ever love me, his mum, the one person who loved him more than life itself? Why would he kill somebody whom I adored, whom I raised as my own? Why would he shatter our family into tiny pieces? What happened to his mental state to conceive and carry out such a horrific act? There is a huge difference between the son I knew and the man he has become, and it terrifies me. One day, I hope to have the courage to visit Nathan in prison and ask him these questions face to face.

I have beaten myself up over and over again, asking whether there were any signs that Nathan was going to do what he did, or if there was anything I could have done differently as a mother. The answer is that I can't think of anything that pointed to this, or anything we could have done to prevent it. If I had known what he was planning, or how twisted his mind had become, I would have been able to stop him murdering Becky. I would have got him the help he needed and we would still be a family. And, despite me having severe MS, if I had been in the house when he attacked Becky, I would have crawled up those stairs to stop him. I would have defended any of our children with my life.

When Nathan stole Becky's life, our world imploded. I feared that Darren would blame me. I was terrified that this might be too much of a burden on our marriage and that he might not be able to be with me any more. But I can honestly say that I did everything I could for Becky and Danny throughout their lives. They were just as much my children as Nathan was, and I think Darren knows that. Our whole life was built around our family, and we always put the children first.

I am grateful for my amazingly strong and loyal husband. I truly believe we are soulmates. When I was a teenager, I always knew I would end up with Darren; I just couldn't work out how. The effort he made with Nathan will forever mean the world to me. We share some incredible memories together. Whatever has happened, I will always be thankful for that.

ACKNOWLEDGEMENTS

When Becky was taken from us, our world fell apart. But the support we received from friends, family and strangers alike has helped to restore our faith in humanity. There are simply too many kind people to mention by name, but there are a few people in particular whom I would like to recognise.

Writing Becky's story has been an emotional and sometimes difficult process, but in many ways it has proved therapeutic for me. As her father, I have so many precious memories of our time together, and I was keen to make sure that Becky is remembered for all the right reasons.

I would like to thank Chantelle Rees for helping me put my story into words, as well as Vicky Eribo, Kate Latham and Gill Paul at HarperCollins. I would also like to thank my agent, Clare Hulton, and Jack Falber at Medavia for making this possible. I would like to express my gratitude to Helen O'Brien and Bede MacGowan for volunteering to read the drafts of the manuscript and for their valuable input into the book. A mention also goes out to Geraldine McKelvie for her essential advice and guidance.

Special thanks must go to the people of Bristol for their incredible support, both when Becky was missing and also during the trial. To the people who came out to help with the search, the people who threw flowers at her funeral, and to those who still support us now – I am grateful from the bottom of my heart, and I couldn't be prouder to be a part of this great city.

We will be forever in debt to the many people who helped bring Nathan Matthews and Shauna Hoare to justice – namely the dedicated officers from Avon and Somerset Police and everyone from the Crown Prosecution Service who worked on the case. In particular, we would like to say thank you to the judge, Mr Justice James Dingemans, and the jury members. Thank you for making the right decision.

A special mention must go out to our family liaison officers, Russ Jones, Jo Marks and Ziggy Bennett, for their kindness, support and professionalism. We do not underestimate your level of commitment, and we know you put your own lives on hold so that you could support us.

To my work colleagues at Power Electrics: I am indebted to you for the amount of support you have shown me since Becky disappeared. I am lucky to work with such kind people, whom I now regard as friends.

To my family, whom I truly believe are second to none, thank you so much for being an absolute pillar of strength for me and Anjie through this terrible year. Your unconditional love and support gave me courage during my darkest hours, and I will always be so grateful. A special mention goes to my son, Danny:

your resilience throughout this ordeal has stunned me, and I couldn't be prouder of you.

Last, but certainly not least, to my amazing wife, Anjie — thank you for being my rock. Without you, I would have nothing.